Praise for THE Missing PIECE

"The Missing Piece is a great demonstration of what enlightened relationship work looks like in today's world."
— **Mike Dooley**, *New York Times* best-selling author of *Infinite Possibilities*

"I'm buying this book for everyone I know. Not joking."
— **Annie Grace**, best-selling author of *This Naked Mind*

"If you've ever felt misunderstood by the humans around you, this book will explain why. This book gives us what we all need, to express in a way that honors ourselves and others. Anyone who leads teams, has a partner, or knows another human needs this book. This is not a business or a relationship book, it's a life book! It is, in fact, the missing piece to effective and efficient communication."
— **Steve J. Larsen**, marketing strategist

"My marriage and my relationships were good, but I had spent hundreds of thousands of dollars on personal development searching for a way to make them great. It wasn't until I found Stacey and Paul that I discovered this missing piece that changed my marriage, my relationship with my kids and with the people I work with every day. I'll be forever grateful that I invested my time to learn their unique methodology on relationship success."
— **Russell Brunson**, *New York Times* best-selling author

"It's not an accident that *The Missing Piece* book found its way to you. As a collective, we're being called to transform our relationships, save our families, and heal our family patterns. The Martinos' life-changing Relationship Development Methodology will empower you to heal your relationships; elevate your family dynamics; break old, outdated relationship paradigms; and support you to create loving, thriving, rock-solid relationships. Read it, absorb every word, and most importantly, put the proven strategies into action—and watch your relationships transform."
— **Linda Joy**, publisher of *Aspire Magazine* and publisher at Inspired Living Publishing™

"As a retired Navy test pilot, I know firsthand the strain military life can put on a family. After years of service and building my real estate business, my marriage was at a breaking point. The Martinos' Relationship Development Method didn't just help, it transformed our family! With military divorce rates far above the national average, the insights in this book are truly invaluable, especially for families who sacrifice so much for our country. This is The Missing Piece that could save countless relationships and our country!"
— **Bill Allen, CDR USN(ret)**, owner of 7 Figure Flipping

"As soon as Stacey and Paul said they were writing a book, I was champing at the bit to get a copy! After just the first two chapters of The Missing Piece, I was hooked. The stories, tools, and action items are clear. This is a must-read for anyone in a relationship, and they are not kidding when they say that one person can make the change."
— **Alison J. Prince**, entrepreneur, Because I Can

Praise for The Relationship Development® Method from Stacey and Paul Martino's Students

"Relationship Development has transformed me from the inside out! Everyone deserves to have this opportunity. Practical and transformative. This is worthy work!" — **Renee R.**

"Relationship Development is a game changer. The tools shared will affect every (and I mean every) relationship, whether it's spouse, parent/child, business, co-worker, neighbor. Each relationship can be completely directed in a positive, uplifting, and loving way!" — **Bryant V.**

"By the grace of God, I found Relationship Development. With Paul and Stacey's guidance, not only was our marriage saved, but it has become better than it ever was before. Our family is joy filled, connected, and there's a newfound peace in our home. We no longer run to the end of our skill set quickly; we are consistently growing together as a family and learning to navigate whatever comes our way together." — **J.S.**

"Relationship Development has transformed every aspect of my life, from my marriage and parenting to work and family relationships. I can now say that I truly love myself. Life's challenges haven't stopped, yet my happiness level keeps on increasing. This method is something every human being deserves to know." — **A.C.**

"I stumbled across Stacey and Paul Martino while searching for ways to start my divorce. I felt that I was trapped in a marriage that I didn't sign up for, with a husband I couldn't speak to without fighting. Fast-forward a couple of years and I am the happiest I have ever been! I single-handedly transformed my broken marriage using the Relationship Development Method. My husband and I talk every day about the topics that we used to fight about." — **Diana**

"Relationship Development has changed my life for the better. I didn't know there was so much to learn about relationships until I met Stacey and Paul. Everyone needs to learn the Relationship Development skill set and take their relationships to the next level!" — **Hillary**

"Relationship Development has completely transformed my life. I first thought it was going to make my marriage better. What I have actually received has been an absolute gift! The level of peace and joy I get to experience every day is something I never thought was possible. This, from implementing the tools and strategies to become the best and most authentic version of myself possible." — **Amanda**

"Relationship Development is the best thing I've ever learned. First, so I can actually love myself for who I am, and second, so I can lead by example and help my kids learn the same. I will be forever grateful to Stacey and Paul for helping me see things differently!" — **Julie R.**

"The best part of using the Relationship Development Method is that only one person has to learn and implement it to transform their relationships. By using all of the tools and frameworks, I was able to bring peace into my household. Thank you, Stacey and Paul, for breaking down this method into pieces that make sense. I am so grateful to be closer to my husband, and that we are raising our girls together as a team thanks to this work!" — **Stephanie Z.**

"Stacey and Paul Martino are world changers! Relationship Development has taken me to my next level in every area of my life. It fundamentally changed the way I approach life, and now I have total confidence in my ability to skillfully navigate whatever comes next. Despite ongoing challenges, I am the happiest and most at peace that I have ever been. I am eternally grateful to Stacey and Paul for the skills and tools they teach with such incredible talent, wisdom, and sparkly joy! They are among the most important people of our generation, and I most enthusiastically recommend their teachings to anyone looking to uplevel their life and evolve their soul. Thank you, Martinos, for all you do, and most importantly, who you are!" — **D.H.**

"Before joining Relationship Development, my partner and I had been in a comfortable but stagnant relationship for seven years. We were content, but we knew something was missing. Relationship Development has completely transformed our relationship. We went from a 'meh' relationship to experiencing love, excitement, and a shared desire to make the most of our lives together. Bonus: Our daughters are witnessing the positive impact of Relationship Development. They see firsthand what a healthy and fulfilling relationship looks like and the mindset/tools required to get there." — **Hannan**

"I was teetering on the verge of despair and divorce after years of trying everything I could to reconnect with my husband for a more fulfilling and fun marriage . . . yet everything fell flat, so I was exhausted! Something was missing and it felt beyond my grasp! Then I discovered the Martinos and their Relationship Development Methodology, and everything changed for the better! I am so much happier and have a stronger love foundation to role model a healthy marriage and homelife for our son." — **S.K.**

"Before we started the Martinos' Relationship Development, my wife said that if something didn't change soon, she was leaving. Then my kids started encouraging her to leave. She was usually annoyed with me, and we fought all the time. Now our marriage is unshakeable, we have fun together, and we can navigate tough conversations." — **Dave**

"Relationship Development transformed our marriage when political tensions were straining our relationship. By implementing the methods, I shifted how I approached our conversations, especially around politics. Remarkably, this change defused the tension, and my husband, without even knowing about the tools, became more relaxed and happier. As we celebrate 30 years of marriage this year, our relationship, which had been under pressure, is now stronger and more connected. Today, we've moved past the political bickering and rediscovered the deep love and passion that first brought us together." — **L.W.**

"When I remarried after my first husband passed away, I was sure this relationship was going to be easier, smoother. But there we were, 20 years later, as my husband told me he'd had it and was moving out. I was desperate. I thought about couple's counseling, but it didn't work for my first marriage. And I knew my current husband wasn't going to go to counseling. So, I gave Stacey and Paul's program a try. And because of that, our marriage is the best it's ever been and I'm so happy! Here's the miracle—my husband has never participated in the program, isn't interested in hearing about what I've learned—and it still works!" — **M.D.**

"I shudder to think what my life would have looked like without finding Relationship Development. I remember the enormous relief when I read Stacey's words, 'It isn't parenting that you hate, it's Demand Relationship parenting that you hate!' And the magic isn't just in the information she teaches, which is so revolutionary that it sometimes takes some time to accept, but the strategies to live it. Prior to this, I had read so many books and attended so many workshops regarding personal development. And after a few weeks, I struggled to incorporate those amazing principles into my life and just felt like a failure. Since doing Relationship Development, I have solved so many kerfuffles for our family. I've been able to navigate a lot of changes at work and have been promoted three times in my position (when I started I was on the verge of elimination). And best of all, I'm able to create this without pleasing or bulldozing, and I'm continuing to uncover my most authentic self." — **K.A.**

"Relationship Development not only saved my marriage but it also saved me! My marriage was in a shambles. We were fighting what felt like every single day, and I had become a version of myself I knew was not me, not who I wanted to be, and definitely not who my family deserved! Stacey and Paul helped me realize that there was a better way! They helped me to see and understand the dynamics that were unfolding in the fights between my husband and me, and taught me tools to actually solve them! And it worked! I believe every human deserves this knowledge!" — **Sarah**

"The Relationship Development Method enabled me to navigate my divorce with grace and improved communication, while rebuilding a friendship with my husband to enable us to be the amazing co-parenting team that we are today. I am a happier, calmer, stronger, and more empowered version of myself today because of these teachings." — **Debra**

"Math was always my favorite subject. Apply the formula and get a predictable result. Learning Relationship Development was mind-blowing. Our home went from chaos to calm. It teaches you the formulas to get predictable results in your relationships with people!" — **Trista**

"It truly does take only one to shift the relationship dynamics. I came into Stacey and Paul's program as a woman entrepreneur transitioning a family business to the next generation. I was determined not to mess up any of the relationships at stake: either the marriage or adult parenting involved. The simple (but not always easy) Relationship Development tools were presented . . . it was a game changer in all the best ways once that missing piece was engaged." — **Anne**

"When I first met Paul and Stacey, I was living in a sad and angry version of myself. I was yelling at my kids and husband daily and held a high level of resentment toward my parents. After working through the Relationship Development curriculum and applying a few of the many tools available, I was able to see a difference. The levels of stress decreased and the peace in our home increased. I worked through past hurts and learned tools to navigate anything that comes my way. Relationship Development has changed my family tree, and my kids get to experience a kinder and more authentic version of their mom." — **R.M.**

"Before I found Relationship Development, I was exhausted! I questioned if I 'made the wrong choice' in my partner, often asked myself 'how did I get here, feeling unhappy and sad most of the time?' When I discovered the Martinos, I started diving into their programs and pretty much every word they said. I was thinking, Wait. What? How come nobody ever told me this? Implementing the Relationship Development Method has changed my life. I found myself and was no longer unhappy and crying every day. I also discovered I didn't make the wrong choice in my partner! I believe everyone deserves to know this. One of the best decisions I ever made!" — **Jenny**

"I started learning the Relationship Development Method because I felt my husband and I could use a relationship 'tune-up.' I had no idea the complete awakening that I myself would receive and that I would not just 'tune up' but transform myself from the inside out! Thanks to Relationship Development I have a much higher level of happiness and peace within; and all of my relationships have improved, from my marriage, to my kids, my family, friends, and even my clients." — **Trisha**

"Relationship Development has, without exaggeration, changed every area of my life. Rebuilding the friendship with my former husband, so we can co-parent as a team, I got what I needed to build a real relationship with my two grown children to an extent I didn't even know was possible. They live Relationship Development every day! And the best: I got to know myself. I am the happiest I have ever been and it keeps getting better and better! There truly is no limit!" — **Andrea**

"With Relationship Development, I feel calmer and happier than I ever have." — **Lori G.**

"Before I found Relationship Development, my marriage was at an all-time low. I really had no hope that things could get better and had chosen to move out of the house with my kids to start the separation process with my husband. In a few short months of learning about Relationship Development, I moved back home and felt a renewed commitment to my husband. Not only did Relationship Development save my marriage, but we are stronger than ever! I have never been happier; and parenting our children together has gotten so much easier." — **Liz**

"Relationship Development has made my marriage and our relationship so much stronger and better. I joined because we were heading into retirement, and I wanted more than just being with my husband and going through the motions. After implementing, I began to see changes, big and small, and every day gets better; my marriage is now fun, exciting, and passionate, and I love my husband so much. There's so much more than just getting by." — **J.W.**

"Relationship Development has been the most impactful training for dealing with life I have ever gone through. It is tremendously freeing to see how, with the Relationship Development tools, I can shift the course of my relationships with others and self. Relationship Development is the best method out there to improve the quality of your relationships. What you learn there won't be forgotten." — **J.S.**

"Before I found Relationship Development, my relationship with my husband was okay, but we were bickering more, and sex was infrequent. With Relationship Development, I found a new perspective and saw my role in the relationship differently. We celebrate our differences now and kerfuffles are short-lived. And our kids are in their teenage years and still talk and hang out with us!" — **H.B.**

"Relationship Development has changed the way I see life. I'm happier, more compassionate, and live life lighter than ever before. Relationship Development has allowed me to see the gifts/talents in my husband and children, instead of what I previously viewed as negative traits or a problem." — **Lori G.**

"I came to Paul and Stacey and Relationship Development broken and in victim mode. My main focus when I joined was to find someone to share my life with and to have better relationships with my two adult sons. And by using their Relationship Development system, Paul and Stacey helped change my life! Because I not only have achieved those two goals but have created an amazing relationship with myself! And I absolutely couldn't be happier!" — **Lisa**

"Before Relationship Development, my marriage was hanging by a thread. I was miserable and my husband didn't even realize there was a problem. Now our marriage is stronger than it has ever been, and I am once again happy to be married. As we continue to work at implementing the Relationship Development Method, life just keeps getting better." — **Melinda**

"Before Relationship Development, my husband and I were headed for divorce; and I didn't really want that. Thank God for Relationship Development. Paul and Stacey helped us. Not only did I save my marriage, but it's so much better than it ever was before. Our kids are happier; there's more rapport and systems in our home." — **K.M.**

"Relationship Development changed my life . . . my entire life. I discovered my authentic self and deepened every relationship in my world. It has changed how I see others and given me so many tools and skills. And just when I think I have everything I need, Stacey or Paul delivers another tool or strategy, which helps me expand my skill set even more. And the best part is . . . my daughter has become a Relationship Transformer by watching me." — **K.V.**

"Relationship Development has given me my life back. My marriage was hanging by a thread; our family was in much pain. I'm so thankful to Stacey and Paul for teaching me how to implement new tools and develop the skills necessary to ascend my life and relationships." — **Andrea H.**

THE Missing PIECE

A Proven Method to Single-Handedly Transform Your Relationship and Create Harmony in Your Home

STACEY AND PAUL MARTINO
Creators of the Relationship Development® Method

HAY HOUSE
Carlsbad, California • New York City
London • Sydney • New Delhi

Published in The United Kingdom by:
Hay House UK Ltd, 1st Floor, Crawford Corner,
91–93 Baker Street, London W1U 6QQ
Tel: +44 (0)20 3927 7290; www.hayhouse.co.uk

Text © The Missing Piece LLC, 2025

Cover design: Milan Bozic
Interior design: Karim J. Garcia

The moral rights of the authors have been asserted.

All rights reserved. No part of this book may be reproduced by any mechanical, photographic or electronic process, or in the form of a phonographic recording; nor may it be stored in a retrieval system, transmitted or otherwise be copied for public or private use, other than for 'fair use' as brief quotations embodied in articles and reviews, without prior written permission of the publisher.

The information given in this book should not be treated as a substitute for professional medical advice; always consult a medical practitioner. Any use of information in this book is at the reader's discretion and risk. Neither the authors nor the publisher can be held responsible for any loss, claim or damage arising out of the use, or misuse, of the suggestions made, the failure to take medical advice or for any material on third-party websites.

A catalogue record for this book is available from the British Library.

Tradepaper ISBN: 978-1-83782-412-0
E-book ISBN: 978-1-4019-9391-7
Audiobook ISBN: 978-1-4019-9392-4

10 9 8 7 6 5 4 3 2 1

This product uses responsibly sourced papers and/or recycled materials.
For more information, see www.hayhouse.co.uk

The authorized representative in the EU for product safety and compliance is Penguin Random House Ireland, Morrison Chambers, 32 Nassau Street, Dublin D02 YH68, Ireland. https://eu-contact.penguin.ie

Printed and bound by CPI Group (UK) Ltd, Croydon CR0 4YY

To our RelationshipU students,
with our love and eternal gratitude.
Thank you.

CONTENTS

The Introduction xiii

SECTION 1: THE SWITCH
Chapter 1: The Closed Loop 3
Chapter 2: The Power of One 15
Chapter 3: The Death of Demand Relationship™ 21
Chapter 4: The Skill Set That Can Be Learned 37
Chapter 5: The Truth about Blame 45
Chapter 6: The Brick Wall Between Us™ 63
Chapter 7: The Hanging-by-a-Thread Moment 81
Chapter 8: The 5% & the 95% Mind 93
Chapter 9: The Relationship Formula............................... 99

SECTION 2: YOU
Chapter 10: The 50% Line™ 107
Chapter 11: The Leash Around Your Neck......................... 125
Chapter 12: The Perspective Shift 143
Chapter 13: The Difference Between Masculine
              and Feminine Perspectives 157

SECTION 3: YOU RELATE
Chapter 14: The Destroyer of Relationships: Compromise 183
Chapter 15: The Win-Win... 193
Chapter 16: The Path to Creating Alignment, Even
              When You Don't Agree 211
Chapter 17: The Faulty Relationship Math™ 233
Chapter 18: The Rebuilding of Trust.............................. 251
Chapter 19: The Differences in Masculine and
              Feminine Communication 269

SECTION 4: THE RIPPLE
Chapter 20: The Keys to Living It Versus Just Learning It........... 289
Chapter 21: The Tools for Your Next Steps........................ 297
Chapter 22: The Ripple 311

Endnotes... 318
The Acknowledgments 319
About Stacey and Paul Martino 323

A NOTE ABOUT THIS BOOK

Please know that Paul and I do all our content development and creating together. While we made a mutual decision that I be the primary writer and voice of this book for the reader's experience, Paul has collaborated on every topic and edited every word, as he does with everything that we do to serve families through Relationship Development.

All student stories, examples, and scripts contained in this book are dramatizations for teaching purposes and based on a synthesis of student examples over our many years of work.

THE INTRODUCTION

We have cracked the code on relationship.

This is not a theory or a guess. Over 20 years ago, I made a discovery that led to our invention of a new relationship methodology that solves relationship issues without pleasing, without compromise, and without couples therapy.

My husband and I have dedicated the past 14 years to the invention of our Relationship Development® Method and hundreds of tools, skill sets, and solutions in our toolbox. We have helped thousands and thousands of students from all over the world to save and transform their relationships with our method, tools, and solutions. Marriages that looked hopeless and people who were told by multiple "experts" or therapists that divorce was their only option have been saved and transformed using our methodology.

But it's even more than that. Our students didn't just save the same old crappy relationship that was defined by fighting, silences, and distance. They built a new rock-solid, passionate, and harmonious relationship, with the same partner.

In a six-year study of our results, the students in our RelationshipU® program had only a 1% divorce rate!

Those results are unheard-of. And that's because what we are doing is unlike anything else.

What you hold in your hands is The Missing Piece. In this book, we'll reveal the invisible problems we discovered and the solution we invented for having a harmonious and thriving long-term relationship.

WHO THIS BOOK IS FOR

This book is for the person who wants real answers, solutions, and a proven methodology to transform their relationship and bring harmony back to their home, without compromise, without pleasing, and without needing to convince their partner to do this with them.

Does that sound impossible? It's not only possible, it's proven; we have already done this (thousands of times).

It pains me to see so many people suffering today unnecessarily. Maybe you can relate to some of these very common challenges that people come to us to solve.

- They feel that the upsets, arguments, and silences are happening too often. It used to just be occasionally, or even once a month, and now it seems like it's happening all the time, even over little things.

- They feel alone in their own relationship, even when their partner is sitting right next to them.

- When they can't see eye-to-eye with their partner, they worry that they are just too different to be together.

- They feel like the things on the "we can't talk about that" list is stacking up too high.

- Even when they show up with the best of intentions and do everything they can, it is disheartening to feel like it's still not enough to make their partner happy (let alone be happy themselves).

- Since the passion fizzled in their relationship, they feel more like roommates living under the same roof, living parallel lives but not *together*.

- What keeps them up at night is what this is doing to their kids. As much as they try to keep it from them, they know they are listening at the top of the stairs.

- They worry that some of their kids' current challenges are a result of the stress in the household.

- Sometimes it seems like their kids pick up on the silence just as much as the arguments, and it breaks their heart not to have the harmonious household they dreamed of for them.

- Sometimes they think it will just be easier for everyone if they got a divorce, but then they fear what that will be like for their kids bouncing between two homes.

- They worry that if they can't resolve their parenting disagreements now, once their kids are out of their house, they will have even less control over how they are parented.

- They start having fears about who will be in the other house with them when they're not there. What about when their partner starts dating, and someone they don't know sleeps in the house with their kids?

If any of that resonates with you, please know that you are not alone. And you are in exactly the right place, reading this book.

Our methodology has solved each of these dynamics. This book is going to reveal the piece that has been missing the whole time and give you the answers you desire for your marriage, your family, and yourself.

IT'S NOT YOUR FAULT

There's nothing wrong with you, your partner, or your kids. There's just been a massive piece missing from what you knew about human relationships. This book will give you that Missing Piece.

As you read this book, please remember my words to you: "You did the best that you could with the skills that you had." None of this is your fault.

THE 5 PHASES OF RELATIONSHIP

This book is for anyone who finds themselves in one of these 5 phases of relationship:

1. Separated, living apart, or hanging by a thread, where one or both partners have thought about ending the relationship. You want either a last-ditch effort to save the relationship or to at least feel like you did all that you could.
2. Passionless and needing to reignite the passion.
3. In a good or even great relationship and you want to do everything you can to grow it, protect it, and feel like you have "divorce-proofed" it.
4. Not currently in a relationship and want to be ready for your forever love.
5. Divorced or heading for divorce and need to heal the relationship with the co-parent so you can have a peaceful and harmonious family for your children, even when you are no longer married.

THE RESULTS OF OUR METHOD

Regardless of the phase that you find yourself in today, our methodology has already helped people and can help you to:

- Save your marriage without couples work
- Create a rock-solid relationship where nothing can come between you
- Reduce and eliminate kerfuffles

- Solve the challenges that have been there for years or decades, even the stuff on the "we don't talk about that" list
- Empower you to bring harmony back to your home
- Create the win-win, so you can both be on the same page
- Heal the disappointments and betrayals that you haven't been able to get past so you can be free of them
- Understand your partner's wiring and how they are wired differently
- Get your needs met in your relationship in ways you could not before
- Feel fully supported as a team
- Navigate any conversation without fighting
- Create alignment, even when you disagree
- Solve the arguments and disagreements without yelling or silence
- Reignite the passion or create passion that you never had together
- Bring the fun and playfulness back
- Gain your calm and confident energy when interacting with others
- Feel ready and skilled to navigate whatever comes your way
- Be the parent each of your children needs you to be
- Create the marriage and the family that you always dreamed of

I understand that you may be thinking, *That's great, Stacey, but you don't know what I'm dealing with over here.*

I have compassion for what you are navigating. I do. And just to give you some perspective, while not an exhaustive list, we have successfully helped people who were dealing with these challenges:

- Separated, living apart, or getting divorced
- Recovering from infidelity
- Navigating the stress of being a first responder or military family
- Different opinions on parenting, money, budgets, religion, health, education, household, where to live, how to spend time, sex, work, family of origin, who does what around the house, and so on
- Medical challenges adding stress
- Having young kids, 10+ kids, no kids, or kids with special needs
- Navigating a partner recovering from addiction
- Dealing with narcissism
- Parenting challenges, getting kids to do what needs to be done without fighting, sibling issues
- Job stress, loss of work, financial stress, or bankruptcy
- Extended family drama
- Blending families and navigating issues with kids, former spouses, and new partners
- A spouse that doesn't support your business or work
- Workplace drama or work relationship kerfuffles

And so much more!

WHAT PEOPLE THINK RELATIONSHIP WORK IS VERSUS WHAT WE ARE DOING

Most people think that "relationship work" is going to suck. I'm aware that you've probably seen the old broken relationship approaches that force one partner to compromise or tell someone to just "let it go."

The old idea of just "staying together in misery" is not what this book, or our method, is about. And I will never tell you that you should stay married. If you want to get divorced, go right ahead. That doesn't change what I'm about to show you in this book.

Whether you decide to transform your marriage and delight in an unshakeable love and unleashed passion together, or you decide to transform your relationship and transition it to a thriving, harmonious co-parenting relationship, that choice is yours to make.

Our Relationship Development Method is used to accomplish both outcomes.

This book will show you that:

- Relationship is a skill set, and it can be learned.
- It only takes *one person* to implement the skill set to create the transformation desired in the relationship.
- Our Relationship Development Method is that skill set.

Relationship Development is a whole new approach to solving the normal and predictable relationship kerfuffles found in long-term relationships. You will not only be empowered to solve the kerfuffles but also can do so in a way that allows you to be the happiest and most authentic version of yourself, without compromise, without pleasing, and without trying to just be okay with something you are not okay with.

WHO THIS BOOK IS NOT FOR

Yes, we have helped people get all those results, given all those circumstances. Still, our methodology is not for everyone.

Relationship Development is a skill set–based method for solving relationship issues. It is not the answer for everything.

Here are a few things that our methodology is not a solution for:

1. **Physical abuse:** Relationship Development is NOT a solution for physical violence. It shocks me that people still think that physical abuse is a relationship issue. That's archaic. Physical abuse is not a marriage or relationship issue. Physical abuse is a violence issue and requires a solution designed to stop violence. If there is physical abuse going on in any relationship, please seek professional help immediately.

2. **Addiction issues:** Relationship Development is not a solution for solving addiction or issues with substances. This method cannot help you to change your own relationship with substances or help another to do so. However, if you are in a relationship with someone who is going through challenges with substances, or recovering from that challenge, the Relationship Development Methodology will give you the skill sets you need to navigate those relationships more successfully.

3. **Couples work:** In Relationship Development, we do not do any couples work, and we never will. If you love couples work, or you are otherwise determined on requiring couples work to be part of your path forward, then Relationship Development is not for you.

4. **Three or more intimate partners:** Relationship Development is only a solution for a two-person relationship. If you have decided to have a polyamorous relationship, Relationship Development is not a solution that will work for you. Note: I'm not speaking about dating or infidelity. Both of those are journeys that our Relationship Development Methodology has been used to navigate successfully.

5. **Therapy or counseling:** As you will discover in this book, the issues you have been experiencing in your relationships are primarily caused by a lack of skill sets, solutions, and The Missing Piece. As such, we believe that marriage is not a mental health issue, despite the outdated and common practice of people seeking mental health practitioners to solve relationship issues.

   Relationship Development is a skill set–based methodology that uses the development of your relationship skill set to solve relationship issues. We are not therapists, counselors, or psychiatrists. Relationship Development is not therapy, counseling, or mental health work. If what you want is therapy or counseling, then Relationship Development is not for you.

IT ONLY TAKES ONE PERSON

To the best of our knowledge, there has never been a book published promising a one-person relationship method before. Relationship Development is designed for one person to get the training and implement the skill sets to create the transformation.

Just because only one person needs the training to create the transformation in the relationship doesn't mean that your partner will not change. They will change, of course, but authentically and in response to you.

This book will also reveal why couples work is destructive to relationships. Until you are further into this book and understand the dynamics, please resist the urge to try to get your partner to read it "with you."

You do not need your partner to participate in this process for you to get the results you want to see in your relationship.

FAMILIES ARE FALLING APART WITHOUT THE MISSING PIECE

Relationships today are suffering. Some statistics show that the current divorce rate in the United States is about 50% for first marriages, 60–67% for second marriages, and 73–74% for third marriages and beyond.[1] The average marriage today in the United States lasts just eight years.[2]

It's gotten so bad that people are giving up on love relationships as a "thing," labeling them as being *just too hard* or deciding it is *impossible*! Although trying to escape one of our most fundamental human needs (love) was never really a viable option, it's an understandable overreaction to people hitting a new low and giving up on fixing their relationships.

In 2023, U.S. Surgeon General Dr. Vivek Murthy issued an advisory calling attention to the public health crisis of loneliness, isolation, and the lack of connection in our country. Among other negative symptoms, he said that loneliness and isolation increased the risk for developing mental health challenges, and that lack of connection increased the risk for premature death to levels comparable to smoking 15 cigarettes a day![3]

Currently, the financial, emotional, health, workplace, and societal costs resulting from relationship failures leading to loneliness are nothing less than enormous. Over the years, various studies and articles have claimed that billions of dollars are spent on divorce each year, in the United States alone.

Even the World Health Organization (WHO) has declared *loneliness* to be a pressing global health threat.[4]

The Introduction

Humans need love, connection, and thriving relationships that last. So do the children that we are raising inside these relationships. We cannot give up on relationships.

I am so happy to tell you that we have cracked the code on relationships, solving this widespread and far-reaching issue.

I'm even more thrilled to tell you that the book you hold in your hands will start leading you out of the fog and confusion that has been bringing others to the point of desperation.

It is possible to have loving, thriving, and lasting love relationships. This book will show you that I'm not guessing. This is not a theory; we've already done it, many times, in real life, for many years.

Using our Relationship Development Method, we have demonstrated that marriages can be saved, transformed, and built to be rock solid. Kerfuffles can be solved in a way that allows both people to be authentically happy and happy together.

Relationship issues can be healed, no matter what has transpired, and families can break the chains of relationship breakdown that have been handed down to us.

Every new generation creates challenges that did not exist before. And each generation also solves issues that were seen as unsolvable before. Everything seems unsolvable until somebody discovers the breakthrough that changes everything. New innovations and breakthroughs do not happen often, but they do indeed happen.

The Missing Piece that was preventing human relationships from evolving and thriving is here.

The old and broken relationship paradigm that I accidentally discovered, combined with our invention of the new paradigm and the Relationship Development Method that Paul and I created, is The Missing Piece to turn this all around.

It's The Missing Piece for successfully relating to other humans in the world who have genuine and legitimate differences in perspective than you do. It's The Missing Piece for your treasured relationships that you hold dear. It's even The Missing Piece for your relationship with yourself.

At a time when technological developments have been outpacing our relationship development, we have a problem. This human relationship breakthrough could not have come at a more critical time.

By reading this book, you are taking the first step toward having the power to choose what your future looks like. You will either perpetuate the old ways and head down the path of upsets, breakdown, and loneliness, or change the trajectory of your family's legacy with Relationship Development.

A RAY OF HOPE

I am both filled with compassion for what you are navigating today and giddy with excitement for the potential in front of you.

As I write this book for you, these are not just words. There are families, all over the world, that are together today. Laughing today. Loving today. Because we showed them our Relationship Development Method, and they single-handedly transformed their relationships and brought harmony back to their home.

Unlike what we have been led to believe, the truth is magnificent relationships are not found; they are created. I wrote this book so that you can start building, because it is so worth it. You are worth it. Your family is worth it.

My dear friend Blue Melnick once asked me, "What will your life be like one year from now, if nothing changes? What *could* it be like if *everything* changes?" You hold The Missing Piece to that opportunity in your hands right now.

While heartbreak may occasionally be part of the human journey, it is my deepest hope that no human ever sits in the agony of a relationship breakdown without knowing that there is a solution, a way forward, and a path into the light.

We are always here for you on this journey.

I don't want you to face one more day without The Missing Piece. (Turn the page.)

SECTION 1

THE SWITCH

CHAPTER 1

THE CLOSED LOOP

When I was 26 years old, I bought my first fixer-upper home. One of the reasons was so that I could move out of my apartment and finally realize my dream of getting a dog. I got a boxer puppy that I named Putty, after the character on the TV show *Seinfeld*. Within a few months, my puppy was already 55 pounds, stood over 6 feet tall on her hind legs, and was hyper, jumpy, and full of energy.

Putty would pull me around the neighborhood and knock people over when she jumped on them. People asked me if maybe she was "too much dog" for me, but the thought of giving her up broke my heart. I was already completely in love with this dog.

So, I watched Cesar Milan, the Dog Whisperer, on TV. I wanted to be able to get Putty to respond calmly, the way Cesar was able to do with "out of control" dogs on his show. Seeing Cesar do it, I knew it was possible, and yet I couldn't get Putty to behave. Was she the *one* dog that was going to be hopeless? I couldn't accept that, so I called a local dog trainer to come help me train her.

The following Saturday morning, we went outside to wait for the trainer. Putty was running around the yard, and I struggled to get her back on the leash. *This better work*, I thought to myself. That's when I heard the dog trainer's giant black pickup truck pulling into the driveway, and so did Putty. Now she was pulling and jumping and freaking out.

This guy stepped out of his truck, and I immediately apologized as Putty started to lunge toward him and jump. To my complete surprise, the trainer stayed right where he was and made a sound, and then I watched as Putty instantly sat down on the driveway in front of him!

What kind of voodoo is this? I thought.

"How'd you get her to do that?" I blurted out. As if on cue, Putty started jumping and pulling on me again.

He looked at me and said, "She already knows how to sit, and she knows how to 'not jump.' I didn't come here to train your dog; I came here to train *you*."

"Holy shit! This just got serious," I laughed. "Teach me, Obi-Wan."

He smiled and took the leash from me. He looked at Putty and told her to sit, and she sat down next to his feet.

"What were you two doing before I got here?" he asked me.

"She was running around the yard. I was hoping she would get some of her energy out before you arrived," I said.

"What about before that?" he asked.

"Before that?" I replied. "Um, nothing, really. We were in the kitchen, I guess."

"Think about it," he said. "Before you came out the door, can you remember where you were standing? Did you put the leash on her in the house? What were you saying to her? Can you show me exactly the way you did it?"

I made a face because I was a little embarrassed. He nodded as if to encourage me to say it anyway.

In my best "mommy talking to a baby" voice, I recreated that moment. Here's how it went:

"Where's my big girl? Where is she? Putty . . . Putty, come on girl! Let's go!" (I said this in my excited, high-pitched voice.)

"Guess who's coming over? Guess? Can you guess? The doggie trainer is coming! Yes, he is. Yes, he is. And he's gonna teach you how to sit and how to walk on the leash like a good girl! You wanna be a good girl, right? Do you wanna meet him? Do you wanna? Do you wanna? Okay, let's go!"

The trainer was smiling. I was super embarrassed, of course.

"Don't sweat it. I already knew it," he said. "Stacey, you took her level of excitement from a level 0 to a level 12 out of 10 in about 60 seconds. Then, you bring her out here, and she's ready to tear the world in two, and then you wonder why she can't just behave, sit, and be calm?"

I started laughing. Damn, this guy was good.

"Putty is a dog," he continued. "She's not a human. She operates the way canines operate. Not the way you operate. She responds to your energy more than your words. So when you take your excitement all the way up, she's going to react to that energy level."

"And when you get upset that she's not listening and you tell her to 'stop it,' 'sit down' or 'don't pull,' but you are yelling and your energy is high, she's still going to react to that increase in energy.

"When I approach her, I am calm. I don't *need* her to listen. I *expect* her to listen, and I'm in charge. And she feels it. Now she understands I'm the leader, and she knows that makes her the follower. And she responds as such. This is how the canine species interacts.

"*She* doesn't need training. She already knows how to react like a dog. *You* needed training for how to get those responses from her. That's all."

He was spot-on right. I was interacting with Putty for how I was wired, not for how she was wired.

I had the best of intentions, but I just had no idea she was wired differently. I had dogs my whole life, as a kid, but no one ever taught me that before.

So, I learned from the trainer how to interact with Putty for how *she* is wired. I kept working with that trainer until I could lead Putty effortlessly.

Within a few weeks, she was walking calmly on the leash. Within a few months, she didn't need a leash at all. Eventually, you could drop a steak on the floor and she wouldn't touch it until I gave her "the nod."

I took her everywhere with me. We were always together. She was an amazing girl and, eventually, the best big sister to our children.

Putty did not need the trainer to teach her anything. I needed the training. And she changed in response to the change within me. And that happens because relationship is a Closed Loop.

> **PRINCIPLE:**
> Relationship is a Closed Loop.

In an inter-action between people, what we put into the Loop (our actions, energy, and language) causes a RE-action to come out of the Loop, back to us.

For instance, if you were talking to someone about something important and they just rolled their eyes at you, would that cause a "reaction" in you?

Yeah, I bet it would.

What if, in that same situation, you were talking to someone about something important and they looked directly at you, nodded their head, and genuinely said, "I'm tracking with you. Yep, I got that." Would you feel and respond differently to that interaction versus the eye roll response? Sure you would.

> **PRINCIPLE:**
> When you change what you put into the Loop, you change what you get out.

Triggers are what go into the Loop.
Boomerangs are what come out of the Loop.

Read that again and take that in. It's both simple and life-changing at the same time.

When someone puts an "eye roll" into the Loop, it creates a reaction from you that boomerangs back to them. When someone puts "understanding and listening" into the Loop, it creates a different reaction from you that boomerangs back to them.

Just like in my example with our dog Putty: I was putting an "excitement energy" Trigger into the Loop and getting a "hyper dog" Boomerang back out from the Loop.

Trigger: excitement energy → Boomerang: a hyper dog

The dog trainer changed what he put into the Loop and got a different output from the Loop.

Trigger: calm, confident energy → Boomerang: a calm and responsive dog

THE CLOSED LOOP

All relationships are a Closed Loop, a Predictable Pattern with a Predictable Outcome.

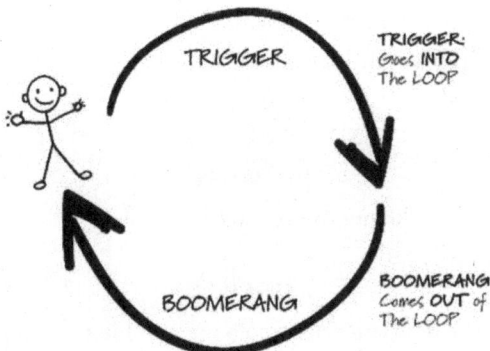

Cesar Milan has been teaching this principle with dogs for decades. I was experiencing the Boomerang of the Loop the whole time. I just didn't know it. I couldn't see the Loop because it was invisible to me. I was missing a piece of the puzzle.

> **PRINCIPLE:**
> Once you have visibility of the Loop, you can choose the output you want by selecting the coordinating input.

Once I got visibility and learned the Loop, then I could choose what I put into the Loop (Trigger) for the output I wanted back (Boomerang).

If I want a calm and responsive dog as the Boomerang out of the Loop, then I know what Trigger to put into the Loop to create that (my calm and confident energy).

What if I said to you, "Well, I don't like that. I'm an excitable girl, and I should be able to be excited around this dog and she should stay calm and listen to me anyway. She's just a bad dog."

Knowing what you know now, what would you say to me? Maybe something like . . .

"She's not a bad dog. She's just being a dog." *or*

"Look, whether you like it or not, it's a fact that's not going to change." *or*

"You can't expect this poor dog to react in a way that she is not wired for simply because *you* refuse to change."

Any of those resonate for you?

The same is true in human dynamics:

> **PRINCIPLE:**
> Relationship is a Closed Loop.
>
> **PRINCIPLE:**
> Predictable patterns create predictable outcomes.
>
> **PRINCIPLE:**
> There are Predictable Pattern Loops that are currently invisible to you based on how humans are wired.

When you change what you put into the Loop, you change what comes out of the Loop. I'll give you an example.

Can you think of a time that your spouse or a family member asked you to do something that you didn't want to do? Maybe they kept pushing or guilting you into doing it. And eventually, you gave in and ended up doing something for them that you really did not want to do, but you decided to do it anyway just to make them happy. Can you think of a situation like that? (I can practically hear you saying, "Which one?")

So, how'd that feel? Not great, right? This dynamic has two common predictable outcomes:

Predictable Outcome #1: They're not happy anyway (it's never good enough) *or*

Predictable Outcome #2: The other person is happy they got their way, and you are unhappy because either (1) they are not grateful, nice, or appreciative of your effort, or (2) when you need something, they don't give back to you.

Typically, when this pattern happens, we end up feeling resentful. Resentment is the feeling that happens when you do something you don't want to do just to make someone else happy, and it still doesn't end happy.

Here's the Predictable Pattern Loop:

Trigger: pleasing → Boomerang: resentment

When you put "pleasing" into the Loop, the Boomerang is resentment. This is a predictable pattern, with predictable results. It's just been invisible to you until now. So, you keep putting "pleasing" into the Loop, thinking or hoping that it will just be better to give them what they want, and you end up feeling resentful later. But because the Loop has been invisible, you don't see the pleasing Trigger going into the Loop. You just feel the resentment Boomerang, and you don't like it.

Maybe you blame the other person by thinking, *There's just no pleasing you.* Or perhaps you decide to give up on interactions with them, thinking, *I don't know why I bother* or *Nothing I do is good enough, so I'm just gonna do what I want anyway.* Those are all very common and understandable reactions to the Boomerang when you can't see the Trigger and the Loop.

Now that you know that the Trigger of pleasing causes the Boomerang of resentment, you can choose whether you want to put pleasing into the Loop next time.

It's not your fault. No one has ever taught us these Predictable Pattern Loops before now. For most humans, the Loop is invisible.

> **PRINCIPLE:**
> When the Loop is invisible, all we experience is the unwanted Boomerang, and it looks, to us, like their reaction is coming "out of nowhere."

BOOMERANG

You've had the experience of being unhappy with someone. You know what it feels like when you don't like what they are doing or saying and you wish they would just stop or do/say it differently.

What most humans do when this happens is what I call "fighting with the Boomerang."

You try to get the other person to change.

You might ask them to change ("Can you not talk to me like that?").

You might beg them to change ("I've asked you not to talk to me that way, please.").

You might yell at them to change ("Don't talk to me like that!").

You may even threaten them to change ("If you talk like that to me one more time . . . ").

All that is fighting with the Boomerang that was already in motion back to you. You are trying to get them to change the output from the Predictable Pattern Loop. Fighting the Boomerang already in motion to you is ineffective at best but often even creates a new fight between you and the other person.

This is what is happening in relationships across the world right now. People are using all kinds of tactics to "try to get their partner to" change. They are obsessed with how to get their partner to change. To stop doing this and do that instead. And their kids, and their family and the people at work, and their friends, and on and on.

How do I get them to stop X and how do I get them to do Y instead?

> **PRINCIPLE:**
> People are not acting toward you; they are *re*acting toward you.

People are reacting to the Trigger you unknowingly put into the Loop. Even after you are fighting with the Boomerang, you keep shoving the same Trigger into the Loop, unknowingly, and generating the same unwanted Boomerang over and over.

It's not your fault. You are not a bad person.

I was doing the same thing, and so were the thousands of students I've trained. No one ever told us any of this stuff before.

I'm here now. And we have solved this. Over the last decade plus, Paul and I have discovered and mapped out hundreds of these Predictable Pattern Loops.

The great news is, this has nothing to do with you or your partner's personality or history. These are Predictable Pattern Loops that humans operate by.

> **PRINCIPLE:**
> It's only a Predictable Pattern Loop if it applies as a principle, impacting most humans.

Please don't confuse these to be a "you and your partner" list of Loops. These are not about the two of you. These are human dynamics. So then, what do we do now?

WHAT DO WE DO?

#1: Get visibility: Get visibility into the Predictable Pattern Loops so that you can see the Predictable Patterns with Predictable Outcomes.

#2: Get the skill sets: Get the skills and training on the Trigger and Boomerang patterns.

#3: Implement: Choose what you put into the Loop for the Boomerang that you want.

STOP putting Triggers into the Loop that create unwanted Boomerangs.

START putting Triggers into the Loop that create the wanted Boomerangs.

This book will begin to map this out for you. We are going to start giving you visibility into the Loops we have discovered and give you our tools, strategies, and skill sets to implement so you get the result you want.

You are not alone. This dynamic is happening in all human relationships. Humans today are unnecessarily suffering because these Predictable Pattern Loops have been invisible to us until now.

IT ONLY TAKES ONE

This is why we say that it only takes one person to transform a relationship.

Relationship is a Closed Loop.

When you gain visibility of the Loops and learn the Trigger/Boomerang patterns, then you can change what Trigger you put into the Loop to change the Boomerang that comes back.

It only takes one person to change what goes into the Loop, which changes the Boomerang.

Relationship is a skill set.

It only takes one person to learn this and implement the skill sets to get the results you desire for your relationship.

You actually do not need your partner's agreement for this to work.

ALL HUMANS CHANGE

All humans change. Not because you told them to. They change when *they* want to. In relationship, humans change in response to you changing what you put into the Loop, both for the positive and the negative. That's not my opinion; that's a fact.

If you continue to unknowingly put Triggers into the Loop that create predictable Boomerangs, it would be ineffective at best to try to get the other person to change their reaction to you. More on that next.

This is not only how I saved my own relationship but also how thousands of people around the world have transformed their relationships with our method and training. And you can do it too. You must start by gaining visibility of the Predictable Pattern Loops and learning the Trigger/Boomerang patterns.

We've covered three Loop examples already:

Trigger: Excitement Energy → Boomerang: Hyper dog
Trigger: Calm & Confident Energy → Boomerang: Calm and responsive dog
Trigger: Pleasing → Boomerang: Resentment

Once you know these Loops, it's now your choice what to put into the Loop.

This entire book will give you visibility into many Trigger and Boomerang Loops. Every chapter will reveal yet another predictable pattern with a predictable outcome, so that you can choose your actions for the reaction you want.

By now, you might have had thoughts, like, *But what about the other person? What if they won't read this book? What if they won't get this training? What if they won't do this too?* Haha!

Luckily for you, everything I'm about to teach you can give you the results you want in your relationships, without you having to convince them to get on board and do this too. I promise you, our dog Putty never read this book either.

I know, it's so hard for people to believe it when we say that it only takes one person to transform a relationship. (Turn the page.)

CHAPTER 2

THE POWER OF ONE

I refer to the 1990s as my Ice Princess days. One night back then, I was leaving the accounting office I worked at after having a heated argument with my manager about what I felt was a very stupid decision he was making that was going to leave me dealing with the consequences. While I was driving home, I was reenacting the argument in my mind the way I wish it had gone down in the office. Saying all the things I didn't say and showing him what a clearly stupid move this would be. I said things I couldn't say in the office or I'd get fired. In my car, I could say whatever the hell I wanted! In my car, I had the floor. Maybe you've had a similar experience of replaying an argument in your mind?

So, I was having this imaginary argument, and of course, I was winning this time, but I was also really riled up about it.

On my drive home, I stopped to pick up a sandwich that I had ordered before having the argument with my manager. I had called in my typical order for a chicken cheesesteak, no cheese, which I had ordered countless times before. At the time, I was living near Philadelphia, and if you're not from around there, let me tell you: Philly does cheesesteaks like nowhere else.

Now, something else you may not know is that when you order a cheesesteak without cheese (anywhere near Philly), you gotta check the sandwich because even though you tell them not to put cheese on it, it's like you're fighting with their life's purpose to make sure there actually *is* cheese on the sandwich.

This time, however, I was so riled up from my argument, I walked out of there with my sandwich and totally forgot to check it. Of course, I get home and what's on my sandwich? Yeah, *cheese* . . . all over it!

So, I call the place and tell them, and they're like, "Oh, so sorry, yeah come on back in, and we'll make you a new sandwich."

Now, I was already in quite a *mood*, so I said to the guy, "Look, I already did my part of this transaction. I came to your place. You made it wrong. You bring ME a new sandwich!"

Keep in mind, this was in the 1990s, and there was no delivery or apps or anything like that. In fact, to paint you a clearer picture, I was having this conversation from a phone that was hanging on my kitchen wall.

So, he laughed and said, "Look, I don't know what to tell you, lady, but we don't do that. I'll make you another sandwich. Just come in and pick it up."

Knowing the futility of my request, I said, "Fine!" and hung up the phone to drive back over there.

When I walked into the place, I guess they could tell by my fiery expression, that it was me. The guy behind the counter looked up and said, "Stacey, right? I'm making your sandwich right now."

I replied, "Fine" as I was standing there, holding their crappy, cheese-covered sandwich in my hand. It was at that moment he said something to me that set this entire interaction in a new direction.

He said, "Your sandwich is almost done, and hey, you can keep that other one, on the house."

At this point, my frustration started to bubble up because he clearly *still* doesn't understand that I cannot eat the sandwich with the cheese on it.

In my desire to both reinforce my point of view and also to "return" his sandwich to him, those two things must have gotten jumbled for me in a way that I am not proud of.

As I said the words, "This sandwich is *useless* to me," the sandwich left my hand and flew directly toward his head. (I know!)

Luckily for me, he caught the sandwich just before it reached his face, and he laughed. Not laughing at me, though. Just laughing because of what had just happened. In a surprisingly understanding tone, he said to me, "Stacey, I get it. It's my bad.

You ordered the sandwich without cheese, and we put cheese on it. That's on me, and I'm sorry. I'm making you a new sandwich right now, the way you ordered it, without cheese. And I know you can't eat this sandwich," putting the old sandwich safely on the countertop.

He continued to say, "Stacey, my name is Anthony, and this is my restaurant. I want to assure you that from now on, I'm personally going to make your sandwich, *every* time, to ensure that it's right. Okay?"

Now, what do you think I did in that moment?

That's right, I apologized. I said, "Oh my God. I'm so sorry. I totally overreacted, and you didn't deserve that. It's not about you at all. I just had a horrible argument at work, and I'm upset about that. I really apologize. You guys are just doing your job. I'm sorry I behaved so terribly."

LET'S LOOK AT WHAT HAPPENED

As horribly as I was behaving, this guy would have had every right to say, "Look, bitch, take your $8 and get the F outta my shop." And he would have been completely justified to tell me to take a hike.

But he didn't do that. Instead, he took personal responsibility, apologized to me, and was gracious about the whole thing.

And what did that do to me? It triggered a response in me. His graciousness caused me to react differently. In a split second, his choice to respond to me that way created a 180-degree authentic shift in me, allowing me to come out of my fog and apologize for my horrible behavior.

Have you ever had that experience? Where you were being totally ugly in the moment and someone showed you grace anyway? Did it change you in that moment? It did for me. Anthony's reaction caused me to go from a level 10 bitch-o-rama to a calm and very apologetic person in seconds.

Even though I was stuck in negativity, still, one person was able to show up differently, and that changed the entire dynamic, the moment, *and* the relationship between the two of us. It only takes one person.

> **PRINCIPLE:**
> It only takes one person to transform a relationship.

As a result of one person becoming the leader, in a moment, both of our destinies were changed.

That is the *power of one*.

That day turned out to be the beginning of a 30-year friendship between me and Anthony, and that never would have happened without his leadership.

When Paul and I started dating, we ate at Anthony's restaurant, Café Antonio's, every Sunday night. Anthony made our kids their first slice of pizza when they were old enough. We watched his girls grow up, and he was there through our children's lives. We've shared important moments in our lives together over the years, including birthdays, anniversaries, and important occasions.

All because, in the heat of a moment, Anthony made the decision to show grace and compassion to a crazy woman who was throwing a sandwich. Now, granted, with a big Italian family and his three daughters, this is probably not the first sandwich-to-the-head that he's ever caught, but he could just as easily gone in a different direction and told me to F-off.

Anthony was making a choice in that moment. His choice changed me. His choice led both of us out of that moment. His choice changed the trajectory of our lives.

Even though it all began in a moment of kerfuffle, it wasn't the circumstances that determined the outcome. It was how he showed up in that moment that set our destiny.

He made a choice to relate to me in a way that built up our relationship instead of breaking it down.

It only takes one person to transform any relationship.

Every human has that same choice. In every moment, you can say to yourself, "I'm going to be the Anthony of this moment."

You already know this, but, just to say it out loud, I didn't deserve his grace in that moment. He could have easily stayed stuck in blame, and anyone would have supported him in that decision. I know it and you know it. But he gave me grace anyway.

How many times in our lives do we stop ourselves from using the tools we've learned, or bringing the compassion needed into a moment, because we've decided the other person doesn't *deserve* it?

That's why I always say that as long as you are stuck in blame, you won't reach for any of our tools, no matter how good they are. When we are stuck in blame, we stop ourselves. Everyone does.

And yet, you can *always* be the Anthony of your moment. We can always choose to respond instead of react. We can choose to build up our relationships instead of breaking them down. It's a choice.

THE SPACE WITHIN THE MOMENT™

It doesn't always feel like we have a choice because we react so fast, right? Like when that person is rude to you, and you react. It feels like, "What choice did I have? They were so rude." It only feels like there's no choice because we have conditioned our reactions and repeated them so many times that they are automatic.

But we do have a choice. There is something Paul and I call The Space Within the Moment. It's the space between the stimulus and your reaction to it, where your nervous system perceives what happens, runs it through your blueprint, and comes out with a program for your reaction.

You run these patterns so many times that, like tying your shoes, you do it automatically and instantly. But what we once wired into our blueprint, we can also unwire and rewire.

The key is to maximize the Space Within the Moment so you have even more time to respond instead of react.

Today, I invite you to be the Anthony of your moment. The tools in our method that we will share in the chapters of this book are designed to help you maximize the Space Within the Moment so you can choose the response that builds up your relationships.

THE Missing PIECE

It's a choice.

Both of you do not need to get this training. Both of you do not need to read this book. You do not need to convince anyone else on the planet to cooperate with you for your experience of your relationships to get better.

You get to choose what you put into the Loop.

You get to choose to be the Anthony of your moment.

You get to choose the results you want to experience.

And it only takes one person. That is the power of one.

So, perhaps by now you are starting to see that this is possible. But how? How is this possible? How are so many of our students doing this? (Turn the page.)

CHAPTER 3

THE DEATH OF DEMAND RELATIONSHIP™

None of this is your fault.

We were handed a broken dynamic by generations before us. To be fair, it wasn't really their fault either. Look at where they came from and what was done to, and modeled for, them.

It cannot be your fault that you didn't know any of this; no one did. No one got an accurate relationship education with the skill sets to inter-operate with other humans in today's world. Including your partner. Even I didn't set out to discover this; it happened by accident.

Once we started helping students, the patterns started to surface. I initially couldn't see it when we were just helping a few dozen students. But once it was hundreds of students and then thousands of students . . . the patterns became clear to me (like in *The Matrix* movie). What I discovered was that there was an actual relationship paradigm that had been handed to us. A paradigm that most humans operated by and were interacting through. This paradigm was outdated, broken, and only worked in an older time when there were different "rules" for how humans behaved.

The old and broken paradigm that was handed down to us is what Paul and I eventually named Demand Relationship™.

Let me explain. Demand Relationship is essentially where a person tries to get someone, or something, else to change in order for them to be able to be happy or be at peace.

Some examples of Demand Relationship are things like telling someone the following:

- "Don't use that tone with me."
- "You can't leave your crap on the counter like that; you need to change that."
- "Don't you want to make Mommy happy and finish your dinner?"

Demand Relationship is where you please, plot, push, demand, or command that someone else do or say things differently for the way *you* want it done or the way that it would feel "right" for *you*. It's where you try to use tactics to get things to change so that you can be happier, more comfortable, or calm.

What you are about to see is that this Demand Relationship paradigm has been the primary relationship paradigm for as long as humans have been on this planet.

Up until the mid-1900s, Demand Relationship "worked" in relationships. When one person doesn't feel free to go, feels powerless to speak up for their needs, or feels they have no choice but to obey or otherwise submit to another, Demand Relationship thrives.

For example, before women had equal rights, they learned to do what they were told and please the man who was in charge (father or husband). If you are not of an age where you remember this time, you can watch shows like *Downton Abbey* and see how things were, not too long ago.

This was not only true for women. It was (and is) unfortunately true for many humans who did not feel they had the power to assert themselves.

It is a predictable pattern with a predictable outcome.

THE 2 ROLES OF DEMAND RELATIONSHIP

There are two roles in the Demand Relationship paradigm. We call them the Power Player™ and the Non-Power Player™. The Power Player is the one who can use leverage to get their way. They may be the one "in charge" and they use tactics like commands, criticism, blame, withholding, and threats to get their way.

The Non-Power Player is the one who does not believe they have leverage, so they must use other tactics to get their way. Tactics like pleasing, compromise, guilt, shame, and manipulation.

What's fascinating about this is that both people in Demand Relationship want the same outcome. Did you catch that?

Both people are trying to get to the same outcome. They are both trying to get their way or get what they need. The only difference is the tactic they use to get there based on their role in the relationship.

You have likely experienced yourself in both roles during your lifetime already.

Can you think back to when you were a little kid, and you really wanted something or really wanted to go somewhere and your parent or other authority figure said no? Can you recall how you felt? That feeling of being powerless to get the outcome you wanted?

Did you try to get them to change their mind?

Maybe you tried convincing them? "But everyone else's parents are letting them go!"

Or maybe you tried bargaining. "I'll wash all the dishes for a month if you let me go."

Or maybe you lashed out. "You are the worst parent, and I hate you."

Or maybe you snuck out and went anyway.

Or maybe you did none of those things but instead pouted or cried.

Whether you have done all those things or none of those things . . . have you seen them done? Maybe you recognize your kids in those examples?

Those are the tactics of the Non–Power Player in Demand Relationship. It's not bad. It doesn't make anyone a bad person to use tactics to try to get what they need or want. It's normal, understandable, and common. It's what made people resourceful and scrappy. And for centuries, it's how a Non–Power Player got things done.

So, when I say that the Non–Power Player uses tactics like pleasing, plotting, or manipulation, that doesn't make them evil—it makes them resourceful in an undesirable situation where they feel powerless. I hope you can have some compassion for yourself, your kids, your mom, or whomever you know that has been the Non–Power Player.

Similarly, the Power Player is also not the bad guy in this story. The parent who tells their kid, "No, you are not going on that class trip to New York City when I don't even trust your teacher not to give you snacks with peanuts in it" is not the bad guy just because they "gave an order" using their leverage.

For instance, maybe your parent didn't let you sleep over at that friend's house when you so desperately wanted to go. Maybe your parent had an "iffy" feeling about someone in that household but couldn't really explain that to you because no one ever trained your folks with the skills to have those conversations back in the day.

Neither the Power Player nor the Non–Power Player is the *bad guy*. They were both doing the best they could with the skill set that they had.

Even with the best of intentions, we run to the end of our skill set and default to using Demand Relationship tactics to get our kids to do what we need done. Like saying, "If you wanna go to that party on Saturday, that room better be clean first."

Demand Relationship is when a person uses tactics to control someone into doing what they want, the way they want it, when they want it. You do not have to have bad intent to use Demand Relationship. It's a default relationship paradigm that has been used for at least centuries, if not forever.

I want to reiterate: we do this even with the best of intentions. You're trying to prepare your kids for life, making sure they are responsible, capable, independent, and contributing individuals, correct?

You are trying to look out for them when you say, "Where's your homework? Is it in your backpack or did you leave it upstairs? Go get it and put it in your backpack. You wanna make sure you get the points for that, right? Why would you work so hard on your homework and then leave it behind and not turn it in? Go up and get it and put it in your backpack."

You are trying to protect them from the negative outcome of not turning in that homework. And when you run to the end of your skill set, you default back to using control, authority, or leverage to get them to do what you think should be done.

The thing about this Demand Relationship paradigm is that it only works when one person does not feel like they are in a position to assert themselves. When that person no longer believes they must obey, Demand Relationship crumbles fast. Eventually the person who has felt like the Non–Power Player hits Threshold: the point where they have had enough. Why? Because no one likes to be controlled. And you already know that, because you hate it when people try to control you.

When someone hits threshold in Demand Relationship, it usually looks something like this: "I've had it. I can't take anymore. I'm done. I will take the kids and figure this out myself. I'll get my own place. I'll take on another job. I don't care. I can't stand this anymore."

And they do the predictable Demand Relationship exit. They leave, quit, or give up.

> **PRINCIPLE:**
> Threshold happens when the pain of staying outweighs the fears of leaving that kept them stuck as the Non–Power Player.

It's the same thing in Demand Parenting. If all that's been done as your child has grown up has been to use shame, guilt, demands, and control to try to shape them, then the minute they are (1) bigger than you (2) financially independent from you, or (3) no longer need to live in your house, they are outta there. They can't wait to get away from you. When that happens, you realize that you didn't have a relationship; you had an arrangement based on control. And when they leave, you don't have a relationship with them; you just have a loss of control.

The truth is, you never really had control because you can't control another human. You can, however, temporarily manipulate or threaten them to do what you want, but that is *compliance*, not control. And the minute they are out from under your boot, they are going to do whatever the hell they want anyway. Why? Because you never actually had control. Very often, the more someone uses control to force someone else into embracing values, teach lessons, or to "shape" them, the less they will have any lasting impact the moment the other person becomes free.

I'll show you why.

When someone doesn't feel free, when they feel oppressed and under someone else's control, what is the one thing that they are focused on? Yeah, getting out. Being free.

They are not thinking, *Oh, thank you so much for that valuable life lesson.* Or, *I'm so glad I have you to tell me what to think. Thank you for showing me the error of my ways.*

Nope, they are not thinking any of those things.

Even if your values and lessons are incredibly important, when they are wrapped in Demand Relationship, the Non–Power Player won't hear it or heed it because they will be focused on getting away from your control. Further, they associate all your perspectives as being "your ideas," not theirs, and you are the bad guy whose boot they've been squashed under. So, they are not internalizing the gifts you're trying to give them, because the gifts are wrapped in Demand Relationship.

Maybe you know this all too well because that's what it was like for you growing up. Perhaps you couldn't wait to get out of there? It's the same in Demand Relationship today. As soon as people can get away from the Demand Relationship arrangement, they do.

You see it everywhere today, a mass of people doing the Demand Relationship exit and leaving. What do they leave for? They try to find a better Demand Relationship player, right? "I'm going to find someone who isn't a selfish ass!" or "I gotta find a partner who is not so miserable to be with."

The workplace is a great example of this dynamic. Someone is unhappy at work but feels powerless to do anything because "what the boss says goes." Until they finally hit threshold and say, "Screw this. I'm gonna get another job, where the boss is not a jerk and they treat me better."

That's when people try to find a better-quality Demand Relationship arrangement, hoping they can finally be happy there. (The grass is always greener on the other side of the fence, right?)

There's also another outcome happening now in love relationships. People don't necessarily have the words for this dynamic, but it's where the Non–Power Player leaves and, because they are sick of always feeling like the victim, they start seeking a new relationship where *they* can now be "in charge," where they can call the shots and have the control, thinking *that* will make them happy. Only to discover that they feel burdened that everything falls on them or their partner is unhappy, and they are miserable, yet again.

You don't have to look far to see this happening everywhere.

Demand Relationship is failing at such epic rates that we have a new epidemic going on today. People are giving up on marriage and even "relationship" as a thing.

They try pleasing, and they're miserable. So, they try being the one in control, and they are still miserable. Then they decide, "I don't want either side of that mess. I'm done with relationships."

Relationship was never the problem to be thrown away; it was the Demand Relationship that was failing.

Demand Relationship will never lead to happiness, and yet that was the only paradigm modeled to us through generations.

We weren't taught how to be in a long-term relationship where both people are free and equal and no one is controlled by another.

That's exactly what Paul and I have been teaching people for years: how to be in relationships with others where you are authentically yourself and happy without controlling others and without pleasing or compromising.

When I mapped everything out and looked at all our years of experience and results, it was very clear . . . our method, our tools, and everything we were teaching people was the opposite of Demand Relationship.

Our empowering relationship model for today's world needed a name. We called the new paradigm that we invented Relationship Development®. And now I get to share it with you, too!

In Relationship Development, you learn to be happy regardless of what's going on around you and how to inter-operate in a way that builds up relationships instead of breaking them down. It's a way of relating without control, compromise, or leverage, even, and especially when you don't share the same perspectives as the ones you are in relationship with!

We believe this has been The Missing Piece in the evolution of human relationships.

WHY NOW? WHY DIDN'T THIS EXIST BEFORE?

People did not need Relationship Development hundreds of years ago because spouses were not seen as equals hundreds of years ago (even less than a hundred years ago).

The unfortunate truth is that until the mid-1900s, we didn't need skill sets to collaborate in marriage because marriage wasn't really a collaboration between equals.

It was the same in parenting. Paul and I often joke that when we were young, kids were treated more like pets who needed to come home and get fed when the streetlights came on.

Thank God those days are over. For many of us, spouses care about each other and see each other as equals now. We care about our children, and we want to do the best we can for them. We care about humanity and want everyone treated well. And we surely wouldn't want our children to be forced into a life of submission or to obey against their will.

Of course, that unsavory history didn't prepare us or train us for how to inter-operate when no one in the relationship is being forced to comply or give in. No one modeled those techniques or skill sets to us because they didn't use them. By the way, that doesn't make them the bad guy either. Please hold compassion in your heart for all those humans who endured the time before now. They not only lived through that but some even fought to end it . . . for us!

That's why Relationship Development didn't exist before. It wasn't needed before. But it sure is needed now! We need a new relationship paradigm for a new time in humanity. A paradigm that works to continually build up relationships, even long term, when people are both equal and free in the relationship.

All humans are equal, and we need newer skills to inter-operate as such. As humans, we know we want to operate from the Relationship Development Paradigm side of that chart. We just never got the tools, training, or skill sets on how to do that (since even just one generation ago, our folks didn't need these skills).

These are the exact skills and tools Paul and I have been developing for many years now, skills that empower our students to inter-operate with humans from the Relationship Development paradigm. To break the chains of Demand Relationship and leave it in the past where it belongs.

In Relationship Development, we use skill sets to create alignment, build rapport, cultivate collaboration, and do all the other things on the Relationship Development side of the chart. The foundation of the Relationship Development paradigm is empowerment for all humans.

THE MISSING PIECE FOR LOVE

Following is our Demand Relationship versus Relationship Development Chart. This tool shows you the Demand Relationship tactics on one side and the Relationship Development replacement on the other side.

THE Missing PIECE

Demand Relationship™		RelationshipDEVELOPMENT®
Win – Lose		Win – Win
Pleasing		Giving
Compromise		Alignment
Control		Acceptance
Blame		Personal Responsibility
Judgement		Observation
Punishing	JUDGEMENT	Rapport
Withholding, Stonewalling		Heartfelt Understanding
Manipulation, Coercion		Collaboration
Guilt, Shame		Empowerment
Nagging, Pushing		Inspiration
Criticism		Compassion
Separation		Unity
Conditional		Unconditional
Frustration		Appreciation
Protection		Connection
Conformity		Evolution
Dominate		Unite
Fear		Love

Look at the Demand Relationship side of the chart. That is not love. And yet, how many times are we showing up in our relationships, that are supposed to be about love from the Demand Relationship side of the chart?

The invisible dynamic happening here is this:

> **PRINCIPLE:**
> You are either building up or breaking down your relationships in the little moments of your day, depending on which side of the chart you are showing up from.

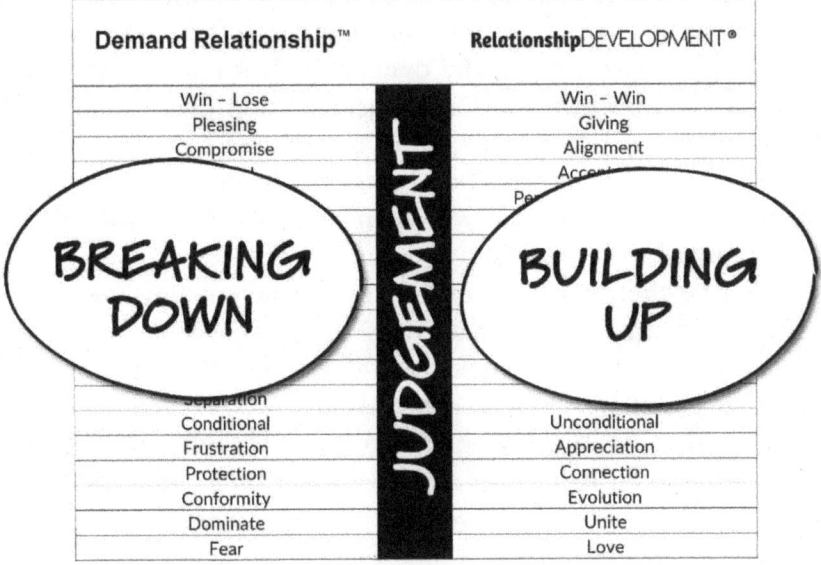

That's why we say that it only takes one person to transform a relationship.

When you show up from Demand Relationship, you are breaking down your relationship. When you show up from the Relationship Development paradigm, you are building up your relationship.

Relationship is a Closed Loop.

The Predictable Pattern Loop that has been The Missing Piece until now is this paradigm shift:

Trigger: Demand Relationship → Boomerang: break down relationship

Trigger: Relationship Development → Boomerang: build up relationship

It only takes one person to transform a relationship because when *you* put Demand Relationship into the Loop, *you* break down your relationship, and when *you* put Relationship Development into the Loop, *you* build up your relationship. *It only takes you.*

When you get the skill sets to inter-operate with your partner by putting Relationship Development into the Loop instead of Demand Relationship, the dynamic between you both will change. Not because you forced them to, told them to, or got them to change. They will change in response to how you are showing up (Relationship Development instead of Demand Relationship). Their reaction will change because the inter-action has changed.

You've already had this experience in your own life. Can you think of a time when you really messed up or created a problem, but it was an accident? Maybe it was at an old job, something you did as a kid, or even in your relationship.

Now, can you think of one of those moments where the other person was critical of you or ripped into you about your mistake? How did you feel? How did you react to them in that moment?

Now, can you think of a time where you made a mistake or created a problem, but the other person was compassionate in response? Maybe they said, "Hey, don't sweat it. Shit happens. Don't worry about it." How did you feel when they said that? How did you react to them in that moment?

Were your reactions to the other person the same in both of those scenarios? Yes or no? No, they were not. How can I possibly know that if I wasn't even there? Because it is human dynamics. It's a predictable pattern with a predictable outcome.

For example, when I was a teenager, I worked at the 10-cent store in our town. Yes, there was a 10-cent store back then. I remember my brother-in-law called me on the store's phone (we didn't have cell phones, yet) and told me that my sister got out of knee surgery and she wasn't recovering as well as he hoped. She was still loopy from the anesthesia, and he couldn't leave her alone. He needed me to come be with her so he could go to work.

I hung up the phone and told my boss, "Sorry, I gotta go. My sister needs me. It's an emergency. I'll make up the time some other day."

My manager said to me, "Stacey, I forbid you to leave."

I swear to God those were her words. I looked at her and said, "You're joking, right?"

She said, "If you walk out that door, don't bother coming back because you're fired."

I replied, "I don't give a flying F&*# if I'm fired from this junk store. She's my sister." And I ran out of there, jumped in my car, and drove to my sister's house.

Fast-forward about 10 years. I was sitting in an airport, waiting to board a flight to a client's location, and my phone rang. It was Paul. He was calling to tell me that our beloved Putty had been lying in the laundry room all morning, hiding from him, and that he felt like she might be trying to tell us that she's nearing the end. Putty had been suffering with cancer for a while. I stood up and ran down the terminal to get a cab home, leaving my luggage on that flight. As I ran through that airport to get home to my beloved girl, I phoned my manager and told him, "I'm so sorry, I can't get on that flight. Paul called, and our dog might be having her last day."

He responded with, "Oh my God, Stacey, I'm so sorry. Please get home safely and quickly and tell me if you need anything." Hearing him, it started to hit me, and the tears started flowing. I could only bring myself to say, "I'm so grateful for you. Thank you." After 14 years together, Putty passed that afternoon, with Paul and I holding her when she took her last breath.

As humans, we respond differently to people who show up differently. Those two situations were almost the same, but my response to each "boss" was 180 degrees apart because of what they put into the Loop. Every moment in a relationship is a choice.

Fortunately for us all, it is not just luck as we have been brought up to believe. It's a human dynamic. We react to people based on how they act toward us. So, when you interact with your partner and others, from Relationship Development instead of Demand Relationship, they will respond differently to you.

It's a predictable pattern with a predictable outcome.

When we learn the skill sets to show up from Relationship Development, we put something different into the Loop and get a different result. We are building up our relationships instead of breaking them down.

Demand Relationship is NOT relationship; it is compliance through leverage. Whereas Relationship Development is transformation through Inspiration that creates real and harmonious relationships that last.

This is how we have helped our students to transform their relationships, save their marriages, and heal their families for years. We have been giving them the skills, tools, and strategies in our Relationship Development Method to empower them to operate from the Relationship Development paradigm.

Don't worry. You won't have to figure out all the tools and skill sets yourself. Paul and I developed our Relationship Development Method and the hundreds of tools, strategies, and skill sets in our toolbox along with all the training to learn and implement them.

Listen, being human can be hard. Being human and being happy is even harder. Thankfully, we have already figured this piece out. Plus, countless students of ours have already experienced the results they desired, which has paved the way for you to be next.

After all my years of working with people, I believe, in my core, that most humans genuinely want to inter-operate from Relationship Development. We want people to interact with us from Relationship Development, and we want to bring Relationship Development to our relationships.

But we come from a history steeped in Demand Relationship. All that's ever been modeled to us is Demand Relationship, and we never got the "training manual" to go with the glorious freedom and equality that all humans deserve.

This paradigm difference is also why everything else you may have tried for your relationships has failed, because it was still based in a Demand Relationship mindset. All the couples counseling, advice-givers, magazine-cover gimmicks, and book after book are trying to teach you how to be a better Demand Relationship game player and how to win at Demand Relationship.

That's why it failed. There's nothing wrong with you. There's nothing wrong with your partner. And there's nothing unique about the two of you together that makes relating somehow impossible.

Demand Relationship cannot work to build up relationships. That's it.

Up until the mid-1900s, humans entered marriage arrangements for very different reasons than they have today. Whether it was for protection, family pressure, to produce an heir to secure your family's assets, or just for survival, Demand Relationship "worked" in those days to simply achieve those types of outcomes (which had nothing to do with the relationship between two humans).

It is my deepest hope that these reasons are not why humans still get married. Today, I believe the majority of humans enter into relationship because they desire the experience of the relationship! They want peace, harmony, happiness, and ultimately love.

Well, Demand Relationship will not create any of those outcomes in long-term relationships. Just look at the chart, and you can probably see why.

Remember, it's not "relationship" that is broken. It's Demand Relationship that doesn't work.

Demand Relationship has caused so much unnecessary suffering. It's an old and broken dynamic that doesn't work when both people are free. The time for Demand Relationship has passed, and it's time for it to die.

The only reason it's still around is because no one has taught us a different way . . . until now.

The truth is all humans deserve to live in an unshakeable love and unleashed passion. All humans deserve to be the parent they want to be and build up their relationship with each child. You deserve to have harmonious work dynamics where you can co-create and collaborate. And you certainly deserve to be the happiest, most authentic version of yourself with thriving relationships and harmony in your home.

This is no longer a dream. It's real. Truthfully, Demand Relationship broke a long time ago. It's now time to evolve and rise into Relationship Development.

Luckily for you, it's a skill set, and it can be learned. It's not magic. It's not just for some people and not others. It's for all people.

> **PRINCIPLE:**
> Relationship Development builds up relationships.
>
> **PRINCIPLE:**
> Demand Relationship breaks down relationships.
>
> **PRINCIPLE:**
> Relationship Development is a skill set and it can be learned.

Our Relationship Development Method and tools will give you the Relationship Development skill set to operate from the Relationship Development paradigm.

This book will empower you to start becoming a Relationship Transformer®, to start breaking the chains of Demand Relationship for your family's legacy and get the Relationship Development skill sets to create a new chain reaction for building up relationships and living in the results of that.

It doesn't matter what's going on in your relationships or what the circumstances are, because that's not where the experience of your relationships will come from. Are you ready to see what evens the playing fields for all of us to have phenomenal relationships, regardless of the players or the circumstances? (Turn the page.)

CHAPTER 4

THE SKILL SET THAT CAN BE LEARNED

Picture this: I'm at the park, and my kids are little, like maybe five and one years old. Our son is playing with this boy who looks about his age, and the boy's mom is sitting on the bench next to me while I rock my daughter, who's napping in her stroller.

Her little boy runs up to us, with his best strongman pose, and says, "I'm a karate master. I'm the best in the whole world." Then he kicks into the air, jumps as high as he can, and runs off playing with our son, leaving both moms giggling on the bench.

I ask her, "Is he in karate?"

She leans over, laughing, and says, "No, not even one lesson, but it sounds like maybe I should sign him up, huh?"

Laughing, I say, "Yeah, maybe you should."

Question for you. Is her son a karate master? Yes or no?

Is he the best in the world? Yes or no?

No, he's not.

Now, another question for you. Is it *possible* for him to be a karate master one day?

Yes, of course.

Okay, last question now. And I really want you to answer this one.

What would he need to do to become a karate master one day?

I'm guessing you have answers like these:

- Take classes
- Practice
- Learn from a karate master
- Stick with it
- How about . . . start learning karate

Anything like that come to mind for you?

Okay, friend, well I am here to tell you that it is the same with relationship skill sets.

You are not a Relationship Development skill set master, yet.

But just like any other human on the planet, it is possible for you to be great at it.

All you have to do is take classes, practice, learn from a master, stick with it, and maybe most importantly . . . start.

See what I did there?

Unlike what we were conditioned to believe through our unenlightened history with Demand Relationship, your success in marriage is not a result of:

- How attractive you are
- How wealthy or poor you are
- Your status or significance
- How well you are aging or not
- How smart you are
- How good a person you are or not

Okay, hold onto your hat . . . your relationship is not even a result of how much you two love each other or not. You might even need to pause for a minute and really take that in.

> **PRINCIPLE:**
> Your relationship is the result of the level of Relationship Development skill set you have or not.

When a person runs to the end of their skill set, they default to their old ways. It's human nature. Like when I can't figure out how to say what I want to say in Italian and I say it in English. I just ran to the end of my skill set, and I already know how to say it in English.

That's what's happening in relationships today. You're running to the end of your skill set for how to operate in the Relationship Development paradigm, because the skills were never taught to us before.

In the moments when you ran to the end of your skill set, you defaulted to Demand Relationship, and the relationship was breaking down in those moments. That's all it is. It's a predictable pattern, with a predictable outcome.

When you get the relationship-building skill sets you didn't have before, you will not only be empowered to *stop* breaking down your relationship in the moments of your day but also even have the skills to rebuild what has already been broken or destroyed.

> **PRINCIPLE:**
> Relationship is a skill set, and it can be learned.

Trigger: Demand Relationship tactics → Boomerang: Demand Relationship outcome (break down relationship)

Trigger: Relationship Development skill sets → Boomerang: Relationship Development result (build up relationship)

Trigger: run to the end of your Relationship Development skill set → Boomerang: default to Demand Relationship

There's nothing wrong with you. There's nothing wrong with your partner. And there's nothing wrong with the two of you together.

And anyone who tells you otherwise is simply showing you that *they*, themselves, just ran to the end of *their* skill set.

Even the most well-intentioned people around you (like your parents, siblings, friends, or co-workers) who give you bad Demand Relationship "advice" have also run to the end of their skill set. The counselors who are handing out divorce prescriptions like Halloween candy have all also run to the end of their skill set to help you.

How do I know that? Because Paul and I have been helping students since 2011, with thousands and thousands of students in our programs and events. And in all those years, with all those relationships, Paul and I have never ever said the words "There's nothing you can do" or "You should leave." Never.

Even after hosting thousands and thousands of hours of Q&A calls with our students for over a decade, we have never once had a student ask a relationship question or present a relationship challenge that the Relationship Development Method, skill sets, and tools couldn't solve or transform.

We believe this is another one of the major reasons why the students in our RelationshipU program have had a 1% divorce rate over a six-year study period of their results. It's not some kind of magic. It's because this is a skills-based method that can be learned by anyone, and it works.

When you have the right skills and tools, there's just no such thing as hopeless.

The key is knowing how to show up from Relationship Development. And even more importantly, how to stop showing up from Demand Relationship.

It's like learning karate. You can't just wing it or guess. Be compassionate with yourself. It requires taking the classes, learning the skills, practicing the tools, and sticking with it. We're going to start showing you how to do that in the chapters of this book.

The Skill Set That Can Be Learned

IT'S A CHOICE

You can choose to start learning this, like the kid with karate, or not. That's your choice.

And the truth is, everyone lives in the results of the decisions that they make, and there are no exceptions.

In my case, English is my primary language, and I don't know how to speak French. Just like any other human, I could learn French. I actually don't have any plans to learn French. That's my choice.

At the moment, I'm totally good with living in the results of choosing not to learn to speak French.

For one, I don't live in France. I also do not live somewhere that I'm surrounded by people speaking French every day. And I don't spend my workdays yelling in English at people who speak French.

However, if I moved to France, worked for a company where French was the primary language, lived in a community where the neighbors all spoke French, and sent my kids to school where French was the primary language, and I *still* refused to learn French . . . well, then I'd be living in the results of that decision too. And that would likely be painful, every single day, all day long.

Let's say I did that. Let's say that you and I sit down for coffee, and I tell you that our family has moved to France. I now live in a community, work for a company, and send my kids to school . . . all where French is the primary language. But I still refuse to learn French. Then I go on to complain to you about how miserable I am and how rude everyone is. I tell you about all the arguments I've been having and how much the people I work with there are just unbearable.

What would you say to me?

Let me guess. Perhaps something about how "I did this to myself"? Or would you maybe tell me to just freaking learn French and stop complaining already?

Hmmm. Interesting.

Dearest, let's sit down with a cup of coffee. I say this with love. You are surrounded.

Your spouse, kids, neighbors, family, work folks, friends, and pretty much every human you interact with are all in *relationship* with you. Every waking minute, of every day.

And you don't yet speak "Relationship Development."

That's not your fault. *And*, once you see it, it's now becoming your *choice*.

My life's work is to simplify this for you, so you can learn it and apply it. But you gotta make the decision to do it.

Kind of like learning how to say, "Un café allongé s'il vous plait," to order a coffee in French.

Your life can start changing from the first time you apply the first relationship skill you learn.

One of our students, Kevin, was facing a disagreement that had been plaguing his marriage for over 10 years. After implementing the tools, he came to a Q&A call and shared a celebration that by using the training, he finally solved that issue. This was an issue he thought would be unsolvable for them for eternity, and yet he applied these skills and within a matter of weeks, had solved it for them.

PRINCIPLE:
Relationship is a skill set and it can be learned.

PRINCIPLE:
Learning the skill set to inter-operate from the Relationship Development paradigm requires training, tools, strategies, and practice.

PRINCIPLE:
When you run to the end of your skill set, you default back to Demand Relationship tactics.

The Skill Set That Can Be Learned

Relationship Development builds up your relationships.

Demand Relationship breaks down your relationships.

The key is to keep extending your Relationship Development skill set so you don't run to the end of that skill set and fall back into old patterns.

So, hopefully you are seeing that it wasn't "relationship" that was the problem to be discarded; it was the old and broken Demand Relationship paradigm that's been making you unhappy *in* your relationships.

But what if you are not the one who needs to hear this? What if it's really your partner who "needs this," but they won't learn it?

I'll just cut to the point . . . what if you are not the one who caused the crap in your relationship? It's not your fault. Your partner did this, and they are the one who needs to hear this. Here's the problem with that thinking: it would be Demand Relationship to shove this book in their face and "make" them read it, right?

So, what do we do about that? (Turn the page.)

CHAPTER 5

THE TRUTH ABOUT BLAME

Take a moment and think of someone you are or were in relationship with who "wronged you" or disappointed you.

One way or another, you probably want that fixed. You probably wish that never happened, but that doesn't change the fact that it did happen, and it left you with a negative outcome.

So, what are your options? If it stays as-is for a long time, how are you going to feel about that?

It's common, in this case, to think, *I want them to make it right, so that I can be happy, at peace, or feel better about this.* Do you resonate with a thought or feeling like that? If so, where does that leave you? Has it been resolved while you have been thinking that way? Why not?

I can tell you why. You are waiting for them to fix it. So you sit there, waiting. Waiting for someone, someone that you are not even happy with right now, by the way, to make things better *for* you.

And you wait.
Waiting.
Waiting.

The seasons change as you look out the window, and the caption reads: "Waiting for my wrongdoer to come fix things." Sadly, you may be waiting forever for them to right this wrong.

You sit there, holding yourself stuck with reasons like, "It's not my fault, so there's nothing for me to do. They did this so they must be the one to fix it."

While that kind of thinking is completely normal and understandable within the Demand Relationship mindset we've all been brought up under, let me ask you these two questions:

Question #1: How has that been working for you?
Question #2: How long do you want to keep waiting?

Ultimately, you are taking your destiny, happiness, and peace and giving it to someone else to handle for you. Maybe they do something to make things better and maybe they don't. Now you're at the whim of another person. Tell me, what are the chances that they are going to somehow right this wrong for you?

This is how stealthy and deceptive blame is. Blame is an invisible force of destruction. Let me explain by making it visible for you now.

The truth about blame is . . .

> **PRINCIPLE:**
> Blame is the act of taking all your power to solve something for yourself and willingly handing it over to someone else in the hope they might choose to fix it for you.

And that's why you feel stuck (let that sink in for a moment). Here's the Predictable Pattern Loop:

Trigger: blame → Boomerang: disempowerment, being stuck

The invisible destruction starts the minute we point that finger in blame. In that moment, we are rendering ourselves powerless to transform the situation.

Let's take a few common example statements to demonstrate this dynamic:

"I can't even talk to him when he's so inconsiderate to me all the time."

"It's not like anything can change when she keeps punishing me for things I didn't even do."

"I'm not the one who broke the trust in this relationship. I don't know what you want me to say. I can't trust that they won't do this again."

THE SYMPTOM OF BLAME: TRYING TO GET THEM TO CHANGE

In every one of those very common dynamics, the speaker has rendered themselves powerless and feels stuck because they cannot get the other person to change. They are blaming the other person and waiting for the other person to fix the problem for them.

I know this may be tough to see or take in at first, so please give me a moment to explain. This Demand Relationship conditioning runs very deep.

OBJECTIVE: DO NOT LOSE

As a society, we have been heavily conditioned to "not be wrong," "do not lose," and "win at all costs." But even more so than winning, don't be the loser.

We have also been conditioned to believe that the person who is blamed is the loser. Meaning, if it's not my fault, then I'm not going to be the one who loses here.

When these two Demand Relationship dynamics (blame and don't be the loser) collide, it creates a very common invisible pattern in human dynamics.

> **One:** I can't be wrong because I can't be the loser here.
> **Two:** It's your fault, so you are to blame.
> **Three:** You lose (if you're to blame, you lose).

Finding who is to blame and "pointing the finger" to clear ourselves from being wrong gives us a false sense of certainty, control, and comfort. It also simultaneously leaves us stuck in a hole we put ourselves in, secretly hoping for someone to help us get out of it.

> **PRINCIPLE:**
> In real human life, nothing actually gets better for you when you declare someone else the loser by blaming them. (Read that again.)

This is a very old and broken Demand Relationship dynamic that stopped working a long time ago. Here's how this used to go in Demand Relationship:

The Power Player would assign fault to the Non–Power Player. The Non–Power Player would accept that fault and fix it (repair). And then the Power Player would feel confident that it was (1) fixed and (2) wouldn't happen again because of the punishment, fear, or leverage they put in place.

This doesn't work anymore, cupcake. It hasn't worked in a really long time. What happens in human dynamics today?

When you blame someone, it's Demand Relationship, so it breaks down your relationship with them. Perhaps they feel misunderstood or unfairly villainized. They create distance from you, your rapport is lost, and your alignment is now broken.

And, in the meantime, nothing changed for you. So, the problem wasn't solved, and you aren't satisfied that it won't happen again. You can turn up the volume on your Demand Relationship tactics, which is what most folks do, but you *still* won't get the result you are after.

You can go from hinting that you need them to fix this, to asking nicely that they fix it, to directly telling them that they need to fix it, to confronting them with "How dare you not fix this?" to distancing from them until they fix it, to withholding things you do until they fix it, to yelling, shaming, and guilting them into fixing it. Until one day you tell their mom, friend, sibling, or neighbor about the audacity of what they did to you and how they haven't fixed it, hoping that someone else can talk some sense into them.

Sound familiar? It's okay. You are not a bad person. You just ran through the entire Demand Relationship side of our chart (impressive). It's called being human, and it's all that was ever modeled to you and everyone else. It's okay and understandable. Have compassion for yourself. And, it is never, ever, ever going to work to build up your relationship or heal the gap now between you and the other person.

No human on the receiving end of the experience of "turning up the volume on Demand Relationship" was ever genuinely more grateful and more in love with the perpetrator afterward.

THE EFFECT OF DEMAND RELATIONSHIP AND BLAME

Yes, it is still possible to raise the volume on your Demand Relationship tactics and get some level of temporary compliance or implied resolution from them as a result. For example, they may say "I'm sorry" and still have no idea why they are apologizing. They may say they are sorry and not mean it at all, because they just want you off their back. They may even say "I'm sorry" because they are genuinely sorry you are so unhappy.

No matter how this goes, however, there is typically no increase in connection and affection for the Power Player from anyone on the receiving end of an intense amount of Demand Relationship being forced to apologize. In fact, after being forced to apologize, most people will probably blame the person doing the forcing for being unreasonable, illogical, or a jerk.

Simple truth: no one loves being forced to comply with someone else's demands and most humans deeply resent it when this "forced compliance" is combined with blame. Ironically, the resulting damage to the relationship from Demand Relationship is often worse than or lasts longer than the original kerfuffle.

> **PRINCIPLE:**
> Blame is Demand Relationship, and it breaks down a relationship.

You already know this because when someone blames you or pulls those Demand Relationship tactics on you, you feel the breakdown in your relationship with them. It doesn't feel good.

WHAT ACTUALLY DOES WORK?

The Relationship Development Paradigm approach is to take the path of personal responsibility, instead of blame.

Now, before you freak out, give me a minute to define what personal responsibility actually is, because the meaning applied today by most people is incorrect in this relationship context.

When I say personal responsibility, it means I'm personally taking the responsibility of solving this.

> **PRINCIPLE:**
> Personal Responsibility DOES NOT equal fault.

Taking personal responsibility does *not* mean that I say it is my fault. Personal responsibility is not self-blame either. One more time: personal responsibility does not equal fault!

The Demand Relationship conditioning runs pretty deep here. Most humans have Demand Relationship wiring in their blueprint that says that only the person who caused the problem should fix it. So, whoever is to "blame" has to clean it up. This goes all the way back to something breaking in your house and your mom saying, "Who did that?" while you and your siblings start pointing fingers at each other, trying to avoid the punishment. We've been conditioned over time through parenting, schooling, sports, jobs, and life to never be "to blame" for something gone wrong. And that the wrongdoer is the one who "cleans up the mess."

This has resulted in humans who are very averse to having anything, no matter how small or even appropriately placed, be *their fault*. They typically don't want to consider even being a part of the problem, let alone the cause of the problem. It's really important to them that someone else is blamed.

No one wants to take personal responsibility, because they falsely think that means it was all their fault, which also makes them wrong, which also means they lose. And now we are back to a cardinal rule of Demand Relationship: never be the loser, so find ways to blame others.

Somewhere along the path in our history with the "don't ever be wrong about anything" garbage, personal responsibility became a dirty word.

See what I mean? This Demand Relationship conditioning is deep. And it wraps itself in disguises that blind us from even seeing its deceptive destruction. That's okay: like a cockroach, when we shine a light on this Demand Relationship junk, it scurries away.

The first step here is to unhinge these old disempowering beliefs around blame, fault, and personal responsibility.

I'll give you an example . . .

JASMINE AND HER DAUGHTER

Jasmine is bringing the tie-dye paints to camp today for her daughter's entire group. The girls have been excited and talking about this nonstop for days. They are making tie-dye shirts for their dance number in the end-of-season show. As soon as they get to camp, Jasmine's daughter runs off to join her friends; they are all full of smiles.

About 90 minutes later, Jasmine gets a call from her daughter, who is now in tears. "Mom, they don't have the shirts for us!" her daughter says.

Now confused, Jasmine says, "What? Why not? They have had weeks to get those shirts!"

Daughter (crying): "My counselor said something about the director saying it was too much money, and we should all just wear the same color shirt instead."

Jasmine hears more girls crying in the background. She thinks to herself, *Maybe he could have made that decision two weeks ago instead of letting these girls get their hearts set on this freaking tie-dye thing, especially since all the parents bought the rest of the supplies. All he had to do was get the freaking shirts.*

Jasmine: "Sweetie, don't cry. Don't cry, honey. You tell your counselor that I will go pick up the shirts myself tonight, and you can all tie-dye them tomorrow. It will be fine."

Daughter: "Really, Mom? Are you sure? It sounds like it's going to be expensive. I don't want you to have to do that."

Jasmine: "Sweetie, it's not that expensive. Don't worry about it. I want to do this. Just tell your counselor to e-mail me the size list and be ready for tomorrow, okay?"

Daughter (smiling): "I will, Mom. I promise. You are the best! Thank you!"

Based on this example, Jasmine did not *cause* the problem.

It was not Jasmine's fault.

Yes, Jasmine could have sat in her righteousness and blamed the camp director for being heartless, setting false expectations, and costing her and other parents money for supplies they weren't going to use.

She could have yelled and screamed and threatened. But, at what expense? Those girls would still be crying and disappointed, and now their parents would be angry too (adding more stress for the kids).

Labeling the person who caused the problem doesn't fix the painful aftermath of the problem. Blaming them doesn't fix it. Waiting for them to fix it doesn't fix it either.

Jasmine decided to take personal responsibility for fixing it because her solution changed the experience for her daughter and the rest of those girls.

You can take personal responsibility to solve things, even when it's not your fault and when you didn't cause the problem. Taking personal responsibility doesn't mean that you are "announcing" to everyone that you accept fault or blame. It just means that you are taking responsibility for fixing it.

LETTING THEM OFF THE HOOK

So, at this point, many folks wonder, "Why should I take personal responsibility while they get off the hook without doing anything?"

In our Relationship Development paradigm, we teach that all humans are 100% personally responsible. You are 100% personally responsible. Your partner is also 100% personally responsible. I want to be very clear. I am not saying that you are responsible, and the other person is not responsible. Both are 100% responsible.

The question is, who is going to take action to solve the problem at hand? My money is on you.

In the scenario above, the camp director is 100% personally responsible for himself and what happened. Jasmine taking personal responsibility does not lift any of the responsibility off the camp director. It just means that Jasmine isn't handing over her daughter's fate to the camp director and waiting to see if he does or doesn't fix it. Instead, in that moment, she's handling it and creating the fate herself.

After she gets off the phone with her daughter, and the girls have stopped crying and are calming down and feeling grateful, Jasmine can still call the camp director and ask him to reimburse her for the shirts.

What do you think the chances are that he will say yes? We have no clue, right? Let's say, it's 50-50. There's a 50% chance that he'll reimburse Jasmine and a 50% chance that he'll say that he just can't do it because they don't have the budget.

By taking personal responsibility, Jasmine created a 100% positive outcome for her daughter and the girls, instead of putting the fate of the situation into the hands of someone who may or may not fix it. She just fixed it herself, so it's done.

Afterward, she can use all the skills she has to try to convince him to repay her, and she may or may not get that money back.

But here is the most important key that I want you to get. Because Jasmine took personal responsibility to solve the issue for the kids, the outcome of him paying or not does not impact the girls anymore. It only impacts Jasmine's cash flow, and she's fine with that.

> **PRINCIPLE:**
> Personal Responsibility is empowerment!

It gives you the power to create the outcome and destiny you want for yourself and your loved ones.

Once you have the skill sets to solve the problem, the big thing holding you back from the results you want is your mindset.

When you blame the other person and hold yourself stuck, waiting for them to fix it, you are letting your own mindset hold you back.

HERE ARE THE 2 PREDICTABLE PATTERN LOOPS

Trigger: blame → Boomerang: disempowered and stuck
Trigger: personal responsibility → Boomerang: empowerment

You can sit in your righteous blame for as long as you want. The Boomerang still applies.

When you are ready to take control of your own happiness and create the outcome you want, you will find your freedom locked behind your personal responsibility!

HOW WILL THEY EVER CHANGE?

What about the deep-rooted aversion we have for letting people like the camp director off the hook when we take responsibility? That's not fair, right? How are they ever going to learn? How would they change if we didn't blame them?

In the old Demand Relationship paradigm, that used to work. When the Power Player blamed the Non–Power Player, there were apologies, reparations, and changes.

You and I both know that it doesn't work that way anymore. Today, when you blame someone, you trigger them into defensiveness.

Whether they say it out loud to you or just silently think it, they are only defending their side. Remember, the prime directive is "do not lose." So, when you blame them, they don't just roll over and accept the loss; they will defend themselves and fight not to be cast as the loser. You already know that because you've been blamed and felt that. And you've likely blamed others and triggered their defensiveness.

Trigger: blame → Boomerang: defensiveness

PRINCIPLE:
Blame breaks down relationships.

PRINCIPLE:
Personal Responsibility builds up relationships.

Personal Responsibility is empowering. It gives you increased control over your destiny. Also, when you are not blaming, you are not triggering the other person into defensiveness and breaking down the relationship.

Just stopping our blame alone can bring so much relief from the downward spiral that we find ourselves on, wondering how things went so badly so fast.

YOUR RESISTANCE

When you find yourself resistant to taking personal responsibility, the first step is to remind yourself that personal responsibility does not mean that it is your fault.

Then, try thinking of it this way . . .

What do you want your kids to do?

Do you want your kids to take personal responsibility, own their crap, and take action to create their life?

Or do you want your kids to blame everyone else and be the victim, begging for others to "fix it for me"?

Well, it's time to take your own medicine.

It's not easy. It's hard work in the beginning. But living your life stuck in disempowerment, begging for others to "fix it for you," is harder. Once you break the Demand Relationship wiring in your thinking that keeps barking at you not to take personal responsibility because you don't want to be wrong, it will get easier and easier.

And the more you take personal responsibility and implement the skill sets to fix the crap you want fixed, it will feel like a whole new life.

Let's take our example statements from earlier to show how you can shift from blame to personal responsibility:

1. "I can't even talk to him when he's so inconsiderate to me all the time."
2. "It's not like anything can change when she keeps punishing me for things I didn't even do."
3. "I'm not the one who broke the trust in this relationship. I don't know what you want me to say. I can't trust that they won't do this again."

I have heard the first one thousands and thousands of times. This is a masculine/feminine difference that causes countless kerfuffles. We're going to dig deep into masculine and feminine processing differences later, so bear with me as I explain this for now.

The Truth about Blame

Labeling someone's actions or words as "inconsiderate" is a meaning you are giving to that moment. And the meaning is based only on your blueprint of what you think "inconsiderate" is. "Inconsiderate" happens inside you. It's a meaning you apply to your experience that causes you to feel a certain way. It's the label you assign as you cast the blame, which leaves you stuck needing someone else to change.

There is no "global definition" of something being inconsiderate or not. You might say "inconsiderate is in the eye of the beholder."

Your partner is wired completely different than you are. One of the masculine/feminine processing differences causing kerfuffles is that the feminine will very often apply the label of "inconsiderate" to things that the masculine organically does because of how he is wired. It's a predictable pattern with a predictable outcome. Other popular labels used to describe this pattern are "rude," "mean," "controlling," and the ever-popular "jerk."

I'll give you an example without using the masculine and feminine differences. Recently, I was watching an episode of *Ted Lasso* on Apple TV, which is a show about a football team in England. The guys were in the locker room when one character, Jan Maas, said, "But I did not make any mistakes. Only you played poorly."

This caused the whole locker room to erupt in, "Whoa!" At that moment, another player, Sam, leaned in and said, "Guys, guys, Jan Maas is not being rude. He's just being Dutch."

All the guys then nodded in a collective, "Ohhh." Showing that they all suddenly understood.

What the team understood, in that moment, was that the Dutch culture speaks very bluntly, and it's not meant to be personal.

Some people are wired to speak bluntly. Some cultures are very blunt and direct, without intending for it to be offensive. Once you learn how others are wired, you can apply a different meaning to what they say and do based on how they meant it. Like Sam saying, "Jan Maas is not being rude. He's just being Dutch."

In the same way, the masculine often speaks directly, without softeners that account for others' feelings. Because masculine to masculine, that's how they operate. How often do you hear a guy say to his buddy, "Hey, is anyone else in here chilly? Anyone need a sweater?" No, he just gets up and gets a sweater for himself.

He's not being inconsiderate; he's just being masculine.

If you refuse to learn the differences and just blame your partner for not being wired like you, then you will stay stuck. By the way, you can swap out your partner for another masculine being, and you'll be dealing with the same shit from a new face within a few months' time.

Or you can take personal responsibility to learn that the masculine and feminine are wired differently and learn the skill sets to solve the kerfuffles being caused by those differences.

See, in the Demand Relationship world, differences are "solved" by making one person wrong (the loser) and making them change.

In the Relationship Development approach, we learn the differences and the skill sets to solve the predictable kerfuffles caused by the difference. No one is wrong for being wired the way they are.

No one has to change who they are when there are differences.

DIFFERENCES CAN BE SOLVED WITH SKILL SETS

Kind of like how we don't settle our differences by shooting each other in a duel in the street like they did in the old days, we don't need to settle our differences today by making one person wrong and attempting to force them to change (or bend to our will).

True personal responsibility is in learning the skill set to solve the kerfuffle caused by the difference. Sometimes it can be as simple as awareness of the difference, like "Jan Maas is just being Dutch." Other times, it is more complicated. Either way, there are still tools and skill sets you can use to solve these kerfuffles.

That's how you take personal responsibility for something that is not "your fault." The choice is yours. You can, of course, continue to blame the other person and keep going through the world, flying blind and unequipped to solve issues, never growing beyond the same problems you're having today. Either way, you will live in the results of your decision. But what about when you feel like there is no way that you can take personal responsibility for something?

I remember when one of our students, Mandie, first came to our program. She was very clear that it was her husband, Kyle, who needed to hear our training because their problems were "his fault."

In fact, when she first heard about our method and that it only takes one person, she thought to herself, *Oh, I wonder if they have anything that will help Kyle fix this for us.*

So, Mandie started our program and started implementing what she was learning. She realized how exhausted she was from constantly policing Kyle to be sure he wouldn't disappoint her again. She was afraid her marriage was on its last breath, and she was worried about how it would affect her children.

When she was ready to face the infidelity from their past, she struggled with taking personal responsibility. Before you freak out, hold on and hear me out.

At this point, Mandie was stuck in blame. After all, she didn't have an affair. Kyle did.

She insisted that Kyle get our training, telling him, "The answers for our issues are IN this program. You need to do this, so you can fix this."

Kyle was willing to do anything to save his marriage. But every time he approached Mandie, he just felt the weight of her blame. The disconnection from her was tearing him apart, and her judgement was insurmountable. Under the weight of her constant blame, he was starting to believe that nothing he could do would ever be good enough to make this right for Mandie, and he was falling further into hopelessness.

For Mandie, some things in their relationship were getting better, but this issue was still unresolved. She was still waiting and expecting Kyle to fix it.

Finally, after watching so many of our students heal their past pains and be free, she hit threshold. She decided she was going to take personal responsibility for fixing this, even if she couldn't save her marriage.

That's when the magic happened. She began to see all the Demand Relationship dynamics she had brought into their relationship that contributed to their breakdown.

She saw, with clarity, all the pieces that created a huge distance between them, long before the breakdown in their marriage occurred.

The truth is, of course, the infidelity was not her fault. And yet, she also unknowingly contributed to the breakdown of their relationship over time prior to it.

Her big breakthrough came when she realized that she could take personal responsibility to be the one to lead them through solving the issues in their marriage.

Instead of waiting for Kyle to do it, she could lead them through healing the damage, brick by brick, to rebuild their relationship from the ground up. And that didn't mean that she had failed or was the loser. It was her way of taking her power back, putting her family first, and freeing herself from the exhausting downward spiral she had been on for so long.

The only way Mandie could lose was by doing nothing to solve things and choosing, instead, to keep doing the same things she had been doing while watching her family fall apart.

She stopped obsessing over what he was doing outside their relationship and started focusing on how to build up their relationship so that it could be unshakeable, even if it was just so that they could heal and co-parent peacefully.

Each piece she led them through solving, using the Relationship Development skill sets, healed her as well. And in the process, she stopped being a victim and became empowered.

Eventually, her healing combined with the tools she was using to inter-act with him differently had a huge impact on Kyle too.

He also had a massive breakthrough and decided to become a student of Relationship Development on his own, to become the man he knew he could be for her.

They didn't just get their old marriage back, the way it was, broken and heading for trouble. They created a brand-new marriage between the same people. Today, they are rock solid, and their children are thriving. In fact, if you asked them, they would each tell you that their marriage was never as good as it is now.

For most folks that are stuck in Demand Relationship, taking personal responsibility to solve infidelity that you did not commit is just unthinkable.

If it's unthinkable, that just means that your blame mindset is controlling your life. It took a tremendous amount of courage for Mandie to lead the way in healing her marriage.

But here's the thing: what's the alternative?

Mandie made the choice to be the one to get the skill sets and lead them through the healing and building. And she's living in the results of that. Kyle is her best friend, biggest supporter, and cherished lover.

The alternative is to sit there and say, "No, I refuse to take personal responsibility for fixing this." And what's the result of that? Also, what does that approach do to prevent it from ever happening again, even if she left and was in a new relationship?

As I always say, it's your marriage. You either have to live in it or live through leaving it. Both take work and courage. Both are hard. As people say, "Pick your hard."

> **PRINCIPLE:**
> You can either struggle for the solution or struggle through the dissolution.

There is work on the upward spiral and on the downward spiral, but only one of them solves anything. Choose.

I choose the tough path of growth and ascension every time. I'd rather struggle to grow than suffer sliding down the drain of despair any day of the week! When I ascend, I get the gift of becoming the version of myself who is equipped to handle whatever life throws my way. That's empowerment, and it's a choice.

> **PRINCIPLE:**
> Blame leaves you disempowered and stuck
> and breaks down your relationship.
>
> **PRINCIPLE:**
> Personal Responsibility leaves you empowered
> and builds up your relationship.

I get it, it's not easy to start with taking personal responsibility. Especially when it appears that you are not at fault.

Perhaps if you could see more of the picture of how you and your partner got to the point that you're at right now (like Mandie did), it would be easier for you?

Let's do that next . . . (Turn the page.)

CHAPTER 6

THE BRICK WALL BETWEEN US™

Imagine that I have a garden in my yard. Let's say, it's four feet long by four feet wide and full of flowers, veggies, and herbs.

I then take 16 cinder blocks and lay them down on top of the garden bed, crushing all the plants and covering the entire garden with cement blocks.

What happens to the plants? They die, right?

So, a few days later, I meet you outside by my garden (which is covered in cinder block bricks) and I say to you, "Oh, these plants are just the worst. No matter what I do, they just won't grow. I come out here to pick veggies . . . but there's nothing. I come out here to cut flowers . . . and nothing. No matter what I do . . . no flowers, no veggies, no herbs grow . . . This garden is useless. I don't even know why I bother."

Let me ask you a question. What do you think? Mind you, we are both looking at a garden bed covered in cement blocks.

Is it the flowers' fault? Did I use the wrong seeds? Maybe there's not enough water? Some people say you have to plant more, that it's all about quantity. Is that what I need to do? Maybe it's because it wasn't organic seed—maybe that's my problem? Or it could be the soil's acidity, right? Maybe that's the problem with this garden? What do you think? Hmm?

Oh! You think I should take the f'ing bricks off the garden?!

Yeah, maybe the solution is to start by taking the cement bricks off the garden so the plants have a chance to breathe, take in the sun, and grow.

Now, do you think that I must remove every single brick before any one of the plants can start growing?

Nope. The minute you take off one brick, the plant underneath will have a second chance at coming alive!

And it's the same dynamic in your relationship.

WHEN LOVE FADES

Regardless of the flavor of the deterioration of your love relationship, it is painful when you feel like love has faded, or maybe there's endless arguing where it's difficult to agree on anything, or maybe it's the passion that has fizzled. It is painful, whether you admit it to yourself or just push the thought away in the back of your mind. Wondering if you even love them anymore (or if they love you) is a common yet haunting question that most folks are afraid to answer.

Over the years, I've seen this materialize in various ways. It could be the woman who blurts out, "Geez, do you even *like* me anymore?" in the middle of an argument because she can't imagine that her husband even likes her, let alone loves her, with the way he talks to her.

Or, it could be the man who feels like he would be doing her a favor by letting her go at this point because she only looks at him with disappointment anymore, and maybe someone else could make her happy since he can't. The right thing to do would be to let her go, so she has a chance to be happy.

Or the parent who is going through a life-phase change when the kids leave the house and is worried about what life will be like when it's just the two of them with no "buffer" from the kids.

As much as we might try to push these thoughts to the back of our mind, they keep creeping in. It used to be so loving when you first got together, and it's hard now not to notice how much things have changed.

Back then, you felt so loved when their eyes lit up as you walked in the room. You knew they had your back. They were your biggest champion, and you felt like you could do anything.

Back then, they were overjoyed to be with you. They would ask you to do all kinds of stuff with them.

But now? Now you dread being around them because all you see is a look of disdain or an eye roll (if they look at you at all). Or maybe you're tiptoeing on eggshells because anything you say might erupt into an argument, criticism, or silence.

And instead of feeling unstoppable, you second-guess everything you do, wondering what will set them off. You are exhausted trying to figure out how to say or do anything in a way that won't create backlash from them, but it's no use. The bottom line is that you just don't feel loved like you used to, let alone feel wanted and desired. This can leave you feeling lonely in your own relationship.

Perhaps you are familiar with the pain of missing that love you used to feel or see on their face and hear in their words. Some days that pain is unbearable, and you can't help but ask yourself, "How much longer can I really do this?" That's when most people try all the old and broken garbage tactics you've heard everywhere. Things like plan a date night, tell the brutal truth, just go back to doing what you did in the beginning, go to couples therapy, or ask a family member or friend for advice.

When none of those outdated, broken tactics work and instead backfire into an argument or an even colder shoulder, the love you remember slips further away as doubts about how much longer you can live this way grow louder and louder in your mind.

I know how painful this is. I've been there myself, and every day I help people navigate forward from this place. I'm not belittling how utterly shitty this feels when you are in it. And, I have fantastic news.

The very ideas about how "love fades" or the relationship "changes" over time were incorrect. The love did not fade. The relationship did not just "change" for no reason. If you have resonated with anything that I have described, the cause of this symptom you are experiencing is solvable. And I'm here to show that to you now.

THE INVISIBLE LOOP (OR WALL)

What's going on when it feels like love fades over time or passion is lost, is what Paul and I call The Brick Wall Between You™.

Think of it this way . . .

Each time you and your partner have an upset, kerfuffle, or pain that goes unresolved, it's like you put a brick down between the two of you. In a long-term committed love relationship, those bricks keep stacking to form a wall.

Sometimes it's a disappointment or hurt feelings, and a brick goes in the wall. Other times, a fight comes out of nowhere, like a whirlwind, and five bricks stack onto the wall!

Over time, that wall gets higher and higher, until one day you look over at your partner, and you don't even see them anymore. You can't feel them anymore. You don't know who they are anymore. All you *feel* is the missing love you used to have. And all you *see* are the bricks on your side of the wall between you. Each one carrying a memory of an unsolved pain or upset.

Everything you or your partner does or says gets filtered through, and flavored by, the pain and upset of each brick in that wall. That is why it *feels* like love fades over time. That's why a friend of yours can say the same exact words to you, and it doesn't trigger you. But when your spouse says those same words, watch out because it triggers the crap out of you. It's not you, and it's not your partner. It's the Brick Wall Between You that everything gets filtered through and flavored by.

Love didn't fade over time. The love you are able to feel, or not able to feel, is just a symptom. The cause is the brick wall. The love did not actually fade, it is just blocked by the bricks. And, like the garden, it can be unblocked. I want to start to make this invisible wall visible to you so that we can start solving each brick, together.

Feeling the "love fade" is a common, practically unavoidable relationship symptom today when Demand Relationship is all that's gone on for years.

This is also a cause for a lot of "bad relationship advice" that's out there. People who are unaware that the Brick Wall is the actual cause will often point the finger to the *incorrect cause*, simply because they ran to the end of their skill set.

Let's say that I'm allergic to strawberries and I'm coughing, my eyes are swollen, and my nose is all stuffy. Then I tell you, "Yeah, all the dust in here is driving my allergies crazy." At the same time, I'm throwing another strawberry in my mouth, and you notice that I'm halfway through the box in front of me. Do you think it's the dust causing my problem? If I keep eating the strawberries but go outside to get away from all this dust, will that solve my problem?

In that situation, I would say that I have two urgent problems. The first is that I'm allergic to strawberries and eating them. The second is that I falsely believe that my symptoms are not coming from the strawberries. Does that make sense?

How much time do you think I have on this wild-goose chase of blaming the dust or hay fever or pollen counts for my symptoms before those strawberries put me in the hospital?

The majority of humans have the same false information when it comes to "love fading" or relationships deteriorating over time. They may think it's because "love just fades over time" or that it's your fault or it's your partner's fault or the two of you are not meant to be together or "people change," or they take the other stance of "people don't change" or the classic "that's just how the cookie crumbles."

Wow! That's pretty awful! All that garbage is useless and old. Like blaming the dust, hay fever, or pollen count, while shoving strawberries down your throat.

No, It's not you. It's not your partner. It's not the two of you together. And no, love doesn't just fade over time.

The Brick Wall Between You is the cause of the day-to-day experience that you currently have of your relationship. (Read that again.)

Think about my garden example again for a moment. Remember when I said to you, "Maybe it's the water? Maybe it's because it wasn't organic seeds? Maybe it's the acidity of the soil? Maybe I just didn't plant enough?"

Remember how ridiculous all those things sounded to you when we were looking at a garden covered in cement bricks? Well, that's how ridiculous it is when people spout the trite "bad relationship advice" like "just plan a date night" or "be the bigger person." Meanwhile, there's a huge brick wall of real unsolved issues standing between the two of you that has built up over time, crushing the love underneath its weight.

I'm not blaming the people spouting that garbage advice. It's not their fault. They do not know about the brick wall, and they clearly don't have the skill sets to see it or solve it either. They ran to the end of their skill set, and they are not qualified to help you solve what you are facing. Of course, it is unfortunate that people continue to dish out bad advice that is harmful to families in these moments instead of saying, "I've run to the end of my skill set to help you solve this."

Now that you understand that the symptom of feeling like the love has faded is caused by the Brick Wall Between You, the question is, What is the solution?

The solution is to solve each brick in the wall, brick by brick.

How? Use Relationship Development skill sets, tools, and strategies designed to solve each brick.

The great news is that solving the bricks in the wall takes a fraction of the time that building the bricks into the wall took—when you have the skill sets, tools, and strategies to solve each brick, that is.

It is simple. But it's not easy. It takes time. There's no "magic pill" for this. It's real work, and sometimes it's hard. But there's another truth that needs to be said here.

Life is hard. Life is really hard. I've been on this journey myself. I've had hard moments that brought me to my knees, and when I did, I always said to myself, "Solving this may be hard today, but being stuck, unhappy, and in a shit relationship every day is actually way *harder, unrewarding, and exhausting.*"

The predictable pattern with the predictable outcome is that if you are going to have unresolved kerfuffles (meaning, you don't yet have the skill sets to solve them), then the bricks are going to keep stacking in the wall between you, getting higher and higher.

Trigger: unresolved kerfuffles → Boomerang: brick goes into the wall

Trigger: solve the kerfuffle with skill sets → Boomerang: brick comes out of the wall

Of course, I didn't have myself to help me back then. Today, our students can follow our step-by-step method to solve the bricks in the wall. It's much easier for them than it ever was for me. And now it can be a whole lot easier for you too.

There are tools and strategies to solve each brick, and even though I can't possibly give you all of them in this one book, we can start with a foundational tool that applies to all bricks to get us moving in helping you to solve yours.

THE RELATIONSHIP DEVELOPMENT TOOL: FACE IT, OWN IT & SOLVE IT™

Each time there is a kerfuffle or pain in your relationship, you have a choice. Most people try to *avoid, prevent,* or *control* the situation to avoid the pain or discomfort. It's like the old saying goes: "Don't rock the boat." That mindset is precisely what keeps the brick stuck in the wall in the first place.

Avoiding, preventing, and controlling are all Demand Relationship tactics, so they all break down relationships. And neither avoiding nor preventing nor controlling things can actually resolve the brick in the wall between you so that it doesn't repeat again. Meaning, these old broken escape tactics don't work to give you the outcome you want.

Let's say there's a topic on the "we don't talk about that anymore" list. You both stopped bringing this up because it caused a fight each time. In day-to-day moments, when something seems like it might cross over into that "topic," you try to prevent it from coming up or you try to control things to avoid it.

Did you solve that issue? Did you fix it?

You may have avoided another kerfuffle in that moment, but did you solve the issue around that topic? No, you did not.

In that moment, you also likely increased distance between you and your partner by further solidifying the things that you two can't talk about without fighting. So, the real outcome was that *the topic* took a hit and *the relationship* took a hit, even when you thought you "avoided" it.

No one ever walked away from avoiding a topic that is important in life thinking, *Oh, I'm so glad that my spouse and I can't talk about that important topic. I feel so loved and close to them right now. And I have so much confidence in us!*

I know that sounds ridiculous, but I just want you to see that avoidance and "not rocking the boat" do not actually heal or improve your relationship; rather both tactics break it down.

Yes, you have not yet learned the skill sets to navigate any topic without fighting and breaking down the relationship. But the fact is that you can. It's all just a skill set, and it can be learned.

The other invisible Predictable Pattern Loop in this dynamic is this:

Trigger: avoidance → Boomerang: repeat experience

Everything you try to avoid in your life is just on a circular path back to you in some form. You can't avoid it. You can only delay it, at best. There's a difference.

Okay, but just so you know, there is also another negative dynamic involved here. Each Loop creates momentum that reinforces the next experience. So, when it circles back to you, it will be more intense than it is now. You might think of it as a "procrastination penalty" of sorts.

As we've already pointed out, each instance of avoidance puts more Demand Relationship into the Loop, adds bricks to the wall between you, and pushes you further down the downward spiral. The next instance will be more painful as it picks up negative momentum.

Remember, if you pick the path of avoidance, preventing, and controlling, you are just signing up for a repeat experience. It's like looking at the thing you are trying to avoid and saying, "Oh, I like this so much, I want to do this again, please!"

If you don't avoid, prevent, or control, what do you do? Great question!

Our tool for this is called **Face It, Own It & Solve It™**:

Step #1. Face it: Don't try to escape it. Be willing to face it. See it accurately for what it is. Get visibility and don't run or hide from it.

Step #2. Own it: Take personal responsibility for the issue. We talked about this one already. Even if it's not your fault, you can take personal responsibility and ownership to solve it. Stop blaming someone else. Stop waiting for someone else to come save you. No one is coming to save you. *You* are going to save you, and we are going to empower you with the skill sets to do that! It's a brick in *your* wall. You own it.

Step #3. Solve it: Get the real skill sets, tools, and strategies that work to actually solve the dynamic. Solving it means that it is resolved, both people feel good about the outcome, and it will not come up again.

Just because the conversation has passed does not mean it's solved. Just letting the moment or topic pass without solving it is called avoidance. Solving it means that it has been resolved successfully. Stay tuned—we will be going through many tools and skill sets for solving common relationship kerfuffles throughout the rest of the chapters in this book.

Trigger: Face It, Own It & Solve It → Boomerang: brick comes out of the wall (does not repeat)

When you Face It, Own It & Solve It, you finally get to take that brick out of the Brick Wall Between You and place it on the ground, on the foundation beneath the two of you. Believe it or not, when this is done right, it becomes a source of strength in your relationship. Each solved brick that comes down in this way transforms into a more solid foundation of your relationship.

Just like with the garden, you do not need to solve every single brick in the wall to experience relief, hope, happiness, and peace. Just solving one brick can bring so much relief for you and your relationship.

I've watched our students do this countless times. They solve the first brick, and the waves of hope that wash over them fuel them to do another and another. Each brick that comes off the wall builds more optimism and hope. With consistency, that hope and optimism turn into belief and confidence. It's inspiring to watch, and I look forward to watching you do the same.

There is no single solution to "bricks" (with an S). Each brick resulted from a specific type of kerfuffle that occurred, and each kerfuffle has its own solution. Don't let that overwhelm or discourage you. You do not have to figure out how to solve each one by yourself; we've already done that part for you.

THE OPPORTUNITY OF ONE BRICK

While each brick has a unique solution, when you do this work, you will see that, at times, you solve one brick and four fall out of the wall. It happens.

For instance, imagine the biggest issue you and your partner have right now. How would it feel if that was genuinely resolved in a way that you feel good about and your partner also feels authentically good about? How would that feel?

I'm guessing it would feel f'ing fantastic! Like a weight was lifted. Like fresh air blowing through or the sun shining in the darkness. Yeah, I've been there, so I know.

And it won't matter to you that there are 19 more things on the list to solve, because it feels so f'ing fantastic to have solved that one thing that you didn't know how to solve before. Each solved brick in the wall fuels you with more energy, excitement, and upward momentum to solve the next one. It's pretty awesome.

I'm excited for you, even if you don't believe it for yourself yet. You're a human. Same as me and the thousands of students who have already done it. If we can do it, so can you.

One of our students—we'll call her Mary—came into our program to get the skill sets to peacefully co-parent because she didn't want her kids to suffer through her inevitable divorce the same way she suffered through her parents' divorce. She started the training in our methodology, and when she got to the experiential exercise where Paul and I role-play the brick wall, seeing how the bricks go into the wall and what it looks and sounds like when they come out of the wall, she had a surreal experience. She said her mind was blown. She saw the wall, her wall, for the first time, and she couldn't believe she hadn't seen it before.

I remember that she asked me, "What's the process for the brick wall if I'm not going to stay married and I just want to heal the co-parenting relationship so we can have a peaceful and harmonious household?"

My response was, "The process is the same, regardless if you are going to stay married or not. Healing the relationship requires solving the bricks in the wall. Married or not, it's the same path, either way."

She started the work and created a massive transformation, not only in her relationship but in herself. She enjoyed the huge relief of solved kerfuffles that used to be fights, and started to enjoy peaceful days of those kerfuffles not repeating themselves anymore.

As it commonly happens, when the brick wall got lower and lower, the love that had been trapped underneath those bricks long ago started to grow again. In the end, she ended up saving her marriage, but not the old marriage with the brick wall. She created a new marriage, with the same person, without the brick wall between them. The beauty of Mary's story, like so many others, is that she also experienced all the benefits of doing this work. The greatest gift goes to the one who does the work.

When we build the Brick Wall Between us and our partner, we not only separate ourselves from them but we also wall ourselves in at the same time. Then, we wonder why we feel dead inside or have a hard time connecting to the love we used to feel, as if it just went away.

When you solve the bricks in the wall between you, and the wall starts to come down, you get not only the relief in your relationship but also your freedom from not living trapped behind that wall.

Sadly, most people still falsely believe that the problem is their partner, themselves, or one of those other false beliefs we've talked about already. So instead of doing the work to take down the brick wall, they just leave that partner, thinking that getting rid of them will solve the problem.

> **PRINCIPLE:**
> You bring "YOU" with you into your next relationship.

You bring yourself, your skill set level, your Triggers, and your brick wall with you into your next relationship and into your next and into your next. As the saying goes, "Everywhere you go, there you are."

THE HEIGHT OF THE WALL

That brings us to another dynamic about the brick wall that I want to share with you: the height of the brick wall.

A low brick wall shows different symptoms in a relationship than a high brick wall does. Said differently, as an expert, I can look at the symptoms in your relationship and know the height of the Brick Wall Between the two of you. The height of the wall creates different symptoms as it goes from low to high.

Think of it this way: in a new relationship, there is no wall (or a very low wall) between you. That's when things feel easy. When you're not so easily triggered. When you're open to them, curious about them, able to make them happy, and enjoy being with each other.

As kerfuffles happen that go unsolved, bricks start going in the wall. When the wall is low, the kerfuffles and upsets seem situational and occasional. In a long-term relationship, without the skill sets to solve the kerfuffles, it's only a matter of time before the brick wall is at eye level, and it now becomes hard to see the partner you once had.

Here are some examples of the symptoms that show up when the brick wall is reaching eye level. You do not need to check every box on this list, of course. It's just to show you some of the symptoms of a brick wall approaching or exceeding eye level.

- No matter what I do or what comes out of my mouth, it's met with criticism and complaints (or eye rolls and disdain) from my partner.
- My partner and I used to just argue over the big things. Now we even argue about the smallest (stupidest) things, like who left the bread tag on the counter.
- The list of things "we can't talk about" is growing.
- There are things I don't share with my partner because I already know I won't have their support.
- It used to be only after a huge blowup that we wouldn't talk to each other or we would go to bed without speaking. Now it seems like it's almost every week that something happens, and we go to bed without speaking.
- We're more like roommates, living lives in the same house but not connected.
- I feel stuck because of the things we can't talk about without fighting.
- I feel lonely in my marriage, even though my partner is right there.
- I can't make them happy, no matter how hard I try.

- There's too much arguing and bickering between us, between us and the kids, and between us about the kids.

- I share things with my friends and feel more supported by my friends than by my partner.

- Even when we are not arguing, the tension and distance between us is obvious. I feel it. My spouse feels it. But what I'm really worried about is if my kids feel it. And what this is doing to them.

Those are symptoms (not causes) of the height of the Brick Wall Between You reaching about eye level. At that point, remember, everything that your partner does or says is now being filtered through, and flavored by, all the upsets and pains you see in the bricks in the wall.

If you find yourself in this spot, do not lose hope. This is where most of our students were before they started our program. You are not alone, and it's going to be okay.

Please, listen to me right now. This is my expertise. This is all we do, all day every day. The list above, that's a humanity list. If I went to the billions of humans in long-term relationships right now on this planet, most of them would have many symptoms on that list. That symptom list is not a "you and your partner" list. How could it be if most people have it, too? It's a human list.

It was never about you and your partner. This was always about Demand Relationship going into the Loop and unknowingly putting bricks into the wall between the two of you.

If you find yourself with symptoms on this list, the great news is that stopping Demand Relationship and operating from the Relationship Development paradigm is the beginning of the cure for every one of those symptoms. You know what would have been worse? Never knowing and never changing direction.

If you're reading this book and you're feeling the harsh weight and breakage that Demand Relationship has left humanity in, just know that we've got you.

THE TIME IT TAKES TO GET TO EYE LEVEL

In my experience, it used to be that once a committed relationship reached about seven or eight years, the brick wall was commonly approaching eye level. These days, it is happening much sooner than that.

What changed?

Remember when I said that when you have a Brick Wall Between You, you also wall yourself in? And remember when I said that you take yourself with you to your next relationship? Well, you bring yourself, and your brick wall, with you into every other relationship.

For example, when someone's date says or does something that lights up one of the bricks in their existing wall, they think, "Oh no. I know that bullshit. My ex used to do that. I'm outta here."

Or their sibling says something to them that lights up one of the bricks in their brick wall, and they say, "I don't have to listen to this crap from you!" And they hang up the phone.

People don't see it, but they are carrying around a big old brick wall with them and dropping it down between them and all the other people they try to relate to.

Some may do personal work to develop themselves and heal. And that's great. But if they never learn how to inter-operate with other people without doing Demand Relationship, the wall is still there. So, each time someone triggers them and it lights up one of those bricks in their wall, they go into Demand Relationship and either tell the other person to change or they leave.

That's the mantra of the old Demand Relationship way: change to meet my demands, or we separate (I can't be around you). That's why I always say, whether you are staying in this marriage or not, these skill sets are for you, not for your partner, and not even your marriage. There is no option not to do this work. Demand Relationship does not work, and it will never work, regardless of how many times you change partners. It's a predictable pattern with a predictable outcome.

> **PRINCIPLE:**
> Your experience of your relationship is flavored by and filtered through the Brick Wall Between You.
>
> **PRINCIPLE:**
> It's not you, it's not your partner, it's not the two of you together . . . it's the Brick Wall Between You that is the problem.
>
> **PRINCIPLE:**
> Without the Relationship Development skill sets to solve the bricks (and ultimately prevent new ones from going in), each unsolved kerfuffle or upset adds more bricks to the wall.
>
> **PRINCIPLE:**
> Each solved brick becomes a brick in the foundation of your relationship, giving you strength that you can stand on.
>
> **PRINCIPLE:**
> There is a Relationship Development solution for every brick in the wall.

This is why we keep saying that Relationship Development builds up relationships while Demand Relationship breaks them down. When you operate from Demand Relationship, more bricks go in the wall, usually until someone gives up.

These bricks go into the wall in the little moments of your day, not just when there is a huge fight. In the small day-to-day moments, when Demand Relationship goes into the Loop and breaks down your relationship, another brick goes into the wall. When we operate from Relationship Development, we can solve the bricks in the wall and prevent new ones from going in.

Hopefully you are starting to see how revelational this discovery and method are. I'm so thrilled to share all this with you so you are never without this fundamental understanding again.

And at this point, I also have to tell you something unflattering about me. The truth is, I never would have figured any of this out if Paul hadn't left me. While this isn't an easy story for me to tell, I do think it's important that you know who I was and how I figured this out. (Turn the page.)

CHAPTER 7

THE HANGING-BY-A-THREAD MOMENT

It was like any other summer evening. I was sitting on our bench under the tree by the driveway, waiting for Paul to come home from work while our dog Putty ran around the yard, chasing squirrels and dropping her Frisbee at my feet.

But this wasn't like any other night. Paul drove up the driveway, and from the moment he got out of the car, I knew something was wrong. Have you ever had that feeling when you look at someone, and you just know something is wrong?

In that same moment, I also felt like whatever was wrong, it had something to do with me. In a split second, I racked my brain, trying to think of what I had done or what this could be about.

He closed the car door and said the four words that no one wants to hear: "We need to talk."

My stomach flip-flopped. For sure, this was about me. I was replaying the last week in my mind, but there had not been any fights or issues I could recall.

We went inside and sat on the couch in the living room. Then, Paul proceeded to drop the bomb . . . he was leaving me. He didn't say that he was "thinking about leaving" or even that "things weren't good." No, he flat-out told me that he was leaving that night.

I sat there, stunned, as Paul told me all the things that were wrong in our relationship. He said that he had been thinking about this for months (I had no idea). He saw no workable solution for us to stay together. At this point, as he described all the horrible things about us together, tears started to roll down my cheeks.

Now that may seem like a very normal reaction to you, but crying was not normal for me. This was many years ago, in July of 2000. Back then, my nickname was the Ice Princess, and it was very well deserved. I was a no-nonsense, kick-ass, nonfeeling, tough-ass, strong bitch, and proud of it. In corporate, they knew to send me in when something had to be bulldozed through or someone needed to be shredded. Why? After getting my heart stomped on one too many times, I had locked my heart away in my icy tower years before. From the day I moved into my ice tower, I went through life unmoved and, *I thought*, unable to be hurt by the world.

The fact is, I had never cried in front of Paul in all our time together. But what Paul didn't even know was that I hadn't cried in many years, long before he came into my life. Not one tear. Not in years.

As I felt the tears rolling down my cheeks, the voice in my head started shouting at me, "Are you crying? Stop crying right now! Are you crying in front of Paul? Oh my God. Pull those tears back in and stop this right now!"

I was terrified. I didn't know how to stop crying. One tear turned into three, and within seconds, I was sobbing.

That's when the voice in my head stopped shouting at me and went silent. I was unraveling and had no idea how to stop the pain. Then I heard the voice in my head, calmly, slowly, saying, "You failed."

"You failed. You failed. You failed."

Not that I failed at the relationship—that was not a surprise. Being an Ice Princess doesn't exactly come with a handbook on love relationships. Besides, every one of my past relationships had failed, so this one was no surprise.

The haunting truth was, however, that I failed to protect myself . . . and here I was with my heart, breaking.

My entire life was built to protect my heart from ever breaking, ever hurting, ever again. Every thought, every word, every action was intentionally selected so that my heart never got hurt again. My whole life was built behind a shield of protection. And here I was, with a heart shattering into a million pieces and destroying me with it.

It was in that instant that an overwhelming realization occurred to me. If I can't protect myself from pain, then I don't know how to navigate life from this day forward.

I began to unravel. Everything I thought I knew about life and how I could get by without suffering was collapsing underneath me. As the pain of my heart breaking collided with my fear of how to navigate life without getting hurt, I began to sob uncontrollably.

Have you ever heard the phrase "some people break down, while others break open"? Well, that must be what was happening to me. As the floodgates of my tears flowed open, I guess the ice tower collapsed with me in it, and I felt this surge of love for Paul that I had never felt before, for anyone.

Honestly, as embarrassing as it is to say this right now, I didn't know that love like that was real because I had never felt love that way before in my life.

Growing up, watching all those movies and hearing those songs, I thought the artists were just making that up for the art. I had no idea they were singing about the pain of losing love that felt like this. I didn't know that real people were feeling something like this, because that was never a part of my life. Until that moment. That moment I unraveled sitting on the couch, with Paul, my best friend and, apparently, the love of my life.

In one unfortunate moment, the worst moment of my life, I realized three truths that devastated me:

Truth #1: Love like this is real, and humans can feel love like this.
Truth #2: I feel this way about Paul.
Truth #3: I'm never going to get to live in this kind of love because, of course, I've ruined it, and he's walking out the door.

I don't know if it was the crying, my heart breaking open, or the desperation of knowing that my ice tower was destroyed and there was no turning back, but the next thing I did was about the most "un-Stacey" thing that I could have ever done.

I looked at Paul and poured my heart out to him. I told him that everything he said about our shitty relationship was 100% true and that I couldn't disagree with a single thing he said. I admitted that I had no fucking clue how to do relationship and that I never had. I said that I thought that day was day one of the rest of my life, and I wanted a chance to live it. I told him that all these years, I was just being who I thought I needed to be, and only now, in that very moment, did I finally realize that everything I thought I needed to be or do was all garbage. I told him that I loved him more than I thought I've ever loved anyone or been loved by anyone and that I wasn't even sure this kind of love was a real thing before today.

And then here's the kicker: I did the thing that I swore I would never do as long as there was air in my lungs . . . I begged.

I begged Paul to give me a second chance. Not to save our relationship (I wasn't going to lie to him; I had no idea how to do that). So, I asked for a second chance to be the real me and figure this out.

With nothing to lose, I told him a truth that I had never even admitted to myself before that moment. Since the day he showed up, I'd had one foot out the door because I was so sure that one day he'd do exactly this . . . leave me.

I told him, "I have no idea if anything I do can save us, but I'd like the chance to try. Just give me a chance. Don't leave this version of me. This isn't even me. I don't know who I really am anymore, but I know it's not this. The only thing I know for sure is that this is not the best of me."

FROM PAUL MARTINO

For as far back as I can remember, I have been hardwired to confront and solve problems. For many months prior to this night, I internally struggled to figure out a solution or even something that would just simply improve the negative dynamics that kept causing the verbal tug-of-war disagreements and regular fights

The Hanging-by-a-Thread Moment

between Stacey and me. The frequency and increased intensity of these battles were getting more commonplace, and, over time, my willingness to even put energy into participating in them was shrinking as a result.

No matter how hard I tried, I simply could not figure out why things kept deteriorating. These seemingly senseless arguments, growing resentments, and my struggle to find a logical way to stop making them worse would constantly seep into my thoughts.

Even though I possessed deep self-confidence in being an independent problem solver, in this case, I simply couldn't identify any solid cause behind what went wrong between us. We used to be so incredibly tight, so seemingly aligned, and we genuinely loved spending all our time together so naturally. Now, instead of loving being together, I found myself regularly needing to keep my growing rage from surfacing, which always caused more damage than the original issue we were fighting about anyway.

At that point in time, the only thing I knew for sure was that I deeply missed the way we used to be together, and I just wanted to do the "right" thing here, for the good of both of us.

After mentally wrestling with this deterioration for quite some time, my logical brain came up with the only thing that made sense to me. That answer was to take the sword (meaning, endure the pain and consequences of leaving) and free her from me so that, at least, she could be happy again with someone else.

Even though I knew that leaving her was also inevitably tied to deep pain and a permanent loss for both of us, and that this would absolutely suck, it was the only thing that made any sense to me at that time.

In effect, the only thing that was clearly within my power to change in this dynamic of the downward spiral was to forcibly break it by removing myself from contributing to it. With no other options in front of me, I slowly became more committed to, and eventually became 100% unwavering in, my resolve to end my relationship with Stacey.

My deepest wish was that I could somehow save the friendship we had that I valued so much. As painful as this was going to be, I believed, in my core, that it was the right thing to do when I got out of the car that night. Expecting a rough time ahead, I strengthened my resolve before saying the words, "We need to talk."

Although our conversation started off as I had predicted, and our mutual destiny of separate lives was assured, time suddenly began to stop when Stacey started crying and broke open. I quickly found myself standing in front of someone else, a version of Stacey that I had never experienced before.

Everything began to change between us in that very moment. And it wasn't because she was crying—that isn't what moved me. The very unflattering truth about me is that I can be nothing less than merciless and icy when I'm committed to a path, like I was that night.

What changed everything, however, was that there was truly something unexpected here in front of me that I had never encountered before. I couldn't put my finger on what was so different about Stacey, but I was suddenly becoming confused and beginning to question the certainty I arrived with that night. The Stacey that was in front of me in that moment was not the Stacey I had always known. And yet, I could simultaneously tell she was also the most real and authentic version of Stacey I had ever met, both in the good *and* bad times.

I found myself moved by this very real and genuinely beautiful heart in front of me, and at the same time, I realized that *I* was the one hurting her. She was open and vulnerable in a way that I had never experienced her before. She was transforming right in front of me. As steadfast as I was coming in the door that night, suddenly I could no longer be so sure that nothing could change between us when I was already witnessing a genuine transformation in Stacey happening before my eyes. I started to question everything.

The shift in Stacey created a shift inside me. The voice in my head started to tell me I was making a *huge* mistake in leaving her. My desire to protect her from this pain that I was now causing her was growing by the minute.

The Hanging-by-a-Thread Moment

Stacey's transformation created an opening for us in our relationship but even more, there was an opening to a different outcome.

Being committed to the outcome before I arrived, I admit that part of me still had an artificial desire to "pull it together" and stay on target to meet the goal I had set out to accomplish that night. That thought, however, lacked any real remaining power, because the truth before me was so undeniable.

That precious and short "hanging-by-a-thread" moment was the start of a 14-hour conversation between us that night and into the next day. While 14 hours of conversation might seem like a lot of time, it is absolutely nothing in comparison to a lifetime that definitely would have been lost if there was no opening at all.

That night could have easily ended up with me walking away from Stacey, sticking to my agenda to end it for our "greater good." Sadly, I'm also confident that with my story of how "unworkable" our relationship was, my well-intentioned friends, family, and the general population would have all readily supported that decision. I could have easily walked away from our relationship very wrongly thinking I had "dodged a bullet" and reasoned away why it was the "right thing to do" and that there was "no other way."

I likely would have reinforced that story for the rest of my life, learning nothing as a result and therefore winning the prize of repeating everything that went wrong between us in my future relationships as well. If it wasn't for that one "hanging-by-a-thread" momentary opening for us that night, because of Stacey's profound epiphany, I would have experienced the most catastrophic loss of my life without ever even realizing that it had happened.

I would have missed out on my life with Stacey, our two amazing children, the happiness and fulfillment of who I have become with her, and the thousands of marriages and families we have now been blessed to help save. All that is what was really hanging by a thread that night. And we could have lost it all in a moment.

But thank God Stacey saved our relationship that night.

After seeing how much Stacey transformed that night, when she asked me to give her another chance to figure this out, I was somewhat optimistic. I'm a little ashamed to admit it now, but back then, my own belief was that I was "fine," and it was just Stacey who needed to "change herself" if this relationship was going to work. We laugh about it now, but back then, I had no idea how much I still had to learn. Luckily for me, Stacey was about to change both of our lives for the better.

Stacey: With my second chance in hand, I dove in on a great journey. I read everything I could about men, women, relationships, love, intimacy, and all the things. Most of it was based on couples work. A lot of things would say, "Get your husband to . . . " and I would think, "Get my husband to? Have you *met* Paul? There is no *getting him* to do anything!" The couples work stuff wasn't an option for me because Paul wasn't going to go near that with a 10-foot pole.

It seemed like when I did try something I found in a book, it would often just backfire and make things worse.

Then I tried something new. I started to reverse-engineer why something didn't work. I would use the results I was getting from my trial and error and figure out things that did work. Then I would reverse-engineer what did work and apply those principles to another situation.

It was very slow going, though, because I had a huge problem. It was like trying to run on a pond covered in thin, breaking ice. Our relationship was very fragile. Every time I tried something that backfired, I was overcome with the fear that this could be the last day. This failure could be the one that made Paul say, "See, I told you this is unworkable. I'm done."

I didn't have any relationship skills back then, so navigating that time was painful and scary. Trial and error was my "method," and it was very risky. But something was happening. Each time I figured out what worked and what didn't, I removed a blind spot and empowered myself with dynamics and principles that worked again and again. I was gaining clarity. I was gaining traction. And most of all, I was gaining hope.

Not hope for my relationship, actually, hope for me. As much as I really hoped that this work I was doing would somehow heal our relationship, there was really no way for me to know if it would, and I couldn't control that. But I for fuck-sure was going to figure out what caused this pain that blindsided me, understand relationships, recover my real and happy self, and stop living in the darkness. That was my commitment, and I was 100% sure I would get there, even if it took me a hundred years.

I want to be transparent with you. I wasn't doing all this for Paul. I was doing this for me. I needed to figure out how to navigate life and be happy. I needed to figure out how to love without being in the dark. I needed to figure out how to be who I really was without being afraid of that. And hopefully, somehow, save my relationship with Paul in the process.

Every week, I was figuring out more about me and understanding more about the differences between me and Paul. I would bring a list of questions to date night with Paul. Yep, I'm fun like that. And he got used to it. I was like a journalist doing an investigation. I was in search of the truth. I would ask him about his meanings for different things and marvel at how different they were from my own. I would find research on the masculine and ask him to validate or invalidate their findings and explain his perspective to me.

I almost cringe to tell you how long this went on. I want to reassure you that it took me longer to discover all this, on my own, through trial and error, than it will take you to learn the step-by-step method that we created. Just this initial trial-and-error phase of discovery took me about a year.

And every day, I was living more and more as my real self, without pain. I was becoming free and happy. And every day, I was leading us through more harmony and less kerfuffles. I was becoming the happiest I had ever been in my life.

For almost an entire year, I kept at this, bringing peaceful dynamics into our relationship, solving issues of the past and present and healing years of past hurts until we were rock solid and unshakable.

I had single-handedly saved our relationship. I had no idea that was even possible when I set out on my journey. And yet that's exactly what I did.

Without realizing it, I made a unique discovery: it only takes one person to transform a relationship.

I don't want you to misunderstand what I'm saying. One person doing what they've always done or what they think might work cannot single-handedly transform a relationship.

However, one person, empowered with the answers, tools, and strategies to solve whatever comes up, absolutely can transform a relationship.

It was a miracle that what I figured out saved us. I was blessed. It was way more likely that I would not save us than it was that I would figure out how to single-handedly save our relationship.

And I didn't "fix" our old, crappy relationship. I built a brand-new relationship with the same partner. Everything I did transformed me and transformed Paul.

The most insane thing about the whole discovery is that everything I did that built up our relationship, and everything I did to stop breaking down our relationship also felt better to me than anything else. I felt happier and more authentically myself than I had in all my years before. I wasn't being something that Paul needed me to be. I wasn't pleasing or compromising. And yet, we were healing, building, and becoming unshakable.

And without doing any of the work, Paul was transforming. He was changing every day. Not because I told him to or instructed him based on my findings. He was transforming in response to the change in me.

It was transformation through inspiration.

About a year after our "hanging-by-a-thread" moment, Paul came to me and said, "I'm happier than I've ever been in my life. I feel more like myself. You gave *me* back to *me,* and I didn't even know I needed that. I don't know what you are doing for us, but I want to know everything. I'm starting to feel like a Neanderthal next to you. Teach me. Teach me everything, so I can start giving to you the way you have been giving to me."

That was over 23 years ago... and Paul and I have been blessed to not only create our own unshakable love and unleashed passion, but we've been blessed to help thousands of others around the world create theirs too.

I used to say that I didn't understand why I was the one. Why me? Why was I the one to go on that journey and figure it out? It would be years before I would get the answer to that question, when I received the "calling" to "tell everyone what I was blessed to figure out." Now it is crystal clear to me. I was blessed to make it through my journey, with all my cuts and bruises, so that I could give my discovery to you.

I was alone, scared, and clueless, but I survived and came out the other side with the discovery... Our Relationship Development Method.

That's why I wrote this book. It's why I built our programs. It's why we provide 24/7 support to our students every day of the year.

This is everything I did not have.

There was no Stacey for me. I didn't have myself to tell me the answers. I didn't have "a Stacey" to hand me the step-by-step solutions. I didn't have support or a community to share in the journey.

I don't want that for you. So, my commitment to God for carrying me through my trials was that I would be here for any human who wants these answers... for as long as I am alive (and hopefully long after).

I am here to give you the answer to "How can I start living this, instead of just learning it?" next. (Turn the page.)

CHAPTER 8

THE 5% & THE 95% MIND

Often, on this journey, students will reach a point where they feel like, "I know better. Why is this still a kerfuffle?" Or maybe there are things that you feel shouldn't still be an issue, since you've been reading this book.

Said differently, at this point, you might be thinking to yourself, *Why isn't this working for me yet?* You might have doubts and be thinking that not much has changed.

And what's even worse, everyone around you is doing Demand Relationship to you! You see it everywhere, and they won't stop doing it, even when you tell them to stop.

This is where many people wonder, "Does this stuff even work?"

I understand completely. At this point, I teach my students the principle of the 5% and 95% minds. Allow me to explain.

Dr. Bruce Lipton (a biologist) teaches that there are two parts to your brain. Your conscious Thinking Mind, which uses about 5% of your brain, and your unconscious Autopilot Mind, which uses the other 95% of your brain.

Your Thinking Mind is the part of your brain that you use to think things through, pay attention, learn, and so on.

Over time, as you learn and practice something through enough repetition, your brain makes a "program" for it in your Autopilot Mind so that you don't have to use your Thinking Mind to do it anymore. This is part of the way the human brain works.

Think of tying your shoes. At one point, you had to learn to tie your shoes. You practiced, over and over again, with your laces. You used the "bunny ears" method or "loop, swoop, and pull" or whatever you were taught. It took effort, practice, and focus. It required your 5% Thinking Mind to be focused on the tying of the shoes. Then you did it enough times that it became what humans refer to as "second nature," which means you knew it well enough for your brain to make a "program" for it in your Autopilot Mind. You could run the "tie your shoes" program on autopilot, without having to think it through.

So now, you can tie your shoes at the same time as talking, and you don't have to focus on how to tie your shoes or even acknowledge that you are tying your shoes. Your mind and body just "do it" for you on autopilot. You understand this and have many experiences of this, yes?

Okay, now let's take an example of the 5% mind function versus the 95% mind function. Have you ever been driving home from somewhere and ended up in your driveway and thought, *Holy crap, I don't even remember getting off the highway.* That's the moment when you realize you were so deep in thought that you don't really remember the exit you took or turning into your neighborhood. But here you are in your driveway, safe and sound (thank God).

Now, have you ever been driving along your route, maybe talking to someone in the car or caught up in your thoughts, and for a moment you realize, "Oh crap, did I miss my exit? Wait a minute. Where are we?"

What happens in that moment?

Typically, we turn down the music or tell everyone to be quiet, and we start looking at the signs on the road to see if we can figure out where we are. I know, it's kinda comical how we all turn the music down when we don't know where we are. But there's a brain science explanation for it.

What is happening?

The moment that our brain ran to the end of our autopilot program for where we were driving, we had to switch to our 5%

Thinking Mind to focus on the task of driving and navigating to get to our destination.

When we couldn't use our Autopilot Mind to navigate us while talking and listening to music, we had to redirect all our focus (5% Thinking Mind) to the task of driving. So, we "turn off" or tune out all other distractions so we can focus with our Thinking Mind.

This is how the brain works.

What does this have to do with relationships you ask? *Everything.*

According to Dr. Lipton, our relationship reactions are stored in our 95% Autopilot Mind. Our Triggers, emotional reactions, feelings, words, and more are all Autopilot Programs that we have created over time.

For instance, when someone rolls their eyes at you, you have an instant feeling or reaction to it. You don't "think through" what that means, how you feel about it, and how to respond. You can instantly react without having to think it through, because long ago, your brain made an autopilot program for your relationship reactions. Like laughing at something you find funny . . . it just happens, automatically.

Our Demand Relationship reactions, patterns, emotions, meanings, etc. are all baked into our 95% Autopilot Mind. So, even though you have learned some of these Relationship Development concepts with your 5% Thinking Mind, your brain is still running your autopilot programs for you from the 95% Autopilot Mind, which is wired for Demand Relationship and all your old patterns.

According to the brain science, just an idea or thought in the 5% mind is not enough to rewrite the 95% mind. Meaning, just thinking and deciding "I'm going to stop judging others, so I don't keep sliding into Demand Relationship" is not enough to rewire your 95% autopilot program.

Which is why, after you have that thought, you are going to realize that you just "judged" about seven things in your mind without realizing it. Even though you had "decided" to stop judging.

Similarly, even though you have read things in this book that you want to be able to do in real life, you haven't been able to "live from" what you have "learned" . . . yet.

It's not that this stuff doesn't work. We've proven that it does. It's just that "reading" it once is simply not enough. Your mind is still operating from your old 95% autopilot program, based in Demand Relationship.

The brain science states that your 5% mind cannot overwrite the program in the 95% Autopilot Mind with merely an idea or thought. It's simply not enough. But make no mistake, you absolutely can rewrite the 95% Autopilot Mind.

This is usually when my students ask, "So, how do we rewrite our 95% mind?" Excellent question.

According to Dr. Lipton, there are two ways to rewire the 95% Autopilot Mind. And Paul and I have discovered a third.

The two ways that Dr. Lipton teaches to rewrite the 95% Autopilot Mind are:

1. Repetition
2. Hypnosis

This means that just "hearing about" Relationship Development versus Demand Relationship once is not enough to rewire the Autopilot Mind after decades of experiences. It requires repetition. Repetition is how your autopilot brain was wired in the first place, so it is required for the rewiring.

Reading this book or even doing our trainings one time is not enough for rewiring the 95% mind. It's not that our content isn't "good enough"; it's just brain science. It requires repetition. Kind of like learning another language, it takes repetition to get it into your Autopilot Mind so it can become second nature for you. It's the same with relationship reactions.

Of course, hypnosis accesses the unconscious mind, so it's also a method for rewiring, when done properly. And in case you were wondering, the answer is no, I cannot hypnotize you to stop doing Demand Relationship and start doing Relationship Development in any given life scenario (and neither can anyone else).

In the over 14 years that Paul and I have been doing our courses and events, we have discovered a third way to enable our students to effectively rewire their Autopilot Mind, break the patterns of Demand Relationship that were in there, and wire in the patterns of Relationship Development so they can get results on autopilot.

3. Immersion events

Think of the magic of movies. Have you ever been in a movie theater and cried, laughed, or jumped in reaction to a movie scene? Sure you have. Yet, you're not *in* the movie. The events of the movie are not happening *to* you. The actors are not even performing the movie live in front of you. And yet, you react with laughter or you are moved to tears or you jump when something startles you. This is the magic of movies. This is the brain science of immersion. Your nervous system is all-in. You are relating to the characters. Your senses are participating in the experience. Both your 5% mind and your 95% mind are in the experience. You are immersed in it.

It's the same when our students attend one of our multiday immersion events. Whether the event is in-person or live-streamed online, they are getting immersion results for their 95% Autopilot Mind rewiring.

This is why you can learn through this book or our courses, but breaking through to living it automatically requires one of the three methods for rewiring the 95% mind:

1. Repetition
2. Hypnosis
3. Immersion

I recommend using all three, which is why we provide all three to our students (and their results support the science).

So, do not give in to the old thinking that "this isn't working" and then give up before you reach your reward. The goal of this book is to show you the paradigm that no one showed you before and for you to see, without a doubt, that there is a skill set you can learn to create the relationships that you want.

You will never again have to go through life blindsided by negative relationships and feeling helpless to do anything about it. And you can start today with everything I could jam into this book! Additionally, if you want them, we're here to give you all the training, immersion events, and support that you desire beyond this book. So don't worry about that now.

Don't worry when you slip into Demand Relationship. It's going to happen, and that doesn't mean that this won't work for you. And for goodness' sake, please stop telling other people when they are doing Demand Relationship (that's Demand Relationship you're doing there).

I put this chapter here for you so that you understand the difference between "learning it" (5% mind) and "living it" (95% mind), so that you aren't so hard on yourself, and so you don't give up before you get results.

I put this chapter here for you, now, because we are about to dive into the strategies, answers, and tools for you to start getting results. And before I start giving you that knowledge, I want you to understand the difference between learning it and living it so you know that you will need both the training to learn it, like reading, and the strategies to live it, like the ways to rewire the 95% mind.

Learning it *is* the first step; it is just not the *last* step to living it.

Just stay with me. I've helped thousands of students navigate this journey. I've got you.

And now you are ready to see the second most critical Closed Loop of relationship. This is going to turn everything you thought about relationship on its head.

And if you thought you'd never hear "brain science" as part of this "relationship stuff," hold on to your hat . . . because the next piece I'm giving you is . . . math! Don't be scared, I got you. It's time you learned the truth about relationship. It's time for me to give you the formula to every relationship. (Turn the page.)

CHAPTER 9

THE RELATIONSHIP FORMULA

Hopefully by now you are beginning to see that relationship is not what you thought it was. Well, hang on, it's about to be an even wilder ride.

Paul and I have been hosting our three-day Relationship Breakthrough Retreat® event for many years. And at the beginning of each event, I will step out and say to someone, "Hand me your relationship, and I'll fix it for you." This usually leads to some puzzling looks.

How can you *hand* me your relationship?

You can't. Relationship is not a *thing*. But make no mistake, relationships are a big deal. They impact you every day. Your happiness, peacefulness, and even your feelings of self-worth and your physical health are impacted by your relationships. But there's no such *thing* as relationship.

Yet people talk about their "relationship" constantly. "My relationship sucks right now." "This relationship means so much to me." "If it wasn't for that relationship, I probably never would have gotten this job."

So, we talk about it all the time, like it's a thing, but it's clearly not a thing. Stay with me. I'm going somewhere with this.

There's an invisible Loop here. Remember how I said that if the Loop is invisible to you, you only experience the Boomerang as if it came out of nowhere? Like "For no reason at all, he was a total jerk about it."

Then I showed you that there is a predictable pattern with a predictable outcome. It's just that the Trigger going into the Loop is invisible to you. So, until I show you the Trigger and make the Loop visible, all you see is the Boomerang. Okay, buckle up, buttercup, because here we go.

Relationship is a Boomerang. It's an effect, result, or outcome; it is not, however, a cause or input. I know. Take a minute.

Okay, are you ready to see the cause of relationships? Brace yourself, because it's math.

YOU + YOU RELATE = RELATIONSHIP

Let me explain. Relationship is YOU plus how YOU RELATE to others in the world around you. That's all relationship is.

We've already talked about how you bring yourself with you into every relationship. You already know that you have feelings, beliefs, meanings, Triggers, pains, upsets, joys, emotions, needs, experiences, and all kinds of stuff that makes up who you are. And you are the one who is hearing what other people say. You are the one who feels what happens to you. You are the one who thinks, judges, decides, and acts. Certainly, you are part of every relationship you are in.

What about the other person? Shouldn't relationship really be YOU plus THEM?

That's one of the oldest, outdated beliefs . . . it's the foundation of Demand Relationship. It's what causes us to push others (them) to give us what we need or change our experience. Falsely believing that it's them.

Let's take a closer look at that together. Let's say you and I meet for coffee (yeah, I use coffee in my examples a lot. I don't know what to tell you, coffee is a gift from God). So, let's say that you and I sit down for coffee.

You had a great day, and you were about to tell me all about it when I start telling you how angry I am about something. You see right away that I'm hoppin' mad.

Question for you: Can I physically put *my* anger inside you? Can I take my anger and shove it inside you and force you to be angry if you aren't angry? If you genuinely do not feel angry, you aren't angered that I'm angry, and you don't feel angry about what I'm saying, can I still *make you* feel angry? Of course the answer is *no*.

Okay, now let's take the opposite situation. Let's say you are very upset. Something awful happened, and you have a lot to figure out about what you're gonna do, how you will deal with this, and how you can recover. The situation is pretty bad. Can I make you feel happy and relieved? Can I take my feeling of happiness and force it into you? Can I just shove it right into you and make you feel happy instead of upset? No.

Here's the truth about human dynamics. No one else can make you feel anything. Only *you* can make yourself feel something, think something, or believe something. (Read that again.)

Yes, if I'm angry and I tell you the story of why I'm angry and you get angry because you relate to my story, or you get angry at me for being angry and crapping all over your good day, then you can also be angry. But it was *still* you, inside you, who became angry. I didn't *make* you angry. You, yourself, got angry by experiencing me.

I'll give you another example. Let's take something that's a big Trigger for some folks, like being late. Maybe you personally have a Trigger around people being late, or maybe you have Triggered other people by being late.

People commonly say it like this: "They triggered me because they were late."

That's incorrect based on how human dynamics actually work. What happens is that a free human made choices with their body in the space and time of their life (freedom). And you experienced their choices, and inside you, had beliefs, judgements, feelings, and energy around their choices and maybe even how it affected you.

Those beliefs, judgements, feelings, and energy all exist inside you. The other person did not put them into you. And I can tell you that not all humans have the same beliefs, judgements, feelings, and energy as you do about another person being "late."

So, they didn't trigger you. Your experience of them living their life set off a Trigger of yours, that you have inside you, and you felt your reaction. It all happened inside you. They didn't really "do" anything to you emotionally. You reacted to something you experienced of them. You fired all that off inside your blueprint, your wiring, and your nervous system.

Your experience of them is happening inside you. You are filtering what you see, hear, experience, and feel through your blueprint. And that is your experience.

If you asked 100 people who experienced the same event to recount what happened, they would give you close to 100 different accounts of the details of what happened because they all filtered their experience through their blueprint (wiring) and applied their own meanings to it.

Furthermore, the brain stores memories deeper when they are attached to emotions. So the emotion you experience, which is very personal to you and happens inside you, also impacts the meaning you give the moment and how it gets stored as a memory.

As far as your nervous system is concerned, your experience of the other person *is* the other person. That's why one person might think, "Oh my God, Stacey is such a bitch. I can't believe she said that." And another person might think, "Oh my God, I love Stacey so much. She told me the truth."

I'm just me, but everyone will have a unique experience of me based on how they are wired and what they experience as a result.

Your relationship with another human is not YOU plus THEM, it's YOU plus how YOU RELATE to them. It's your internal experience of them, what you believe about them, how you feel about them, what meanings you apply to what they say, and so on. How you relate to them is really what results in the relationship.

Relationship = YOU + YOU RELATE

The Trigger going into the Loop has been invisible to you before now.

Trigger: YOU + YOU RELATE → Boomerang: Relationship

The YOU plus YOU RELATE was invisible as the Trigger going into the Loop. So, all you experienced was the relationship (Boomerang), and it looked like it was erratic and "out of nowhere."

The relationship is the Boomerang. It's the effect of the combination of YOU plus how YOU RELATE to others in the world around you.

And that is the most empowering revelation I can give you right now. For thousands of years, people have been using Demand Relationship tactics, trying to change their relationship. But remember what I told you about trying to fight with the Boomerang already in motion back to you? It's ineffective at best but often destructive and leads to more fights.

But what choice did people have when they couldn't even see the Loop? It's understandable. And it's old, broken, outdated, and over. Just like people used to think that putting leeches on a sick person could cure their illness or that if you sailed to the edge of the horizon, you would fall off the earth . . . it's old, broken, outdated, and over. And so is Demand Relationship.

Demand Relationship is always disempowering because you are constantly trying to fight to change your partner, or to change your relationship, and feeling stuck because you can't really control either one.

Here's the empowering revelation: since the Relationship Development Formula for Relationship equals *YOU* plus *YOU* RELATE, who is the common denominator in both pieces of the equation that creates relationship?

You!

That is outstanding news! Because while you cannot control anyone else, you *absolutely* can change you and how you relate to others in the world around you, if you desire to.

As the transitive property teaches us, you can either change you or how you relate, and the relationship will change as a result.

Change either of the two ingredients, and the output changes. Yay! That's excellent news, too, because we're going to transform them both.

That's why the Relationship Development Paradigm results in two predictable outcomes: (1) a happier, more authentic, and peaceful "you" and (2) you empowered with skill sets to relate in a way that builds up relationships instead of breaking them down!

That's why I always say it only takes one person to transform any relationship. It's math. Now you know.

So, the next two sections of this book are going to be divided into YOU and YOU RELATE. It's time to dig into the "YOU" and "YOU RELATE" tools, strategies, solutions, and skill sets of our Relationship Development Method for you to evolve yourself and how you relate to others in the world around you so that you can transform your relationships.

Ready? (Turn the page.)

SECTION 2
YOU

CHAPTER 10

THE 50% LINE™

Have you ever had this experience? You are in a good mood, your day is going just fine, and then your partner comes home in a crappy mood. They start complaining, bitching, moaning, and saying everything sucks.

Question for you. What happens to *your* mood when they come home like that? Are you still in a good mood? If you're like most humans, your state starts to drop. You might even get triggered to react to them for bringing their crap to you, the kids, and into the house. Like, "Hey, get your shit together and calm down, please."

Or, perhaps you try to help them by saying something seemingly helpful like, "Hey, it's not so bad" or "You know, it will all work out." And the next thing you know, they are coming back at you with "You have no idea what's going on" or "Don't come at me with your 'look on the bright side of life' bullshit." Or perhaps they say, "You don't even care about what's happening to me" or "You have no idea what you're talking about."

Now you're defending yourself to them, and before you know it, the two of you are in a fight. And this thing didn't even start out by being about the two of you! Have you ever found yourself in that situation? Yeah, it's not pleasant.

For most humans, this just becomes another crappy moment to let pass or to sweep under the rug. But not for a Relationship Transformer like you! With the empowerment you are getting from this book, you don't have to keep repeating this pattern of misery.

Let's slow this down for a moment and look at the dynamics through our Relationship Development lenses.

What really happened in this interaction? You were fine. Nothing changed in your world. They came home in a crappy state and they triggered you. This caused your state to drop, and you reacted.

> **PRINCIPLE:**
> When you are in unrest, you add unrest to a situation.

In the scenario above, the person coming home was already in unrest. So, when they interacted with you, they added unrest to the situation. The Trigger going into the Loop is their unrest, and the Boomerang back is your negative reaction. Your reaction is either you getting upset with them for bringing their unrest to you or you trying to appease them into feeling better, whichever your blueprint is wired to do. You are reacting (Boomerang) to their unrest (Trigger), either way.

It's a predictable pattern with a predictable outcome. When you are in unrest, you add unrest to a situation.

Hang on now. Before you freak out, I'm not saying you can never get upset. I'm never saying that. So, before you react, give me another moment to explain this. No one is saying that you must have "good behavior" all the time. I can't have good behavior all the time (just ask Paul). And the concept of having "good behavior" is Demand Relationship. I'm going to show you the dynamic and then give you a tool that you can use to get better results than you have been getting.

THE DYNAMIC: THE INVISIBLE LOOP

Remember, relationship is a Closed Loop. The Trigger and Boomerang patterns in the Loop are at work, whether you like it or not. I'm here to give you visibility into the Loop.

By making the previously invisible Trigger of "unrest" (input) visible to you, you can preselect the outcome (response) you want from people. You do this by selecting the input that predictably creates what you want *before* you enter a situation.

That is power. Knowing, beforehand, what input creates a negative output and what input creates a positive output, then choosing which one you put into the Loop is empowerment.

The opposite approach is the way it is right now, where this predictable pattern still exists and is happening but is invisible to you and it's throwing you around. When it becomes visible, you will have the power of this dynamic in your own hands.

Trigger: you in unrest → Boomerang: add unrest to the situation

Trigger: you in peace → Boomerang: no added unrest to the situation

How many times in a day do you feel like you are getting triggered by someone else's unrest?

How many times in a day do you feel like you are bringing unrest to another person and experiencing the negative Boomerang?

How many times in a day do you feel like this is coming up for your partner? Your kids? And others whom you interact with?

This is a huge dynamic that is impacting you every day of your human experience. Learning new skill sets to navigate these moments differently can be life-changing.

Even if you could transform 20% of those moments from unrest to peace, what kind of difference would that make for you?

What if it was 50% of those moments that went from being triggering to feeling genuinely and easily peaceful? Would that make a difference in your life experience? In your marriage? In your household?

Our students consistently and quickly reach the point where the majority (more than half) of the moments that used to trigger them into unrest and fighting are genuinely gone and are now peaceful and harmonious instead.

It's a skill set, and it can be learned.

As you become more empowered with this skill set, it becomes your choice, in any situation, to decide what you want to create by choosing what you put into the Loop. That is freedom.

RELATIONSHIP DEVELOPMENT METHOD TOOL: STATE-O-METER™

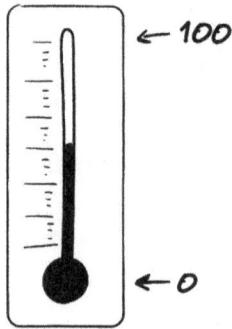

Look at this thermometer for a moment; Paul and I call this the State-O-Meter. The bottom (0) is your low state, where everything feels like crap. The top (100) is your high state, where you are rocking it.

Right across the middle of the State-O-Meter is an invisible line that has more to do with your daily happiness than you have ever realized. We call it the "50% Line in Your State."™

You already have a sense of what it feels like when you are below your 50% Line. And you already have a sense of what it feels like when you are above your 50% Line. In fact, you can sense it in others, too, right? You know when someone's in a bad mood or they are in a great state. Yes? It's wired into us as humans to pick up on this and be aware of our own and others' states.

THE INVISIBLE LOOP FOR STATE

When you take action from below the 50% Line, you get a negative Boomerang reaction. Just like in our scenario from before.

That person came home and started inter-acting with you from below their 50% Line, yes? And that triggered a drop in your state, too, maybe even dropping you below your 50% Line.

Trigger: take action from below the 50% Line → Boomerang: negative reaction/result

It's a predictable pattern with a predictable outcome. When we inter-act with someone from below the 50% Line, we are putting a negative input into the Loop, and we are most likely creating a negative Boomerang (output) coming back at us.

Now, I wish I could tell you that every time you take action or inter-act from above the 50% Line that you will get a positive outcome. You and I both know that life doesn't always work like that. Sometimes, even when you are above the 50% Line, someone else is just pissed off and they are going to react to everything negatively. However, it's also true that, when you inter-act from above the 50% Line, you're giving yourself the best chance of creating a positive outcome.

Trigger: take action from above the 50% Line → Boomerang: best chance for a positive reaction/response

Think of it this way. When we inter-act from below the 50% Line, the most common outcome is triggering a negative reaction or outcome.

When you show up from below the 50% Line, you often trigger people to drop their state and react to you. There are other times, like in my inter-action with Anthony, when you show up from below the 50% Line and they are gracious back to you. They are reacting positively to you. And that sounds like it is contradictory to the Loop I defined. But it's not.

Even when you lash out from below the 50% Line and someone else is gracious or kind in response, it leaves you either feeling bad about yourself for being a jerk (like I felt about how I treated Anthony) or it just has no impact on you, and you keep yourself below the 50% Line. Either way, there's a negative Boomerang from acting from below the 50% Line.

By harnessing the power of this human dynamic, you can preselect the response you desire by choosing what to put into the Loop. If you'd rather *not* have a negative reaction from someone, don't inter-act with them from below your 50% Line.

It's at this point that most people will say something like, "So, what do we do, then? Never get upset?" Nope, I'm not saying that (I'm never saying that). That's a super common Demand Relationship thought, though. It's very understandable, and it's not your fault. We've been conditioned to think this way. So, if I'm not saying to just stop getting upset, then what is the answer?

The Relationship Development Method solution is to use the 50% Line as a tool. This tool is focused on giving you a way to time your interactions to not cause unwanted negative boomerangs.

The 50% Line Tool for YOU: When you are below the 50% Line, get back above the 50% Line first and then inter-act or take an action.

The 50% Line Tool for OTHERS: When you observe that someone else is below the 50% Line, that is not the time to engage them in conversation or action if you want the best results.

That's not what most people do, though. Is it? Most humans get upset about something and feel angry, frustrated, sad, hurt, or whatever your flavor of upset is. Then they go right into it with the other person. They want to feel better about it, or they want the situation fixed, so they "bring it" to the other person when they are below the 50% Line.

Often, we feel "justified" that it is reasonable and understandable for us to be upset. The truth is, you may very well be justified. And it may be entirely reasonable for you to be upset. And yet, the truth remains that when we are in unrest, we add unrest to a situation.

So, bringing yourself to the other person when you are below the 50% Line results in a negative Boomerang back to you. When you do that, you now have doubled your problems. Hear me out.

Problem #1 is whatever upset you in the first place. After you inter-act with someone from below the 50% Line, you have now triggered them negatively. You just created problem #2.

Problem #2 comes in different flavors, but most commonly it's something similar to this list: (1) they are now in a bad mood, (2) they are below the 50% Line too, (3) they are upset with you, (4) you damaged your relationship or rapport with them.

We've all been in that situation, right? You go to someone about something you are upset about, and before you know it, they are talking about how *they* are upset! And you're like, "How the F did we circle back to you? This is about me being upset. You always make everything about you!"

Sound familiar?

Now, when you begin to use this tool consistently, you will become free from this crap. And you will start to free your children from inheriting this crap, too, as they witness your Relationship Development skills in action every day.

I'm not saying this to make you feel bad about all the times that you unloaded on your spouse, or even your kids, from below the 50% Line. It's called being human. It's okay. You're okay.

I'm teaching you this principle because when you inter-act with someone from below the 50% Line, it's not a surprise when they react negatively and things go further down the downward spiral.

It wasn't a fluke. It's not a personality thing. It's not them and it's not you, nor is it the combination of you and them together that is the problem. It's a predictable pattern with a predictable outcome.

This is one of the reasons why so many people say that "counseling made things so much worse." Because, among many other reasons why the couples work approach fails, when you put two people together and a third party asks them to share their upsets, they go below the 50% Line. Then they trigger the other spouse and the outcome is predictable . . . and not helpful.

So, if you do not want to trigger that negative reaction, what can you do? The first thing is to use the 50% Line as a guidepost for your actions.

For example, when you are below the 50% Line, get back above the 50% Line and then take action or have an interaction.

Get above the 50% Line and then use the tools to have a conversation to solve whatever happened.

Get above the 50% Line and then use the tools to take action to resolve the dynamic so it doesn't happen again.

Get above the 50% Line and then . . .

Why? Because not only does interacting from below the 50% Line Boomerang into a negative reaction, but also you are not operating at your best when you fall below the 50% Line.

Besides, even if you knew all the tools in our toolbox, you wouldn't reach for them or use them accurately when you are below the 50% Line. Even if you know the situation calls for you to be compassionate and patient, but you are below the 50% Line and upset, are you going to be compassionate and patient? Not likely.

That's why I say that it takes emotional maturity to use the 50% Line tool to time your interactions.

By the way, I'm not telling you to suppress how you really feel and wait until you can be calmer before unloading on someone. We are going to share real tools with you so you can do the work to transform how you genuinely feel. Then you can rise above the 50% Line and interact from Relationship Development for the best outcome.

And as hard as it may be for you to manage your state in the beginning, it's even more difficult, if not impossible, for the other person.

Look, the person you are upset with does not actually have the relationship skill set to solve your upset for you. And they don't have the skill set to keep themselves above the 50% Line when you come at them from below the 50% Line. How do I know that? You don't even have that skill set, yet, and you are reading this book. They aren't even doing that (yet).

If you want someone outside of you to solve something inside of you that you, yourself, have not yet been able to solve, then you do not have the skill sets needed to solve the problem yet.

Why would you expect them to have a higher level of relationship skill sets than you have?

I get it. You want them to fix it. That Demand Relationship thinking has been conditioned into us for thousands of years.

And from time to time, when you are below the 50% Line, the very unhelpful chatter in your head (your drunk monkey) is going to chime in with some version of . . .

WHY SHOULD I?

"I'm pissed, and I shouldn't have to keep this inside."

"They deserve it, so I'm gonna let them have it."

"This is their fault! They did this!"

Remember that Demand Relationship program is in your Autopilot Mind, so it's gonna keep coming up until you rewrite it.

By the way, my answer to that "Why should I?" question is . . . then don't.

You read that correctly. So don't get above the 50% Line. Go ahead and let 'em have it. That's your choice. You always have the power to choose whatever Boomerang you want. I'm being sincere, not sarcastic. Each moment is a fresh start. You get to choose.

It doesn't matter to me which option you choose. My job is to show you the predictable patterns and the predictable outcomes so that you stop living your life being blindsided by something invisible to you. We have already proven that it is a predictable pattern that you can know in advance.

I'm not being cheeky. I'm being realistic and earnest.

You get to pick your outcome. That's free will. Sometimes you are going to go ahead and unload on them and deal with the negative Boomerang. You and I both know that's going to end up in a fight. It's gonna happen. That's okay. Now you understand WHY it's happening. It's no longer a surprise.

Other times, you will do the work to get above the 50% Line, then take action to resolve the issue and give yourself the best chance at preventing an unnecessary fight. And it's going to feel great, and you're going to feel proud of yourself for doing so!

The choice is yours, always.

Just keep in mind that your goal is to inspire others to inter-act with you in a way that you like. More love, more peace, more kindness, more harmony . . . whatever it is for you.

Here's the Predictable Pattern Loop:

Trigger: inter-act from below the 50% Line → Boomerang: inspire negative reactions

Trigger: inter-act from above the 50% Line → Boomerang: (best chance to) inspire positive reactions

It's a choice. And it's your choice to make in the moment . . . that is, if you have the skill set to get or stay above the 50% Line.

When you're upset, however, this can be easier said than done, right? So, what can we do in these real-life moments? You don't need to be a superhero or somehow impervious to every upset or annoyance. It comes down to using the right skills for the right moment to make it easier for you and everyone around you.

RELATIONSHIP DEVELOPMENT TOOLS

That brings us to how. How can you stay above the 50% Line or get back above the 50% Line when you drop below it? While Paul and I have loads of tools for this in our methodology, too much for this book, I'll share just three with you that you can use right away.

Just being aware of your own 50% Line is already a game changer. You can finally have control and power over choosing your own outcome by choosing what you put into the Loop based on the Boomerang you want back.

State Management Tool #1: The 50% Line

The first tool is the 50% Line itself. Your role is to become aware of your 50% Line and to get above the 50% Line first and then take action or interact with others. Once you are below the 50% Line, you only have one job to do: get your state above the 50% Line! That's it. You don't have to worry about using our hundreds of tools. You only have one job: get above the 50% Line first, and then act or speak.

If we're not going to "pretend" that we are unbothered by something, because it would be Demand Relationship to pretend or "please," then what can we do to become peaceful or undisturbed in those same life moments?

This is the key to unlocking your authentic and genuine peace regardless of what's going on around you.

State Management Tool #2: Drop Your Sail™

The tool I'll share with you for this is something we call Drop Your Sail.

Picture a sailboat in the middle of the ocean. Imagine that the boat is sailing north when a strong opposing wind blows in and pushes on its sail, driving it backward toward the south. The boat's sail is up, so it's catching all the wind, and even though the captain wants the boat to go north, it's being pushed south because its sail is up.

What if the captain lowers the sail? Now that opposing wind can blow right by and the sailboat can keep heading north or, at least hold steady, until the wind blows by.

It's the same when someone is coming at you from below the 50% Line. Simply Drop Your Sail.

If you catch all the crap that they spew your way, you take it all in and feel it all. You are choosing to keep your sail up. And by catching all that negativity in your sail, you are letting it toss you around. It can easily push you back or throw you below the 50% Line.

Instead, Drop Your Sail!

Whatever someone says when they are below the 50% Line is either garbage (they are simply upset) or it's so heavily flavored in their upset that it won't be productive in that moment anyway.

Let that crap blow right by you, like the wind. Don't take it in. It's not a *requirement* for you to take it personally. The minute you start taking it personally, you are putting your sail up and catching it all.

The unfortunate truth is that most people are only focused on themselves. They are just trying to get through their day and deal with what's going on for them. They are venting, complaining, or trying to get others (including you) to soothe what's disturbing them (Demand Relationship).

Even the stuff they say that sounds like it's about you isn't really about you anyway! It's about their own internal discomfort that they would like soothed.

Remember, Relationship = You + How You Relate. And in that moment, when someone is spewing stuff your way, you just got caught in their "You Relate." It's how they are relating to you because of how they feel inside.

You do not have to respond to everything someone else says. You don't have to evaluate what you think about what they say every time someone else speaks.

Are there real upsets being vocalized that need to be solved sometimes? Sure there are. All we need to do is circle back later with that person when they are above the 50% Line to address it.

You do not have to react to something inside the moment of a kerfuffle. It takes emotional maturity to be strategic with your timing.

It's not rocket science to know that there's a good time and a bad time to talk to someone. It takes work and practice, however, to rewire yourself to be calm and confident when someone else is unloading. And it also takes skills to be able to bring the topic up outside the moment of kerfuffle, when it can be solved.

For example, later, outside the moment of kerfuffle, you can say something like, "Hey, I know you were pissed off earlier when you got home from work, but I just wanted to check in. I know the kids' toys were everywhere by the end of the day. Is that really an issue that you wanna solve together, or was that just about what's been going on at the office?"

Then the other person has the opportunity, from above the 50% Line, to respond. Maybe they will say something like, "Yeah, I was so pissed from work. It really wasn't about the LEGO bricks that I stepped on. I mean, yeah, maybe we should come up with a way to handle the toy issue in a way that doesn't get outta control. But no, it wasn't really about the toys. It was a rough day."

That was an actual interaction that Paul and I had many years ago.

Drop Your Sail. It's so worth it.

Someone in your family will need to lead when it comes to these inter-actions. You have this book now, so the leader is you. The peaceful and harmonious household you can create is absolutely worth it.

State Management Tool #3: Be the Observer™

This brings us to the third tool: Be the Observer. When you are inside the moment of a kerfuffle and the other person is below their 50% Line and you want to Drop Your Sail, it begs the question, What *do I actually do* in the moment instead?

Your brain needs something else to focus on other than the other person's anger or upset. If you don't give it something to focus on, then the whole time you are trying not to react (because your sail is actually up, even though you are telling yourself it's down) your drunk monkey brain will be saying things inside your head like, "I can't believe you're not saying something to this jerk right now" or "Are you just gonna take that?"

You need a tool so that your brain can focus on something that can actively help you create positive progress in your relationship. Otherwise, there will just be more of a downward spiral to recover from later.

We created the Be the Observer tool for this purpose. When someone is interacting with you from below the 50% Line, focus on observing them with curiosity, instead of reacting to how you personally think or feel about what they are saying or doing. Said differently, instead of making it about yourself, make it about them and their why.

The best way to understand this tool is to think of a neighbor or an acquaintance, someone that you know but you don't really have a friendship with. I'll give you an example.

Let's say it's Saturday afternoon, and you're walking down your street, enjoying the sunshine and feeling a warm summer breeze in the air. You walk past your neighbor Amy's house and notice that she's in the front yard, working on her flowerbeds. She sees you and gives a quick wave. As you walk by, you say, "Great day to be outside in the garden, huh, Amy?"

You're just making polite conversation. It is a nice day for it. In fact, now you're thinking about going to the home store later and picking up those plants you have been wanting to plant next to the mailbox.

Just as you get caught up in your own thoughts, you are jolted out of them when Amy responds with, "Well, it would be a nicer day if I could get my *own* crap done, but no one else around here even lifts a finger except me."

Noticing now that you don't see her hubby, Dan, or any of the kids in the yard, you call back compassionately, "Aw, sorry, Amy . . . If it helps, your flowers look really great."

She half-smiles, half-frowns, and says, "Thanks, I appreciate it."

As you walk away (at a little faster pace to get away from that awkward conversation), you think to yourself, "Whoa, what's with Amy today? I wouldn't want to be Dan right now."

What just happened there? You were easily able to make Amy's bad mood about Amy and not take it personally, right?

Your first thoughts were about Amy. First observing that Amy was in a bad mood. Then maybe observing that Amy feels unsupported. And, you also now know that Amy has other stuff to do and believes that someone else could have been doing that gardening instead of her! You were able to observe quite a lot about Amy in that short interaction. And yet, you didn't get pulled below your 50% Line or react negatively toward Amy.

Your sail was down, and you were already in the seat of the Observer. You observed Amy and what was going on *for her* instead of making it about you or taking it personally.

By the way, do you see how much easier it is to do this when you don't have a brick in the wall between you and Amy?

If it was your mother instead of Amy and you walked by and she said *the same words* to you, you might react or think to yourself, "Gosh, Ma, how about you give me a freaking break? You're not the only one with a ton to do today. I got three kids I gotta take to a million sports things. I can't just drop everything because you want some flowers planted."

Just a hunch.

It wasn't your mother, though. It was just a neighbor you barely know. And you were able to keep your sail dropped, let her negativity blow by you, and stay in the seat of the Observer by observing her behavior as being *about her* and what was going on *for her* (not you). So, you have just proven to yourself that you *can* Be the Observer when someone else is below the 50% Line, yes?

Will you be able to keep your state above the 50% Line now for the rest of your life? No, that's ridiculous! Stop being so hard on yourself. That's old self-demand thinking (judging yourself).

Remember, your relationship reactions are stored in the 95% Autopilot Mind. So, both your reaction to other people who are below the 50% Line and your Trigger to unload on others when you are below the 50% Line are just on autopilot right now. It will take repetition to rewrite that autopilot program for you to get that control back. But it can be done with practice, and it's so worth it.

Mastering this is just one of the many reasons why our students report that they are authentically happier than they have ever been. For one thing, they are genuinely not being yanked below the 50% Line all day long.

Think about the number of fights that have happened over the years because either you or your partner were below the 50% Line. It's a lot, right? How about your kids? Yeah, it's a lot.

Now look forward. Imagine the rest of your years without that same number of fights. Even if all you did was eliminate the fights that happened from below the 50% Line and nothing else, that would be a different life, right? No worries, we are going to show you how to solve all the other stuff too. It's worth it. You are worth it. Your family is worth it.

> **PRINCIPLE:**
> When you are in unrest, you ADD unrest to the situation.

As a human, there is a way to talk about things that genuinely upset you or a challenge that needs to be solved without getting upset during the interaction. You can plan a productive conversation with another person for a time when you are genuinely calm. You don't have to "get upset" just to talk about when you were upset.

CAUTION: A word of caution about this, so you don't fall into a trap.

There's a difference between coping and solving. Coping tools allow you to stop a bad situation from becoming worse. They mitigate the damage inside the moment of a kerfuffle. We all need coping tools because real life happens, and we need the skills to navigate the moment, as it happens.

The 50% Line on the State-O-Meter, Dropping Your Sail, and Being the Observer are coping tools in the beginning.

And if all we do is cope through moments when they happen but never solve the dynamics that caused the kerfuffle, then we are still on a path of misery.

> **PRINCIPLE:**
> Coping happens INSIDE the moment of the kerfuffle.
> Solving happens OUTSIDE the moment of the kerfuffle.

Don't just get stuck in coping and never solving. It's exhausting. There are not enough funny cat videos on the planet to get you above the 50% Line every time you get triggered in this life if you refuse to solve your Triggers or the bricks in the wall between you.

If you are upset about something, then that thing needs to be solved. If it remains unsolved, it's just another brick going into the wall between you.

Remember, the old broken Demand Relationship model tells you to "just don't let it bother you." The Relationship Development Method empowers you to Face It, Own It & Solve It in real life.

> **PRINCIPLE:**
> Demand Relationship breaks down your relationships.
>
> **PRINCIPLE:**
> Relationship Development builds up your relationships.

So, the best way to get back above that 50% Line, or better yet, not get knocked below at all, is to understand what is causing the upset and solve it.

Don't pretend it's not there. Don't make yourself wrong for being upset. Look at it and get the skill set to solve the dynamic.

If you refuse to do the solving part, then that upset is set on REPEAT, and it will circle back to happen again in 3, 2, 1 . . . (just so you are not surprised).

It's a predictable pattern with a predictable outcome.

> **PRINCIPLE:**
> Unsolved kerfuffles repeat themselves.

It begs the question, then: How do we *solve* these dynamics?

I'm so glad you asked! In the next two chapters, "The Leash Around Your Neck" and "The Perspective Shift," we are going to cover that. (Turn the page.)

CHAPTER 11

THE LEASH AROUND YOUR NECK

Imagine this: Marcie is waiting outside the movie theater for her friend Carla. They agreed to meet at the theater at 7:10 P.M. for a 7:20 P.M. movie and already had reserved seats.

Marcie looks at her phone. It's now 7:11 P.M. And there's no sign of Carla yet. It turns to 7:12 P.M. Then it's 7:15 P.M. Now Marcie is thinking, *Crap, the movie starts in five minutes, and I want to go inside. Carla always does this. She's always late. I should have told her to meet me at 7 P.M. instead of treating her like a responsible person who can be somewhere on time.*

Marcie decides to head into the theater to sit in her seat for the show and now her internal dialogue goes something like this:

Carla is so selfish. She only thinks about herself. She always does this. The fact that I wanted to see the previews and sit down means nothing to her. She never considers what matters to anyone else; it's always about how busy she is and how she couldn't get here in time.

If she gave a crap about anyone other than herself, she could be here by 7:10 P.M. like me and every other human. It's my own fault. Why do I even make plans with her? You know what? That's it. No more. I'm not inviting her anywhere anymore. She can take all the time in the world for all I care.

Carla shows up 15 minutes into the movie, trying to explain to Marcie, but Marcie tells her to be quiet because she doesn't want to let Carla ruin any more of her evening because of her selfishness.

Now, if you are the one who is usually late to stuff, you might be feeling either guilty or defensive right now. If you are the one who gets triggered by people being late, you might feel vindicated or validated right now.

While this was just a story, it is a pretty accurate representation of a common dynamic.

In this example, Marcie gets triggered when people are late. And her flavor of that Trigger is that the other person is being selfish and thinking about themselves instead of considering the other people affected by the schedule and timing.

So, in this case, Carla triggered Marcie by being late, right?

Before I reveal the answer to that, let me ask you this: Does it regularly trigger *you* when people are late? Okay, answer this question, then, please: Are *all* humans triggered when someone is late?

Careful! I did not ask if all humans "should" be triggered when someone is late. I asked you if all humans are actually triggered when someone is late. Are they?

No. The fact is, not all humans have a Trigger when someone is late. And further, among the humans who are triggered when someone is late, there are thousands of flavors of that Trigger.

For instance, some people aren't triggered because it's inconsiderate; they are triggered because there is a right time to be somewhere and a late time to be somewhere, and late is the wrong time.

Others like to be perfect and not make mistakes. Being late is a mistake that is imperfect, which makes them uncomfortable.

Still other people feel it is out of integrity to promise someone you will be there at a certain time and then fail them, so it's a sign of distrust if someone doesn't honor their commitment.

Other people get uncomfortable when they feel like they are missing out, so when people are late, they start to feel unrest.

The Leash Around Your Neck

Still others see disorder in lateness because if one thing is late, it creates a second thing running behind schedule, and before you know it, it's chaos.

I could go on and on.

So, the facts are that some people aren't triggered at all by lateness, while others are triggered but not in the same exact way.

When we are triggered by something, what do we typically do? Some common answers are:

- Try to avoid it
- Try to prevent that circumstance from coming up
- Attempt to control our circumstances so that it doesn't come up for us again
- Ask people to stop doing the thing that triggers us
- Distance ourselves from people who refuse to stop triggering us

Whether it's a tone of voice that we can't tolerate or someone being late or our kids who left a mess downstairs while they are now sound asleep, we try to get the circumstances (external) to change so that our experience of it (internal) can be peaceful or happy (not triggered).

If you look at the Demand Relationship side of the chart, we go through all the levels of tactics to try to get others to change so we are not triggered. When the "nice stuff" doesn't work, we increase the intensity and start using leverage, pushing, or making threats like, "If you talk to me like that one more time . . . "

We exhaust ourselves trying to get people (and things) around us to stop triggering us. Or we start to isolate ourselves from everything that triggers us until the only person on the planet we can be with is ourselves (and maybe our dog).

Which brings me back to my original question: Did Carla trigger Marcie by being late?

The answer is no. That's not how Triggers actually work. Carla cannot make Marcie feel a specific way.

Here is what really happened . . .

Marcie has a Trigger inside of her that gets disturbed when someone is late. Marcie attaches a meaning to that Trigger that being late is inconsiderate. This meaning makes Marcie feel upset about how she believes Carla is "treating" her.

The entire process happened inside Marcie. Carla was merely the catalyst for Marcie's existing Trigger. Marcie observed the catalyst moment (Carla being late), and Marcie set off a series of experiences inside Marcie that caused Marcie to feel a certain way.

This is further proven by the fact that another human can experience the same situation, of someone being late, and not have the same experience as Marcie.

> **PRINCIPLE:**
> Your Triggers are only inside you. You own your Triggers.

No one is "triggering" you. You are only experiencing your Trigger that is already inside you based on your observations of the outside world and the people in it.

The Demand Relationship response to a Trigger is to tell the world what your Trigger is and request that they stop triggering you, "or else [insert your own threat or punishment here]." You can't control the nearly 8 billion people on this planet. In fact, you can't control the hundreds of people you interact with. In fact, you can't control even one other human, other than yourself!

This is usually where people wonder, "Why not?" You might be thinking, *Well, if they love me and committed their life to me, is it so much to ask that they not trigger me?*

Let me ask you this: How many items are on that list of "things that bother you" about what other people do or say? I mean, what kind of volume are we talking about?

And what if they forget or just slip up? I mean, they are not wired to either see it or do it like you, so anything they do to serve life up to you in the way you need it is going to have to be something they will need to *actively work and think about* just to do, right? But still, *maybe* they can do that.

Now, what about each of your kids? Will they also agree to your list of Triggers and commit to near-perfect performance of not triggering you? How about your co-workers? Your folks? Your siblings, friends, and others? Should we distribute your list worldwide and make sure that no one triggers you?

Okay, fine. Then get ready because your partner has a list for you too! And so do each of your kids. And your folks, siblings, co-workers, friends, and everyone else!

Are you ready to serve life up to them, each one of them, individually, so you don't trigger any of them? After all, you thought it didn't seem like too much to ask of them, right?

Let me catch you up on something. This is exactly what people have been trying to demand of each other for hundreds of years, and it does not work.

Humans have *had it* with being told to change and to *stop this* and *don't do that*. People are *sick and tired* with being ordered around. So, demanding that no one trigger you is out of touch with reality, at best.

In fact, if you think about the previous outcomes you've had when you tried to tell someone to stop doing or saying something that triggered you, you may realize that they didn't respond well to you in those moments. People hate being controlled. And they usually take it personally and get upset. They may get upset with you for "bossing" them around or being dismissive of their own wants or needs. Or they may get upset because they feel like you are constantly telling them how they are failing you. Does any of that sound familiar?

The truth remains that trying to get people to stop triggering you is Demand Relationship, and it breaks down your relationship.

Trigger: Demand Relationship tactics for our Triggers → Boomerang: break down relationships

Trigger: control others because of our Triggers → Boomerang: ineffective at best (they take it personally instead)

Even though it doesn't work, and even though it breaks down relationships, neither of those are the number one reason why we must STOP trying to get other people to stop triggering us.

The number one reason is this: Why are you protecting your Trigger?

(Pause and read that again.)

Why are you imprisoning yourself by protecting that Trigger?

Why would you want to keep defending and protecting your Trigger (keeping it inside you)? Why would you want to try to (ineffectually, anyway) get everyone around you to change just so they don't disturb your Trigger?

Your Trigger is inside you. Why are you prioritizing the Trigger over your own peace and happiness? Why are you prioritizing the Trigger over your spouse and children? Why are you prioritizing the Trigger over the greatest feeling of all, love?

Even when you get other people to "comply," and stop doing the thing that triggers you, the prize you win is that you get to keep that Trigger inside of you. (And double bonus, you also break down your relationship with that individual!)

So, yes, 1, maybe even 10 people, might be temporarily convinced not to disturb your Trigger. But that still leaves 7 billion people who can come up to you and pull on that Trigger and set it off any time they want.

Every Trigger that you have inside you is like a leash that you have put around your own neck.

Yes, you might be able to get 1 person, even 10 people, not to grab that leash. But all of humanity can easily and accidentally jerk you around in seconds just by grabbing that leash and yanking it.

WHAT'S THE SOLUTION?

Solve the fucking Trigger and be free!

Solve it! Solve the Trigger and take the leash off your neck. Instead of exhausting yourself trying to make people conform to your needs, just solve the Trigger.

Of course, the majority of humans right now do not have the skill sets required to solve their Triggers. So, they run to the end of their skill set, and instead of taking personal responsibility for their own Triggers and solving them, they just blame everyone around them for "triggering them" and use Demand Relationship tactics to try to get them to stop.

This is an epidemic right now. Especially in the personal growth space. People are becoming very aware of their Triggers (which is lovely) and doing personal awareness work (which is great).

But . . . then they just run to the end of their skill set in solving their Triggers, so when they have to inter-operate with *other* humans, they blame the other person for triggering them and say, "Stop triggering me, or I can't be in a relationship with you." This is the mantra of Demand Relationship and why relationships are falling apart at epic speed. It's not that personal growth work is bad or a problem—it's not. It's just that Relationship Development has been The Missing Piece from personal development.

Your Triggers can be solved. We've been helping people solve their Triggers for over a decade. It's a process that requires work, and it's so worth it.

The old, broken tactic of telling people to "do this" and "don't do that" is just never going to work to give you internal peace and the happiness you actually want. It is also never going to create long-term relationships that are rock solid and thriving.

PRINCIPLE:
The people on this planet are not actors in your play.

You can't just tell them where to stand, how to dress, and what to say. They are free humans, and they are here to have their own lives too.

Relationship Development is learning how to be happy regardless of what goes on around you (solve your Triggers) and relate in a way that builds up your relationships instead of breaking them down.

In Relationship Development, we also teach the skill sets to successfully interact with others for how *they* are wired. Doing the "YOU" work of solving your Triggers and becoming happy is the first part of Relationship Development. It can't be the only part, or we would never get the skill sets for the inter-actions to build up our relationships. But we must do the YOU work before the YOU RELATE.

In other words, solve your shit and stop telling others what to do.

Trigger: trying to control your external environment to protect your Trigger → Boomerang: you get to keep your Trigger

Trigger: solve your Trigger inside you → Boomerang: freedom from that Trigger (authentic healing)

Yes, it's possible. It's not just possible—we've proven it, working with students for years to help them solve their Triggers and be free. Everything is possible when you don't have to do this alone or figure out how all by yourself.

It's real work. It's not a trick or a gimmick, and this book alone is not enough to solve all the Triggers in your blueprint today. But we're going to start right here with one of our Relationship Development tools to solve Triggers.

The first step in solving your Trigger is to accurately understand what it is. Let's do this exercise together.

RELATIONSHIP DEVELOPMENT METHOD TOOL: TRIGGER FRAMEWORK™

Trigger Framework, Part I:

Question 1: Think of something that happened in the last 24 hours with another person that made you unhappy.

Question 2: Was there any part of you that had this thought: *If they had just done things differently, this would have been so much better for me?*

Question 3: What specifically about "their way" or how they did what they did felt like a problem for you or made you unhappy?

Example:

This example is from over 20 years ago, when Paul and I were first together. I hope it will illustrate this framework for you.

At that time, I had a big Trigger around Paul not moving fast enough.

My answers to those three questions back then would look like this:

1. I am waiting in the kitchen to go to brunch and not only is Paul not ready to walk out the door, but I think he's still in the shower and not even close to being ready to leave.

2. Of course, if he would just hustle, we could be out the door already. I need to be at brunch before 10:30 A.M. After 10:30 A.M., we will be waiting for like an hour to get a table. If you think I'm bitchy now, wait until you've made me wait another hour to eat. Plus, the candle lady is at the farmer's market that I wanted to go to after brunch. But if we get delayed, the market will be closed, and then I'm not going to have the candle I want for movie night tonight (true story).

THE Missing PIECE

3. My only problem is that he is not ready to leave right now. He refuses to rush. He only has one speed—slow. That's it. That's the only problem.

Now, for your same Trigger, answer the following three questions in Part II of our framework.

There are two different versions of each question simply because people are wired differently, so please answer the question that resonates most with you.

For many humans, if your core is feminine, you will probably be able to easily answer/resonate with version 1 of each question. If you are masculine core, you may find it easier to answer/resonate with version 2 of each question. But either way, please use whichever version resonates with you.

Trigger Framework, Part II:

Question 4
Version 1: What are you afraid of losing or trying to prevent from losing?
Version 2: What are you trying to protect?

Question 5
Version 1: What are you afraid of being blocked from?
Version 2: What obstacle are you trying to remove or unblock to get to your goal?

Question 6
Version 1: What is it that is really upsetting you about this?
Version 2: (same question)

Example:

These were my answers for my Trigger back then.
Question 4: I don't want to lose out on going to the farmer's market. I don't want to miss out on getting a table at brunch and have to spend valuable time waiting around on a Sunday.

Question 5: I don't want this day to be wasted. It's Sunday. I go back to work tomorrow. I have to get everything in today. Sunday is for brunch and farmer's markets and fall leaves and everything that we do on Sunday. This is my vision of my weekend. The rest of my week is spent in an office, doing taxes and being frustrated by people who move too slow. This is Sunday. It's time for brunch. It's now actually past the time for brunch.

Question 6: We could get so much more done in a day if he would just move faster. If he would just pick up the speed, we could get loads of things done in a day. We're not going to get enough done at this pace, and I'm getting more upset by the minute. It also really bugs me that Paul refuses to be rushed. I mean, what is that? When I pick up on the fact that he doesn't like how chatty I'm being, I shut my trap. Why does he sit there, unaffected, refusing to be rushed? Do other people notice this? OMG, is he making other people uncomfortable? Should I say something to them to make them more comfortable? What would I even say?

So, just in case you didn't believe that I drove my relationship into the ground, there's a little glimpse into the old Stacey with the old blueprint, full of Triggers and unrest. That example was 100% accurate for how I felt and thought over 20 years ago.

If you look at my answers to the questions above, you can see more clearly what my REAL Triggers are. Paul being a "slow mover" was just the catalyst to my "bag of Triggers." And he wasn't the only one in my world who set off those Triggers for me. Did you catch that?

Before doing this work, I would have said, "My Trigger is people moving too slow." You probably also have a statement like that, from the first three questions. But when you look at the answers to questions 4, 5, and 6, you see the real Triggers. I'll show you a few of mine from my answers above.

Accurate Identification of Triggers from the six-question Trigger Framework above:

(Stacey's examples of her actual Triggers)

- I am attached to my vision of what a Sunday should be for me (without making room for the other human).
- I am unhappy at my accounting job and using a specific Sunday experience as a coping vehicle.
- I'm in unrest over not getting enough done in a day.
- I'm in unrest over "missing out."
- I have a false belief in the scarcity of time.
- I'm holding invisible expectations of Paul that I never communicated to him, and I'm experiencing the Boomerang of them not being met.
- I'm lacking the internal confidence and worth to assert what I will or won't do (and I'm uncomfortable with someone else's internal confidence when I see it).
- I'm worried about what other people might think about my partner's pattern.

Can you make a list of your actual Triggers that were revealed through this Trigger Framework exercise? For now, let's look at my example. Look at that list. Are those things that lead to a peaceful and happy life full of love for me? Nope.

So why would I defend my "right" to keep those Triggers inside my blueprint? Why should I try to get Paul to move faster (it's impossible; don't bother) when even if I did, all I would get in return is to KEEP these Triggers that are making me miserable? And in the process, I would make him miserable trying to be something he is not just to please me.

Why in the world would I want to keep these leashes around my own neck?

Even back then, my younger self decided to work on solving my Triggers one at a time. The truth is, I knew that I loved Paul, and I didn't want to live alone my whole life. I didn't want to be jacked up by my unrest and continue running on a hamster wheel at a thousand miles an hour. I wanted to make room in my life for Paul, and I also wanted to find peace inside me about this. So, I pulled my false beliefs and Triggers apart one by one.

For instance, if I'm unhappy at my job and trying to use my specific "picture perfect" Sunday to somehow make up for that, maybe I should look at my job in corporate tax and make a change so I don't need that other coping vehicle.

The big scary one for me was, "If he doesn't hurry up, I won't get enough done in a day." Then I asked myself one question: "Enough done for WHAT?"

And at first, I couldn't answer that question. So, I dug deeper. I just knew that there was this churning inside me to get more done in a day so I could feel like the day was worth it, like this was good enough. Like I was good enough. Oops, there it is.

Maybe that's why Paul's confidence in his worth also bothered me. I was trying to prove (to whom, I have no idea) that I was worthy through my achievements. And if I didn't have enough achievements at the end of the day, I didn't feel "worthy." So every day, I hustled to move fast and get those achievements, like Mario collecting coins in Super Mario Bros.

I never saw it before'I forced myself to Face It, Own It & Solve It. Doing the work allowed me to start solving those pieces in my blueprint so that I could be free of that unrest. It wasn't serving me to have that in my wiring. It wasn't making my life better; it was making it worse.

Is that Paul's fault? Nope. Is that the fault of all people with a slow pace? Nope. And would rushing Paul do anything to solve the wiring of unrest that was in my blueprint? No.

Our Triggers are inside us. They are usually created from false beliefs, lies, or fears in our blueprint. Solving them removes this piece from our blueprint that is causing internal pain and then replaces it with peace.

> **PRINCIPLE:**
> Find the lie in your blueprint and replace it with the truth.

A great way to start solving Triggers is to find the lies and replace them with the truth. It takes time and real work because those Triggers are baked into your 95% Autopilot Mind, but the beginning of the process is still to identify the lie and the truth that replaces it.

Don't be hard on yourself. Most humans cannot do this in isolation. Because those false beliefs are inside your blueprint, it is nearly impossible to see them and figure this out without the perspective of someone who does not also have those same false beliefs in their blueprint. So have patience and compassion for yourself. It's much easier for our students to do this work with us because we can offer the alternative perspectives. Go easy on yourself as you begin this journey.

Here were a few of the truths that I replaced in my blueprint back then to solve those Triggers:

Truth #1: I need to stop making this about me. His speed is about him. I don't own him. He is a free human. His speed is in his wiring. I need to observe his wiring as being about him and stop sliding into the old thinking of "What does this mean for me?" It's not about me.

Truth #2: My Triggers about scarcity, worth, and "being enough" are mine to solve. I refuse to be driven by fear. I will not make other humans bend to my will so I can avoid my own discomfort. I will solve these one at a time and be free.

Truth #3: My need to get as much achieved and accomplished in a day has definitely caused me to make mistakes and run right past them to the next thing. I need patience. *Patience* is not a dirty word. Being patient will not cause me any harm, and avoiding it is causing harm for me. Paul is infinitely patient. I need to seek his insights and guidance on how to develop patience, practice modeling patience, and being at peace in that.

Truth #4: My worth is not tied to my achievement. My worth is inside me and not "given" to me or taken away. Paul's worth is inside him (clearly). I need to learn more about that from him, to see what I can use or model.

Truth #5: I don't need Paul to speed up to make me more comfortable. And I don't need to slow down to be more like him either. I'm not wrong for moving fast if it's making me happy. There are times when I'm moving fast, not because it makes me happy but because I'm trying to avoid pain. Those are the things I need to solve.

Ultimately, after years of doing the real work to solve the Triggers, I learned emotional patience. I found my calm and confident center and connected with my internal self-worth. Because I struggled to do this on my own for so long, it created a passion within me to give our students the step-by-step solutions, so that it turns years into weeks for them.

To this day, I still move fast. It's who I am. But my motivation for moving fast is positive and not causing me pain. And Paul is still methodical and calm, and I love it! He's the best balance to the tornado that is me. The two of us together are such polar opposites, it really is perfect.

So, how do you solve TriggerS?

First of all, there is no one solution for TriggerS (with an S). Each Trigger went into your blueprint individually, usually as a reaction to an experience you had. For the most part, each one needs to be solved, individually, to come out. But rest assured, there is already a solution for every Trigger.

Accurately identifying your Triggers is the first step. Most people have not yet accurately identified their Trigger. If you haven't done that, you have little chance of solving it, so that's the starting point.

I'll give you this as a guideline for knowing if you have accurately identified your Trigger yet or not: if the way you state it points to someone else being at fault, then you have not accurately identified your Trigger yet.

Example: I have a Trigger when people are late. Wrong!

Your Trigger is inside you, so it can't be someone else's fault. This is where you would use the Relationship Development 6-Step Trigger Identification Framework™ to accurately identify the Triggers set off by that catalyst.

Once you can accurately identify the Trigger (Face It), then you need to take personal responsibility for it (Own It) and start solving it.

I know it's a deep pattern to want to get other people to stop setting off your Triggers. It takes work and time. Lack of personal responsibility is a huge cause for pain in this dynamic. Everywhere you look today, someone is screaming "Trigger!" and demanding that you stop doing the thing that triggers them instead of taking personal responsibility for their own Trigger.

> **PRINCIPLE:**
> Your Triggers are inside you. You own them. They are yours.
>
> **PRINCIPLE:**
> It's your partner's job to *show* you your Triggers, not solve them for you. That's *your* job. (Read that again.)

That's why your partner is your biggest gift. They will show you all your Triggers. It's like the Universe is saying, "Hey, here's another Trigger lighting up inside you. Solve this, so you can be happy, peaceful, and free."

But instead of saying, "Thank you for showing me that so I can solve it," most people say, "No! Don't disturb my Trigger. You change who you are being when you approach me and let me keep this leash around myself, making myself miserable and breaking down my relationships in the process." Or something like that.

We started off this topic of Triggers talking about something that bothers you and how you were blaming the other person for that upset and feeling stuck because they won't change.

Using the Relationship Development paradigm, we are uncovering the empowering truth of the Triggers inside our own blueprints and freeing ourselves from the leashes that were around our necks.

> **PRINCIPLE:**
> Demand Relationship breaks down relationships.
>
> **PRINCIPLE:**
> Relationship Development builds up relationships.

Now that you see it, we can start solving these, together. We've been doing this for a long time and solved what feels like millions of Triggers. You are so close. There's not only hope—there is certainty that it's already been done.

And the number one best way to solve any Trigger is to start by seeing it differently. (Turn the page.)

CHAPTER 12

THE PERSPECTIVE SHIFT

I have a scenario for you to explain this next piece. Let's say you and I meet for coffee. While we are standing in line to place our order, we run into my friend Diane, whom we invite to join us. Once we find a table and sit down together, Diane proceeds to make nasty, snarky, negative comments and chatter about what is going on in her life right now. Maybe you find yourself wishing we had not run into Diane. Part of you might be thinking, *Doesn't this bitch have somewhere else to be? Someone else to make miserable?* Is it fair to say that you wouldn't be hoping that she stays longer or starts hanging out with us regularly?

Okay, take two. What if it happened like this instead . . .

I call you and say, "Hey, I know we have a coffee date today and I'm so psyched to see you. Listen, would you mind if I invite my friend Diane to join us? Before you say yes, I want to let you know that you can totally say no, and I'll completely understand.

"Here's the thing: Diane lost her mom last week, and she's in a really low place right now. To be honest, I'm kinda worried about her. I was hoping that if we could even give her 30 minutes of distraction, it might help to lift her spirits. Diane is one of the sweetest women I know, but right now you can practically feel her heartbreak. She's not coping well. So, I completely understand if you'd rather I not pick her up and bring her with me."

Knowing that, do you think you would feel differently if Diane had a negative reaction or two during coffee?

Why? It's the same words and same energy. Why would your reaction to Diane feel different to you in scenario two?

It's because you are applying a different meaning to her words, energy, and actions. Maybe you feel compassion for her in scenario two? Maybe even empathy? But certainly some kind of understanding, yes?

What happened between scenario one and two to cause that genuine (not forced) shift inside you?

You experienced a perspective shift.

Experiencing a genuine perspective shift creates an authentic shift inside you. When that happens, you don't have to try to be nice or force yourself to do something differently. When you see it differently, your own feelings, beliefs, meanings, energy, emotions, and words shift inside you, automatically, to match the new way that you see it. And your actions, words, and energy follow. Does that make sense?

> **PRINCIPLE:**
> Until you see it differently, the tools and strategies do not work.

Let's look at scenario #1 again, where you just run into Diane and she's bitchy "for no reason." What if I asked you to stay above the 50% Line, Drop Your Sail, and be kind anyway? Uggh. That's gonna be really hard, right? Maybe you can do it, but maybe you won't be able to, right?

That's what most people wrongly think Relationship Development is going to be like. They think that they are going to have to try to have "good behavior" and use all these tools, when inside, they are still feeling bad about the situation but can't be true to themselves.

That's not Relationship Development; that's Demand Relationship. Having "good behavior" is Demand Relationship.

Pleasing, being inauthentic, and compromise are also all Demand Relationship tactics. Staying miserable out of obligation is also Demand Relationship.

> **PRINCIPLE:**
> Seeing the situation in a way that makes you feel negatively makes all attempts at "good behavior" strenuous.
>
> **PRINCIPLE:**
> Forcing yourself to behave "well" is Demand Relationship.

Most folks think that this relationship work is a big struggle of trying to suppress yourself and doing what you don't want to do (compromise) to make others happy. That's also Demand Relationship. That's not what Relationship Development is.

I'm not asking you to have good behavior (on the outside) and still feel the way you feel now (on the inside). I'm never asking you to do that. Never.

In scenario #2, you learned something new about Diane. It gave you a perspective shift. You assigned a new meaning to her same behaviors, and the switch happened inside you, authentically and genuinely. That's Relationship Development. We're giving you The Missing Piece, so you can see what has been missing from the full picture. That gives you an authentic perspective shift, which creates an opening for real change.

It's the moment that you say or feel, "Oh wow. I didn't know that. Okay, what can I do?"

That moment is a perspective shift.

> **PRINCIPLE:**
> A shift in perspective is the opening for the tools and strategies to be effective.

> **PRINCIPLE:**
> Having a genuine perspective shift makes shifting your thoughts, feelings, and actions easy and authentic.

It's a predictable pattern with a predictable outcome.

Trigger: seeing it the same way → Boomerang: wind up on the Demand Relationship side of the chart (forced behavior)

Trigger: genuine perspective shift → Boomerang: opening for use of Relationship Development tactics and tools

The thing that creates the perspective shift is revealing to you The Missing Pieces. This is why the number one exclamation that we hear from our students is, "Why the heck did no one tell me all this before? They should start teaching this in kindergarten!" (I couldn't agree more, and I'm working on it.)

There is a crap-ton of Missing Pieces from your current view. There's nothing wrong with you, it's just that people didn't know this stuff before.

Once you have The Missing Pieces that shift your perspective, you authentically see it differently than you did before. And while new habits and skills take time and practice to develop, it's not the painful forcing or suppression that you probably thought it would be. It's more of a revelation and relief. This is another reason why our students say that they are the happiest they have ever been.

Without a shift in your perspective, you will often feel like everything you are forced to do is difficult and brutal, and it will not work to transform your relationship.

Without the shift in your perspective, the tactics people use are typically based on either (1) trying to have good behavior or (2) trying to get the outcome they want from the situation. Both of those are Demand Relationship, so they break down your relationship. It doesn't work.

THE MISSING PIECES

We teach hundreds of these Missing Pieces in our method. The invisible Loops are pieces that were missing. There are also loads of Missing Pieces that show you how humans are wired and how they are wired differently than you are. There are also dozens of masculine and feminine wiring and processing differences that have been pieces missing from your perspective. And so much more. Each piece that you get into your perspective is like adding pieces to a jigsaw puzzle that were missing before. As these new pieces are added, everything looks so much clearer.

In fact, it's very common to hear our students say, "Oh my gosh, that explains SO much!"

I'll give you an example using human processing speeds.

There are generally four types of processing speeds that humans have. I did not invent these. The research for this discovery goes back to Julius Caesar during Roman times, and I, unfortunately, can't even cite a person who specifically invented this. I will do my best to explain this in a way that is relevant for you.

These processing speeds are wired into each human. It's not really a personality thing; it's more like a human's energy or vibration. Most people are born with one of the four processing speeds, and like it or not, based on my last 14 years of experience and results, unlike most things in your blueprint, it appears that this processing speed doesn't change over a human's lifetime.

It's not a limitation or a scarlet letter. Your human processing speed is your natural tendency. But all humans can learn skill sets to complement their wiring to create any outcome that they want in life.

THE FOUR TYPES OF HUMAN PROCESSING SPEEDS IN ENERGY

1. Quick
2. Chill and easygoing
3. Fast and pushing to get it done
4. Methodical and patient

At first, you may find it difficult to tell the difference between 1 and 3 or 2 and 4. But as I explain them, you can likely identify yourself, your partner, and each of your kids.

The type 1 is the "quick like bunnies" energy. They are fast movers, fast talkers, fast thinkers; quick to change and bounce from thing to thing. They have a quick and light pace.

Type 3 is the "pushing to get it done" energy. This is the person who is bulldozing forward to get things done. They are fast, yes, but not fast just for fast's sake. They are fast because that enables them to push more things forward so they can get more done. Their focus is on getting shit done. They have a pushing, heavy, forceful energy and plow through things.

The commonality between type 1 and type 3 processing speeds is that they are both fast. The difference between type 1 and type 3 is that with type 3, you will feel a pushing or bulldozing strength in the energy, while type 1 energy is light and bouncy.

Type 2 is a chill and easygoing processor. It's that comfy, laid-back, calm, and cozy person. This is the person that does not like to be rushed, but it's because rushing is not chill. They are typically happy to go with the flow. They get stressed when they are being pressured to speed up or rush.

Type 4 is the methodical and patient processor. They are also slow in processing speed, but the energy is different. They are slower to process because they are taking their time to specifically get it right. They are orderly, methodical, and exacting. They are *not* chill. They are definitely not laid-back. They end up externally actioning at a slow speed, but internally, their minds are processing, and they are working to get it right. They are very patient and will measure 72 times to cut once.

The commonality between type 2 and type 4 is that their processing speed is slow, and they don't like being rushed. The difference between type 2 and type 4 is that type 2 is chill and laid-back, while type 4 is more precise, structured, and orderly.

Do you see yourself in one of those descriptions? What about your family members? Maybe you had an aha moment about someone who triggers you a lot, seeing that they are wired opposite from you? I get that.

I am a type 1 "quick" processor. When our son was an infant, before I knew about these processing types, I would just pick him up and head out to wherever we were going that day. By the time he became a toddler, I noticed that he would start crying when it was time to go somewhere. I felt frustrated at the time because I not only felt helpless to help him stop crying but also we could have been there already if he wasn't melting down.

After I learned about these human processing speeds, I had a huge aha. He's a chill and easygoing processor. No question about it. Even in the womb, I would have to drink a cup of apple juice once in a while to get him to move just so I knew he was okay.

So, when he was a toddler and I came at him with my "quick like bunnies" energy, bouncing him from thing to thing, I was literally stressing him out. Once I realized this, I started a practice of taking three deep breaths to calm my energy before interacting with him. I also started giving him a 30-minute heads-up (calmly) before transitioning to the next thing. I would say something like, "Hey buddy, in about 30 minutes, we are leaving for the grocery store."

Then I started giving him something to attach to for the next phase of our day. Instead of "taking him away" from the playroom, I would focus him on picking out a comfy blankie for the car ride and a DVD that he could bring to watch. I started linking him to future coziness without stress, and he began to move from thing to thing happily and calmly.

Notice that I didn't have to make myself or him wrong for our different processing speeds. One is not better, and one is not worse.

Another big key here is that in order to solve the kerfuffle, I didn't have to change who I was, and he didn't have to change who he was. I didn't have to stop being quick, slow down, and be more like him. He did not have to speed up and be more like me.

I solved the kerfuffle caused by our differences with a skill set. That's the Relationship Development paradigm approach. In Demand Relationship, people try to force others to change or make themselves change to be more like the other to eliminate the kerfuffle. In Relationship Development, we honor each person for being who they are and how they are wired and use skill sets to solve the kerfuffles caused by those differences.

> **PRINCIPLE:**
> Differences in wiring can be solved with skill sets.

It's a predictable pattern with a predictable outcome.

Trigger: conflict with someone's processing speed → Boomerang: resistance and triggered reaction (they resist you)

Trigger: skill set to work with their processing speed → Boomerang: ease and cooperation (they respond well to you)

Our son is now a 20-year-old who works long shifts six days a week. He has his own apartment and two jobs and just bought himself a new car. He can use skill sets to get his work done and keep up with the speedy demands of his job. In fact, at one of his jobs he is timed to deliver on the result . . . and he nails it.

And, when he's not at work, he knows to give himself lots of time to slow things down and recover, in his way. It's not that he can't move fast; it's that he learned skill sets to complement his wiring and allow himself to be who he is. He didn't make himself wrong for being chill. He uses a skill set at his work to move fast (for the job), and when he's not at work, he doesn't have to use that skill set and can rest and move at his desired pace.

I encourage you to do the same. Please don't use any of what we teach you as another barrier between you and other humans. Please do not tell people, "I'm an X processing speed, and that's why I can't . . . "

Your wiring is not your limitation; it's an element of who you are. It's not everything you are. You can learn skill sets to complement your wiring and to interact with others who are wired differently without making yourself or others wrong.

Paul is a Type 4 processor; he is methodical and patient. Knowing this now, when you look back on my story of Paul refusing to be rushed, it may make more sense. Here I am, trying to bounce through lots of activities on a Sunday, being "quick like bunnies," and Paul is moving slowly and methodically to get it right. Without relationship skills for navigating differences, this could easily cause a huge clash.

The solution was not what most people think. Most folks would try to get us to "agree" by either asking me to slow down or Paul to speed up (that's Demand Relationship).

Demand Relationship is where you see a difference between you and another, and you try to figure out who is right and who is wrong. Who is being reasonable, and who is unreasonable? Who is the winner, and who is the loser? Then the loser has to change to be more like the winner or do it the winner's way.

That doesn't work in today's world.

Sure, a hundred years ago, the Non–Power Player was always the loser and did what they were told. That's not relationship building; it's just survival. It was what it was.

But today, that won't fly with people. Thank goodness! People are sick and tired of being made wrong or feeling like the loser, and they won't accept it anymore. That's why Demand Relationship is failing at such epic rates.

Trigger: try to get them to → Boomerang: resistance to you and triggered reaction from them

Paul is not wrong for his processing speed. And I'm not wrong for mine. When I understood and accepted him for his processing speed and started using skill sets to solve the kerfuffles caused by our differences, I created harmony and built up our relationship.

Once I discovered The Missing Pieces about these processing speeds, it was so easy for me to implement the tools and skill sets to bring more harmony to my relationships and reduce kerfuffles.

If I never learned that Missing Piece, I'd still be struggling to "get them to" cooperate.

These Missing Pieces give us a genuine perspective shift, change the entire experience, and remove the struggle that we thought relationship transformation would require.

THE GIFTS WE WERE MISSING OUT ON BEFORE

I will also say that my husband has taught me a ton about patience. I used to say, "I was born without patience. I guess they skipped me when they were handing that out." But thanks to being with Paul for almost 30 years now, I have learned the skill set of patience. I don't have patience wired into my processing speed, but I learned how to use it as a skill. That approach can be used for anything and everything. All organic wiring can be complemented with learned skill sets that can be used when it's helpful to you.

> **PRINCIPLE:**
> When we stop making either them or ourselves wrong for being different, there are so many gifts to be enjoyed from the other people in our life.

Just like our son who learned the skill set of getting himself into fast motion to get his work done by the deadline because that's what he wanted to do. And how I learned the skill set of patience, because there are times when that really serves to help me get a better outcome. The result is that I'm benefiting from the gifts that other humans bring into my life.

THE MISSING PIECE

Think of a jigsaw puzzle. Maybe it's a 1,000-piece puzzle, and you've been working on it for days. It's getting close to the end. You have about 40 or 50 pieces left to place. Then you get to the very end. There's only one piece missing and . . . you don't have any pieces left. You look under the table to see if a piece fell on the floor. You look under the rug. You get up and look in the seat cushion.

Question for you: Do you want to find that last Missing Piece? Why? Maybe because you worked hard on the puzzle, and you want to complete it. Maybe because without that Missing Piece, the puzzle seems ruined. Maybe you want to see the whole picture. Maybe it just feels like a bummer after all this time. Whatever the reason, you desire to find that Missing Piece, correct?

Then, let's say you spot The Missing Piece on the floor, and you complete the puzzle. Do you feel better?

It's done. You love it. Maybe you'll glue the back this time and frame it. It looks awesome! You might even leave it there and admire it for a bit.

Question for you: Now that the puzzle is complete, look at it. Seeing all 1,000 pieces put together, can you tell me which piece is the best piece? Which piece is the worst piece of the puzzle?

Which piece shouldn't be in the puzzle? Which piece needs to be removed and discarded? None, right?

Why? Because we need every piece of the puzzle to make the beautiful picture. It's the same with humanity. Every human on the planet is a piece of the puzzle. When we all come together, we create a magnificent tapestry called humanity. No one piece is better than any others. No one piece should be discarded as "not good or needed."

Yes, some pieces have commonalities. All the edge puzzle pieces have that flat edge in common. Yet each edge piece has a different shape or picture on it. Even when there are many pieces with a single color, each one still has a different "innie" and "outie" to its shape.

As humans, we are not all wired the same. We are actually different. We have some commonalities and other differences. We need *all* the pieces of the puzzle to complete the picture.

No one starts a jigsaw puzzle by saying, "I hope there are pieces missing," or "I really hate this picture, so let me get started on this puzzle."

No puzzle piece is wrong. Every puzzle piece is different. When those differences come together in harmony, it creates a beautiful picture. Earth is the same way. All 7+ billion of us are unique. No two are identically the same. No one is wrong or better than anyone else.

Yes, our differences cause kerfuffles. But instead of the archaic approach of settling our differences with a duel in the street, suppressing someone's freedom, or making someone wrong, we can evolve and solve the kerfuffles caused by our differences with skill sets instead. Notice, I said *solve*, not *settle*.

Our Relationship Development Method is that skill set. You and every other human deserve to have these skills. You are a valuable piece to the puzzle of humanity and so is everyone you inter-operate with.

I deeply hope that this starts to help you see it differently. Yes, our differences cause kerfuffles, and no, those differences don't mean that "we can't be together." That's primitive thinking.

Your partner, and each of your kids, is wired differently than you are. Instead of butting up against each other, you can solve the challenges.

It's a fact that these differences are causing kerfuffles. Demand Relationship would tell you to either make the other person change or just "suck it up." Neither one of those approaches is solving the real kerfuffle. You can't live a real life while pretending that there is not a kerfuffle or hoping that the kerfuffle doesn't happen again.

People who just sit and hope don't see the Predictable Pattern Loops, so they falsely think the Boomerang came "out of nowhere." They fictitiously hope that the other person will just have "better behavior" in the future.

The Perspective Shift

That's all false. It's old, broken, and outdated. There is a real Loop there. And these differences do and will cause kerfuffles.

A solution to this dynamic is to get The Missing Pieces and perspective shifts. You can think of it in three steps:

Step #1: Learn the Predictable Pattern Loops.
Step #2: Understand the differences in how humans are wired.
Step#3: Get the skill sets to solve the kerfuffles caused by those differences.

Like the difference in human processing speeds, Paul and I have documented hundreds of differences in how humans are wired that are impacting you day after day.

After all these years working with so many different humans, I can tell you that one set of differences impacts relationships more than any other, and that is the set of masculine and feminine core processing differences.

Masculine and feminine core beings are wired very differently. We have found that at least 50% of all marriage issues are caused, at least in part, by masculine and feminine differences. I have also discovered that even though the kerfuffle may not be caused by one of those differences, once you start trying to talk to your partner about the kerfuffle, the masculine and feminine differences in your communication will often cause new challenges. Meaning, you start fighting about how you're fighting.

The biggest perspective shifts you are likely to have, that will allow you to get to the biggest relief, will probably be around masculine and feminine differences. So, in the next chapter, we are diving into those! (Turn the page.)

CHAPTER 13

THE DIFFERENCE BETWEEN MASCULINE AND FEMININE PERSPECTIVES

For this chapter, I need to start with a disclaimer. When I say masculine and feminine differences, I am not talking about differences between males and females, nor am I talking about male roles versus female roles. All of that is old, broken Demand Relationship garbage.

We are talking about the commonly observable "wiring" and processing patterns of masculine and feminine beings that result in legitimately having different perspectives on the same situation.

The kinds of commonly recognizable differences that story writers and comedians have leveraged in their own work because they are so relatable.

All humans have both masculine and feminine "energies" inside them. Most humans on the planet have a primary core energy. It has nothing to do with the physical body you came in. It's a core energy.

There are feminine core energy beings and masculine core energy beings. They come in all kinds of bodies, and your core energy is not directly tied to your sex or gender identification.

Core feminine and core masculine energy beings have certain common wiring and processing patterns. Let me explain for better clarity.

Do you remember when I showed you how most humans have a processing speed? Well, each processing speed has patterns that help us understand ourselves and others and how we relate to them. It's not a limitation or a life sentence in any way. It's just a way of understanding common tendencies.

It's similar with masculine and feminine wiring and processing. Each have patterns that we can use to help us understand ourselves and understand others in a way that helps us build up our relationships and solve the kerfuffles caused by these differences.

I've been doing this for a lot of years. A lot. And plenty of people have yelled at me, insisting that there is no difference between the masculine and the feminine. When I ask them why that's important, it usually comes down to some form of "I can do anything they can do" or "they are not better than me."

Both of those are Demand Relationship thinking and definitely not what we are talking about.

In Demand Relationship, when a difference is perceived, a winner and a loser are declared, and no one wants to be the loser. When there is a difference between two people or two things, one is typically deemed superior while the other one deemed inferior.

Understandably, those who were made to feel worse for so long are defensive about anything that they feel is implying that something or someone else is better than they are. In other words, if you say that I'm different, then you could be saying that I'm inferior.

I'm not saying that at all. But Demand Relationship thinking runs deep! Sometimes people incorrectly interpret it that way when I speak about differences. But I'm not saying that, and I'll never say that.

I get it. We have a long history to overcome here, and those feelings are very real.

When someone feels upset or challenged by us pointing out the common differences between masculine and feminine core

The Difference Between Masculine and Feminine Perspectives

being perspectives or processing, it is usually tied to their own Demand Relationship meanings.

They are the ones who think that if there is a difference, then one is better or one is worse. Or that *different* means that "you can't." I'm not saying that at all, but many people (most people) do think that way, because they *think* through the lens of Demand Relationship.

Let me be 1,000% clear on this: masculine core beings and feminine core beings are equal. All beings are equal. No one on the planet is any less than any other human. Any idea to the contrary is barbaric and archaic.

But I understand that the conditioning of our unsavory history runs deep. So please take as much time as you need to process this and allow the old false beliefs about inequality to fall away and the wounds to heal.

The other question I get a lot is, What about same-sex couples or gender-neutral people, or all the beautiful colors of the rainbow? Relationship Development is based on human dynamics for all humans. We believe that all humans should be free, and the only way humanity wins is when everyone is free to be loved for exactly who they are, all of who they are.

In my experience, I have found that most beings have a core masculine or feminine energy. It doesn't matter if you are a same-sex couple or not. This is not about personality, orientation, sexuality, or gender.

I'm lucky to have served students over the years who are in same-sex relationships, and they have all been able to see themselves and their partners in the masculine or feminine processing patterns I have shared with them. That doesn't mean that everyone will be able to, but I invite you to consider learning it, if you want to. See how it speaks to you. The goal is to see the Predictable Pattern Loops and understand the pieces that have been missing. Then use skill sets to solve the kerfuffles caused by the differences without making anyone wrong for how they are wired or who they are.

All humans are equal, just like every piece of the puzzle is worthy and needed. And we are also all different. These differences are nothing to be afraid of. When you have the training, skill sets, and tools to navigate life with people who are wired differently than you are, you'll see how all pieces of the puzzle fit perfectly, just as they are.

The world is a big place. The goal of love is not to try to find someone who is wired just like you so you can love them easily. (Don't bother, by the way. People have been trying to do that for decades, and it doesn't work.) The goal is to learn how to navigate life with people who *are* different than you while being happy inside yourself and building up your relationships with others. That's harmony. That is peace and happiness within. That's what Relationship Development allows you to do.

VOCABULARY DISCLAIMER

At times in my writing or examples, I may use the words *she, her,* or *lady* for feminine core energy beings and the words *he, him,* or *guy* for masculine core energy beings to make it easy to digest, explain an example, or tell a story. Please do not let my vocabulary trip you up.

It's just that *feminine core energy being* is a mouthful to use in every instance, so sometimes it is shorter or easier to read as "she, her, or lady." All energy beings come in all body types. I am not trying to exclude anyone. I assure you, it's just vocabulary.

If your energy core being and pronoun are different than my example, just make the flip or translation in your mind as you read. It's all beautiful and great.

My dear reader, I wrote this book for YOU, for all of who you already are and everything you will ever be. There's not a cell in my being that wants to exclude you or anyone from anything. I love you and only have the most positive intentions for you and for all.

Let's dive in.

Now, imagine that you and I work in an office with a whole team of people. We've been at this job together for several years, and you and I are the managers of the team in our department.

The Difference Between Masculine and Feminine Perspectives

A new employee, Anne, gets transferred into our department. Before she arrives, we're told that she's smart and hardworking and has great follow-through. For the last four years, she's worked in a department just like ours but in another location, so she knows this role and can hit the ground running.

Anne's first week is a very hectic week for us. We're working 70 hours a week, facing a deadline, and we really can't stop. This morning, you tell me that you're kinda grateful now that Anne has experience because neither of us has time to babysit someone new this week. I couldn't agree more. Since you have a huge client call in 12 minutes, I tell you that I'll stop by and welcome Anne to the team by myself so you can go get ready for that call.

I walk by Anne's desk and say, "Hi, Anne, great to meet you! I'm Stacey. I know this week is crazy but make yourself at home here. Here's the research reports for the build-out. Please get these compiled with slides and get this back to me by Thursday, end of day, so we are ready to present it to the customer. If you have any questions, Neal sits right next to you, and he's awesome, so be sure to ask him. I'm heading into the morning team meeting, so please come join us there. Welcome aboard."

Anne smiles and nods, and I walk away. But I don't have warm-fuzzy confidence that she's got it. Call it intuition. Then I'm in my office at around 7 P.M. packing up to leave for the day and figure I should check on Anne, just to be sure she's "got it." I walk by her desk. Not only is she gone, but it doesn't look like anything has moved since she arrived this morning.

The next day, over coffee (of course), I tell you, "I'm not sure about Anne. I'll keep an eye on this."

Later, I stop by Anne's desk and say, "Anne, I know you just got here, but I'm told you have done the research compilation reports many times before. Just show me what you've got done by lunch today, so I know we're on the same page with this. Do you have any questions that I can answer?"

Anne smiles and nods.

"Okay, great. What are your questions?" She just looks at me, confused. I pause for a minute, but she doesn't say anything.

"Alrighty, then. If you have a question, you know where I sit." I walk away. I'm pretty sure Anne is going to be a disaster. So, I stop by your office to discuss. You make the decision to ask Mark to do the compilation for Thursday because we can't risk relying on someone who might not pan out. As usual, that's a great call, and I couldn't agree more.

Lunch comes and goes and I get nothing from Anne. I wait until 2 P.M. Still nothing. So, I go over to Anne's desk and see that her laptop isn't even open. "Anne, look, I get it. It's tough to start in a new office, but this is not a new job for you, right? If you can't do the project, then we're going to need you to say something. We're a team in this office. I know we move fast, but we get the job done. It's fine if you have questions. It's even fine if you can't do what we're asking. But you gotta say something. We can't just have trees falling in the woods in silence, and no one knows, right?"

Nothing, no response from Anne.

I think to myself, *That's it. This bitch is wasting my time. I don't know why they loved her in that other office. She's useless. We gotta cut her loose.* And I start to walk away.

A moment later, Jeff from accounting walks by and says to Anne, "J'ai vu que tu as déjà rencontré, Stacey" (I see you've already met Stacey).

And Anne replies, "Oui, mais j'ai l'impression qu'elle est en colère après moi" (Yes, but I think she's angry with me).

My jaw falls open. She doesn't speak English! I'm laughing so hard now that I have to sit on the floor. Anne is laughing too.

"You don't speak English?" I say to her. She shakes her head no.

I pull out my phone and open my translator app. I select English to French. I speak into the phone what I need Anne to do with the compilation report. She speaks back into my translator asking a very good question that I hadn't considered. I answer her through the translator. She then opens her laptop and goes to work.

Wow! Turns out I was kinda wrong about Anne, huh? No matter how often I checked on her, even if I turned up the volume, she wasn't going to understand me.

The Difference Between Masculine and Feminine Perspectives

Is she wrong for speaking French? Nope. Am I wrong for speaking English? Nope. Is one right and one wrong? Nope.

And yet, the difference between us caused a very real kerfuffle. There's no point in pretending that there's no kerfuffle. It's real.

How did I solve the kerfuffle caused by our differences? Did I demand that Anne become English speaking? No. Did I make myself wrong for speaking English? No. Did I have to stop speaking English, learn French, and pretend I am French just to solve this? Nope.

Neither one of us had to become something that we are not just to solve the challenges between us. I used a tool to solve the kerfuffle caused by the difference. Using that tool does not make me wrong for speaking English, and it doesn't make Anne wrong for speaking French. The tool simply solves the kerfuffle caused by our differences. It's a bridge-builder.

The translator allows me to use a tool so that my listener, Anne, understands what I mean, in her language.

It's the same with masculine and feminine core beings. Our Relationship Development tools are like the translator that allows you to frame what you are saying for your listener, so that they understand what you mean, in their language.

> **PRINCIPLE:**
> If you want to build up your relationships, speak for your listener (the way they are wired).
>
> **PRINCIPLE:**
> If you want to break down your relationships, keep speaking for yourself (the way you are wired).

It's a predictable pattern with a predictable outcome.

Trigger: speaking for YOUR wiring → Boomerang: misunderstandings and upsets

Trigger: speaking for your LISTENER → Boomerang: clarity, calm, and collaboration

By the way, in my story, how were you feeling about Anne? Did you also feel the discomfort of "Anne's not going to work out" as I was describing the situation? Did you have some judgements about Anne?

I just want to illuminate the picture my story painted.

Trigger: invisible → Boomerang: (all I see) confusion, inaction, kerfuffles

When the Loop is invisible, we can't see the Trigger going into the Loop, so it looks like the Boomerang coming back to us is unwarranted and "out of nowhere." Like in my story, the Boomerang of "confusion, inaction, and kerfuffles" seemed like it was happening for "no reason."

But truthfully, the Trigger was me speaking English to someone who didn't understand English. Now that the Loop and Trigger become visible, the Boomerang is not just understandable but obvious, right?

Trigger: speaking English to someone who speaks French → Boomerang: confusion, inaction, kerfuffles

When it comes to the dozens and dozens of masculine and feminine processing and wiring differences, you are missing the Predictable Pattern Loop. Therefore, you are assigning *your* inaccurate meanings to the Boomerang coming back to you, just like I did with Anne.

> **PRINCIPLE:**
> Without knowledge of the Predictable Pattern Loop, the other person is inaccurately blamed for the Boomerang.

When I have no visibility or knowledge of the Predictable Pattern Loop, I will inaccurately blame the person instead of the accurate cause of the kerfuffle, which is the differences between our wiring. (Read that again.)

In my example above, the Loop was invisible to me. I only experienced the Boomerang (confusion, inaction), which seemed to come at me "for no reason." And when I experienced a Boomerang that seemed to "come out of nowhere," I inaccurately blamed the person, Anne.

That's what's happening in relationships all over the world right now.

It would change things tremendously for you if, from now on, when it seems like someone's actions or words "came out of nowhere" or were for "no reason at all" you would just PAUSE. Take a minute and say to yourself, "There's likely a Predictable Pattern Loop here that is invisible to me. It's critical that I do NOT inaccurately blame the person. Instead, I need to find out what this Loop is."

That's not what most people do today, however, is it? In most cases, someone "behaves" toward you in a way that you don't like. You have no idea that they are reacting in a Predictable Pattern Loop, so you try to get them to change the Boomerang (how they treat you). And if that doesn't work, you increase the volume on your attempts to get them to change until you give up trying and move onto phase two of Demand Relationship, which is separation or removal.

THE 2 PHASES OF DEMAND RELATIONSHIP™

Phase 1 of Demand Relationship: Get them to change

Phase 2 of Demand Relationship: Separation or removal

Within these two phases are many layers of variation, going from low intensity to high intensity. For example, in phase 1 (Get them to change), a low-intensity variation is "asking nicely." As the low-intensity variations fail, people stuck in Demand Relationship tend to turn up the intensity. Eventually you end up in a high-intensity variation like "manipulation or threats."

When people run to the end of their Demand Relationship skill set for trying to get the other person to "get on board," they often come to the place where they feel like they have "no other choice" but to separate or distance themselves. It can often sound something like this: "If, after everything I've tried, you're not going to see things reasonably, then I guess this is over, and I can't be around you."

It's the oldest Demand Relationship dynamic that exists. If you won't submit to my way, I will have to distance myself from you, or you will be "removed." Just think about this clearly for a moment. Submit or exile is ancient, archaic, and obsolete.

I'll share one simple masculine/feminine processing difference as an example of the differences that are causing kerfuffles today. It will take me a few minutes to frame this out for you in a full explanation, so if you really want to learn this, please just give me a chance to explain and demonstrate this dynamic to you. Meaning, read this section all the way to the end of the chapter before you either make a snap judgement or give up. You may not love everything about this explanation, but I invite you to give me a chance to teach the full concept before deciding if you want to use this specific tool or not.

THE EMOTION & MIND SHIFT TIMELINE DIFFERENCE™

The feminine processing: The feminine core being can typically shift between emotions rather quickly. She can shift from being upset to feeling relieved when there is "cause" to do so. When her thinking genuinely changes, she changes the emotion that goes with it. Either the emotion will shift soon after the mind, or the mind and the emotion can shift at pretty much the same time. This is very normal and expected for the feminine.

The masculine processing: The masculine core being typically does not process the same way. First, the masculine core being doesn't typically experience a lot of emotional shifts in a day. Their emotions are pretty even throughout their typical day. Every once in a while, the masculine experiences a big emotion or spike in their energy. The masculine processes big emotions very differently than the feminine does and on a different timeline.

For the masculine, the mind (understanding) can change with logic and reason, but if it was a big emotion, the emotion or energy does not necessarily change at the same time. It is more like it gets stuck for a while.

The mind and emotion are often unhinged from each other on the timeline for the masculine. He may genuinely change his mind from being angry to it being *resolved*. But if the negative emotion was a big negative emotion, that emotion will not usually leave him at the same moment that he changes his mind. It will take more time for the emotion to "wear off."

The best way for me to illustrate and teach this difference is with an example.

LANA AND BILL

Lana's 16-year-old daughter was late coming home. She was supposed to be home by 10 P.M., and it was already 10:30 P.M. Lana texted and called but got no answer. She checked her app to see her daughter's location, but it said that her location was unavailable. Lana is now both worried and angry. It's 10:45 P.M., and there's still no word from her daughter.

Bill, Lana's husband, says, "That's it. I'm going out looking for her." Lana keeps checking her phone while Bill is out driving around, trying to find their daughter. As you might imagine, they have stories running through their minds that are making them angry, like "How could she not respond to us?" They also have thoughts going through their minds that are terrifying them about why she might not be responding to them.

At 11:00 P.M. Lana's phone rings. It's their daughter.

Lana yells into the phone, "Are you okay? Where are you?" Their daughter says, "Mom, I told you that we were going to a movie that ends at 11 P.M. and I wouldn't be home until 11:30 P.M., and you said it was okay. I had my phone on airplane mode in the theater. Everything is fine. I told you the plan this morning."

Lana vaguely remembers something about this and says, "Okay, okay. I forgot that, and I thought you were supposed to be home at 10 P.M. I'm just glad you are fine. Drive safe and I'll see you soon." Lana breathes a deep breath of relief, so grateful that's over.

Lana calls her husband and says, "Bill, she's fine. Everything is fine. She was at the movies. I guess she told me about it this morning, but I was doing a million other things, and I forgot. She's fine. You can come home."

Bill is silent.

"Bill, did you hear me? She's fine. It was just a mistake. Come on home."

Bill says, "I'm coming home."

Lana hangs up the phone but feels like he's mad at her.

Her thoughts start questioning, *Is he mad at me for forgetting? That was an honest mistake. He didn't know about it either. Why should this be on me? I'd like to see him keep track of all the shit I keep track of. Besides, I never told him to go out looking for her. This is ridiculous.*

Half an hour later, Bill walks in the door, walks past Lana without a word, and goes out to the garage to work on something. Lana follows him.

"Excuse me," Lana says, "are you mad at me for this?"

"I'm not mad," Bill says, and he keeps working on his project without looking at her.

"Clearly you are mad." She continues, "You know, with everything that I manage around here, I'm going to forget things from time to time, Bill. I'm not a secretary; this isn't my job. I didn't see you keeping track of where she was or when she was supposed to be back. And now you're mad and you're gonna sit out here for hours, tinkering on that old motor and come to bed without talking to me. Just great.

"You know, next time I'll just worry about my kid by myself instead of even telling you. Geez, you'd think you'd want to know if something might be wrong. But no, you're just gonna make me pay for it later. I don't know why I bother."

The Difference Between Masculine and Feminine Perspectives

"I'm not mad. If you want me to get mad, however, keep talking, and I'll get mad," Bill says, getting mad now.

"Oh, forget it!" Lana says, and she goes inside and goes to bed.

Can you resonate with any piece of that example? Maybe you have been on one side of that or the other?

While there are many dynamics at play in that example, we see an excellent demonstration of the Emotion and Mind Shift Timeline Differences between the masculine and feminine beings.

When Lana found out that it was just a misunderstanding between her and her daughter, she was relieved pretty much instantly. As soon as she got new facts that corrected the misunderstanding, she went from mad or scared to relieved. While it would probably take her a little bit to unwind from that stress, she wasn't still mad or scared once she found the information that assured her there was nothing to feel mad or scared about.

When her mind changed (new information), her emotions shifted (from upset to relief/calm) shortly after.

That's often how the feminine being operates. For the feminine, changing the emotion quickly when the mind shifts is rational and makes perfect sense. In fact, feminine to feminine, if Lana had found out the facts on the phone with her daughter and then said to me, "But I'm still so mad," I would probably respond with, "What? Why are you mad? It was a misunderstanding. The girl did nothing wrong. Don't be silly. There's nothing to be mad about." If you are feminine core, can you resonate with that, perhaps?

The masculine core being doesn't operate the same way. He has a different timeline processor for strong emotions and energy. Once he goes into a strong emotion, he likely will not release that emotion at the same time he changes his mind. The two are seemingly not linked in his nervous system, so it just doesn't work that way for him.

In the example above, Bill got the information from Lana that their daughter was fine. He rationally understood there was nothing to be mad or worried about. He logically resolved it in his mind when Lana gave him the information. Since he is masculine core, the logical change of the mind does not flip the emotion at the same time. So, he still had this big emotion of anger/worry/protection vibrating inside him.

RELATIONSHIP DEVELOPMENT TOOL: THE BELL TOOL™

Think of it like a big gong that you hit with a mallet. Once you give that gong a strong whack to make a big sound, it will take some time for it to "ring out" as the sound dissipates. It's the same process for the masculine core being with a big negative emotion. Not every emotion, but this is definitely true for the big emotions.

It's like his bell was rung, and it's going to take time for his bell to ring out, to come to a standstill of no emotion again. Because of the way the masculine processes, his bell will typically not stop ringing in the same moment that his mind is changed.

When Bill came back to the house, his bell was still ringing from the big emotion of anger and protection that his Trigger for his daughter's safety had caused.

Since the feminine does not operate this way, she will sense that he is still mad and assign her own meanings to why he is angry. Think of it as her filling in the blanks, but inaccurately.

Notice Lana's internal dialogue. She was triggered that Bill didn't seem relieved, calm, or fine when he received the information about their daughter. She sensed that he was still mad and assigned her *own meanings* as to why.

That is very common and understandable. If the Trigger going into the Loop is invisible, most humans default to assigning a cause based on how they, themselves, are wired.

Lana doesn't process the same way Bill does. Lana doesn't need time for her bell to ring out. So, Lana had no idea that's what was going on for Bill. Understandably, she assigned the meaning that Bill was mad at her and created a story about that. Since she believed the anger was "directed" at her, she assumed it was "about" her.

The Difference Between Masculine and Feminine Perspectives

When in fact, his bell was still ringing from the big emotion that he felt over the situation with their daughter. He had to process that emotion to release it and get his bell to stop ringing.

Without training and tools, the masculine organically needs time and space to let his bell ring out. This means time alone, with silence. The masculine instinctually knows this, which is why Bill went out to the garage. This is why when your son gets angry and stomps up the stairs, Mom will get up to go after him, but Dad will say, "Leave him be. Let him cool down."

The masculine and feminine beings process big emotion very differently. The masculine needs space (alone) and time to let his bell ring out and for the emotion to fade away. The feminine does not and has no idea this is the case for the masculine.

The way the masculine organically processes his big emotion is actually very difficult for the feminine to handle without training, especially when she falsely believes that he is mad at her.

Thus, the most common outcome is that feminine core beings approach their masculine partners to try to get reassurance that everything is okay or to resolve the issue. I call this *poking the bear.*

She might approach him, asking, "Is everything okay? I thought we resolved this."

And he tells her, "Yep, it's fine." But she feels his anger or intensity, so she will often reapproach him with a heightened energy, saying, "Clearly, it's not fine. What's going on now?"

Every time she engages with him when his bell is already ringing, she smacks that gong with the mallet again and the bell increases, intensifying the original emotion within him, requiring more time to ring out.

I know. It's a miracle we even made it this far. Our processing and wiring are so opposite. Without training about how the other is wired, we are destined to encounter kerfuffles, even with the best of intentions.

In this example, Lana and Bill went to bed angry, and they weren't even fighting about the issue that came up that evening (their daughter being late). They were now fighting about how they were fighting.

This is what most humans are doing because The Missing Pieces are invisible to them. So, they end up fighting the Boomerang of how they are reacting to each other. They walk away from these moments thinking they have a relationship problem when all they really had was a lack of visibility and lack of skill set problem.

Neither the masculine nor the feminine is wrong.

The masculine core being is not wrong for having wiring that has a timeline difference between a change in mind and a release or change in emotion.

The feminine core being is not wrong for having her mind and emotion change simultaneously.

One is not better, and one is not worse.

And it's not their fault for not knowing that about each other, assuming the other person is wired the same as they are and applying their own meanings, because no one ever taught us this.

In fact, just to prove it, I'll give you another example.

If two masculine core guys are hanging out and one of them goes from happy to angry to crying and back to happy within 10 minutes of talking, I can almost guarantee you that everything will stop as the other guy looks at him and says something like, "What the fuck is going on right now?"

Those kinds of fluctuations are not "common" for a masculine being. They simply do not shift from big emotion to big emotion like that naturally. Just observe it for yourself. Masculine to masculine, you don't see that. And if a guy demonstrated fluctuations like that, another masculine being would assume that he was flipping out, losing it, or something catastrophic was going on.

This is a very real difference between masculine and feminine core beings. Neither of you is wrong. Neither of you needs to change who you are. And, this difference causes some big kerfuffles. In fact, I'm willing to bet that some of the biggest fights you have had were when his bell was ringing out and you went and "poked the bear" while he was trying to let it ring out.

If you are feminine and have a daughter, I'm also willing to bet that there have been times when your husband's bell was ringing out, unbeknownst to you, and your daughter approached him and he snipped at her or was unkind, and mama bear came out.

It's a predictable pattern with a predictable outcome.

Trigger: poke the bear when the bell is ringing → Boomerang: anger and frustration reactions

Trigger: silence and solitude when bell is ringing → Boomerang: comes to peace within when his bell rings out

> **PRINCIPLE:**
> Once his bell is ringing, the masculine core being requires time and space to let his bell ring out.

Just like you don't want to be judged for processing your tough stuff as best as you can, no one else wants to be made the bad guy for processing their tough stuff the best they can either.

HOW TO SOLVE THIS KERFUFFLE

Either the masculine or the feminine being can solve this kerfuffle when it comes up. You both do not need the skills to solve this. And you don't need to go running to your partner with this book, telling them how to fix this going forward. That's Demand Relationship.

The Relationship Development approach is that only one person needs to implement the tools and solutions to apply the skill set that solves the kerfuffle. Either of you can solve this. So, I'm picking you.

I'm including the list of solutions below that the feminine core being can implement and then a list of solutions that the masculine core being can implement. Use whichever one is suited for you.

RELATIONSHIP DEVELOPMENT SOLUTIONS FOR THE FEMININE CORE BEING

Solution #1: Understand and accept that he is wired with a timing gap between changing his mind and releasing the big emotion.

Solution #2: Observe when he has a heightened emotion and his bell is ringing, so you know when to use your skill sets.

Solution #3: Change your meaning to be accurate for the masculine: He's not mad at you. It's not personal. His bell is ringing. It's a process.

Solution #4: Set your goal: Allow his bell to ring out.

Solution #5: Stop yourself: When his bell is ringing out, stop yourself from interacting with him just to get comfortable that everything is okay. Remind yourself, "If I poke the bear, I will just be extending the time for his bell to ring out."

Solution #6: Give yourself the reassurance and certainty that you need. Try repeating a mantra like, "We're fine. It's just his bell ringing out."

Solution #7: Solve the Triggers that come up for you when he is upset. Why is him being upset a problem for you? Solve that (this is usually a huge source of Triggers for the feminine, so be compassionate with yourself).

Solution #8: Allow him to lead the timing. When his bell has rung out and he interacts with you again without the strong emotion, that's when you know that it is resolved for him.

RE-ENTRY WHEN THE BELL HAS RUNG OUT

When the masculine is done processing that big emotion, he will typically just interact with others normally. From his blueprint, there is nothing to address or say. This can be a huge Trigger for the feminine who feels the need for the distance or silence to be addressed and a reconnection to be formed.

Unfortunately, without training, the feminine will often re-trigger the masculine when he starts organically interacting with her again as if nothing happened. She feels the need for a reconnection after the distance or an apology for the silence. Feminine to feminine, this is organically how we would interact with each other.

If one of my feminine friends wasn't talking to me for some reason and then suddenly started talking to me again, it would be normal and expected for me to say, "Hang on, are we just not going to talk about the fact that you have ignored me for the past three days? What is going on?" To which the typical feminine reply would be something like, "Yeah, I'm sorry about that. I was really upset when you didn't stop by on Saturday, and I wasn't ready to talk about it. But I understand completely, and I'm sorry I didn't reach out sooner."

The feminine expects the masculine to interact the same way she does. But it's not the same for him. For him, there's nothing to talk about. There was nothing "wrong." He just needed the time to process that emotion and let it go. The last thing he wants is to go back to that and think about it again.

Without understanding and accepting that there was nothing wrong, he was just processing the emotion. During his bell ringing out, she will often assign meanings like:

- He's punishing me.
- He's icing me out.
- He's withholding from me.
- Or worse.

I understand from the feminine blueprint these meanings feel true to you, but it's not accurate to apply that meaning to the masculine core being. He's not doing anything *to* you; he's just processing the only way he knows how. I invite you to stop making it about yourself and do the "you" work to shift how you feel inside to get to a calm and peaceful state. This is no small task. So, be patient and compassionate with yourself.

RELATIONSHIP DEVELOPMENT SOLUTIONS FOR THE MASCULINE CORE BEING

Once you know this about yourself, you can stop the negative spiral that it causes in your relationship using skill sets. You are not wrong for how you process. And you are not the bad guy for any kerfuffle that it causes. It's just a difference in processing, and you can use skill sets to solve the kerfuffles that are caused by this difference.

Solution #1: A Golden Tool: Reassurance

There is a golden tool that the masculine can use for his feminine core partner. When your bell is ringing, offer her reassurance. I know it's hard and doesn't feel necessary or applicable for you, but she is not wired like you, and this will help her a lot. For instance, you could say something like, "We're okay. Everything is fine. I just have to let my bell ring out. I'll be back."

The more you can practice this skill, the easier it will become for your partner to be calm when your bell is ringing out. It's likely not easy or natural for you to do this, so it will take time, practice, and work. But you can do this, and the result is so worth it.

If your bell tends to ring out for longer than a few hours, you will likely need to offer her reassurance multiple times, at least daily, for her to try to stay calm while your bell rings out. She has very good reasons for her discomfort that you don't have (it's part of her wiring and not yours). But you have the power to give her peace, which is what you want to do for her. So I invite you to try it.

You are not wrong for needing time and space for your bell to ring out. There are lots of skills you can use to shorten the length of this experience for yourself. But in the meantime, know that just offering her consistent reassurance that this is just your way of processing, and that the two of you are *okay*, will go a long way.

For the masculine, I want to be very clear that this reassurance needs to be offered to your feminine partner even when the cause of your bell ringing out has nothing to do with her or your marriage. I know that in your rational mind, if it's not about her, then there's no reason to include her. Be careful not to try to apply your thinking and processing to her blueprint; it doesn't apply.

When you are silent toward her and upset in your energy, she's likely to apply the meaning that it's about the relationship or her. So even when your bell ringing has nothing to do with her, please still use the golden tool and give her reassurance, for as long as it takes.

The truth is, the calmer she is, the easier it will be for your bell to ring out and for you to feel peace within again. So, on every level, it's productive to use this tool.

Solution #2: Give Her The Missing Piece

If you reach a place where enough bricks in the wall have been solved that you can have a conversation about this processing difference with your partner, I encourage you to take personal responsibility and explain your wiring and the "bell ringing out" concept to your partner. Not in a way that asks her to change for how you process, but in a way that gives her a Missing Piece that she can't possibly guess about how you are wired.

It's best to explain this outside the moment of the kerfuffle, because when your bell is ringing, your "words" are the first thing to leave you, and that's not the time for a productive conversation.

Here's a summary of this masculine and feminine difference.

THE PREDICTABLE PATTERN LOOP: EMOTION AND MIND SHIFT TIMELINE DIFFERENCE

Feminine core beings: When the mind shifts, the emotion shifts quickly or at the same time.

Masculine core beings: The mind and emotion are not on the same timeline. Big emotions take time to process long after the mind has changed. Masculine processing requires space (alone) and time (usually in silence).

PREDICTABLE PATTERN LOOPS

Trigger: poking the bear → Boomerang: retrigger his big emotion and the bell starts all over again

Trigger: when the feminine applies feminine meanings to the masculine behavior (he's still mad or he's mad at me) → Boomerang: kerfuffle

Trigger: when the masculine applies masculine meanings to the feminine (there's nothing to talk about; silence) → Boomerang: kerfuffle

Could you see yourself in any of the examples in this chapter? Did that give you a shift in your perspective? Do you genuinely see it differently than you did before?

With this new understanding, you got another Missing Piece. Did receiving this Missing Piece shift how you see the situation? Did getting this new understanding make you feel even slightly more likely to want to shift how you are interacting so that you get a better result?

> **PRINCIPLE:**
> The perspective shift from The Missing Piece is the opening for the tools and strategies to work!

This is why we offer hundreds of Missing Pieces to give you perspective shifts. Plus, it's such a relief to learn what has been invisible to you all this time. Especially when that lack of visibility has caused so much unnecessary pain.

I understand that some of this may be difficult for you to believe because the masculine and feminine beings are wired so differently.

The Difference Between Masculine and Feminine Perspectives

A great way to help increase your belief is to share this concept with someone who is the opposite core energy of you and ask if they can relate or share their perspective and experience.

In our programs, it's so much easier to integrate these differences quickly because when the masculine core beings in our group all say "Yep" or the feminine core beings all say, "That's true," then you get immediate confirmation. So, you may need to seek that out for yourself if you find it hard to believe. Or you could just observe your partner interacting with people who have the same core wiring as your partner has. Masculine to masculine or feminine to feminine, it's easier to spot the wiring.

I hope you can have more compassion for yourself and others. Without this training, we have had no choice but to apply our own meanings and labels to what we see in others. Yet, others are wired so differently than we are.

Masculine and feminine differences have been causing kerfuffles in our marriages, in our parenting relationships with each child, in our family, with our friends, and especially in our work relationships.

There are dozens of these that can be easily solved with skill sets.

Remember: It's not you. It's not them. It's not the two of you together who are the problem. It's a kerfuffle that's caused by a difference in wiring and processing. And that kerfuffle can be solved with a skill set from our Relationship Development Method.

Remember, when you put Demand Relationship into the Loop, you break down the relationship.

When you put Relationship Development into the Loop, you build up the relationship.

When you learn about these masculine and feminine differences and the tools and skill sets to solve the kerfuffles caused by them, not only do you heal and rebuild your relationship, but you also understand yourself at a new level.

There are many times that we blame ourselves for how we show up. Or we take in other people's criticisms of us then feel badly. Or we wish we wouldn't be like THIS and could be more like that.

That's all Demand Relationship.

You are a being with a particular processing and wiring combination. You are wonderful and worthy and awesome. You are an important piece of the puzzle of humanity. And the pains and bumps that you have felt along your journey can be solved with skill sets.

There's nothing wrong with you. And there's nothing wrong with your partner either.

We just never got this training before to understand these differences. Once you get this visibility, you can not only have more compassion and acceptance for yourself and others but also be empowered with the skills and tools to create the peace, harmony, and happiness that you desire.

An amazing side effect of learning and implementing our Relationship Development Method is that your children will learn this just by watching and hearing you. They won't have to unravel decades of crap when they are your age because they've already learned Relationship Development organically by watching and modeling you.

We have the greatest opportunity in front of us. Not just for our own relationships, but we are on the precipice of changing the trajectory of our family's legacy for our children and grandchildren.

Of course, if we are going to make a huge change for ourselves, our kids, and humanity, we are going to have to eliminate one of the biggest lies in love relationships today.

Ironically, the ONE thing that everyone tells you to do in relationships is actually killing relationships everywhere.

Compromise.

Everyone tells you that you must compromise in relationship. The truth is that compromise destroys long-term relationships. What?!

So, what do we do about that? (Turn the page.)

SECTION 3

YOU RELATE

CHAPTER 14

THE DESTROYER OF RELATIONSHIPS: COMPROMISE

Think of the last time you felt like you *lost, gave in,* or were steamrolled into losing "your way" in your relationship.

Did it feel good?

Did it strengthen your relationship or break it down?

Did it pull you closer to your partner or push you further apart?

Did you feel more at peace afterward or more in unrest?

Do you think that, perhaps, a brick went into the wall between you?

Now, think of the last time you felt like you "won" and actually got your way in your relationship. You convinced or steamrolled your spouse into agreeing with you and giving up "their way."

Do you think they felt good afterward?

Reread the list of questions above but from their perspective. After they felt like they lost, what do you think their answers to those same questions would be? Probably similar to your answers, huh?

When we lose, nobody says, "Oh thank you so much for showing me the errors of my ways. I love you even more now."

See, it ultimately doesn't matter who wins and who loses in a long-term committed relationship. Regardless of who the winner is, someone in that two-person relationship always feels bad, it breaks down the relationship, pushes you farther apart, leaves someone in unrest, and puts a brick in the wall.

When we stay stuck in this win-lose dynamic in our long-term committed relationships, someone in the relationship loses every single time. In other words, the relationship takes a hit every single time.

Compromise is nothing more than a pattern of alternating between who gets to be the winner and loser. Compromise is a commitment to do the win-lose dynamic as a way of relating on repeat.

With compromise, someone loses something they wanted, every single time. In a long-term relationship where there are only two people, that means that every time, one of the two people is the loser. When someone loses, it breaks down the relationship. So, compromise is a commitment to break down the relationship every single time.

Therefore, compromise destroys relationships in the long run.

Compromise erodes relationships slowly under the false pretense that it was somehow a "good thing" to do.

But you already know that in your heart and gut because compromise feels like crap when it happens. In fact, that is yet another reason why people hate couples therapy because it's often a compromise machine.

> **PRINCIPLE:**
> Compromise destroys long-term relationships.

Compromise is based on the win-lose paradigm, which is one of the oldest human relationship dynamics that exists.

Wars are fought based on the win-lose dynamic. Sports are played based on the win-lose dynamic. Who is the winner? The person or team who is not the winner is the loser. Even spelling bees are based on the win-lose dynamic. You can't just be a good speller, there needs to be a winner.

The Destroyer of Relationships: Compromise

Competition is your human experience of the win-lose dynamic.

Competition in the workplace shows up as "who is the best" or "who gets promoted" or "who makes the most money." Everywhere you look, from the boardroom to the classroom, there is competition to see who wins and who loses.

We are taught from the earliest age to win. "Win at all costs." And even more than winning, whatever you do, do not be the loser. Siblings argue over who got there first or who jumped the highest.

The lenses that you use to see the world are tinted by the win-lose paradigm (Demand Relationship paradigm). There are winners and losers, and you don't want to lose.

This is one of the reasons why, when we teach that there are observable common differences between masculine and feminine core wiring, people get angry and say, "No, we are the same!" That's because they don't even see how deep this win-lose dynamic is conditioned into their blueprint.

Here is how it goes . . .

If I can spot a difference between A and B, then one is right and one is wrong, or one is better and one is worse.

When there's a difference between person A and person B, then one of them is right and one of them is wrong.

And I can't be wrong, so let's fight to see who wins.

With people who you interact with, this shows up as "my way" versus "your way."

For instance, if I say, "I think we should meet at 7:00 P.M. so that we are not late." And your response is, "We have plenty of time and we should meet at 7:15 P.M." What now? We argue until someone compromises, gets convinced, or gives up.

If I say that we should punish our kid for lying about having done his chores and you say that we should talk to him and help him get it done. Game on! Who wins? Who loses?

Right there is where a huge percentage of relationship disagreements get stuck. Right there in the "my way" versus "your way." It is all rooted in the win-lose dynamic.

Now, let's be clear. Competition and the win-lose is not inherently "bad," though. The win-lose dynamic is not "the bad guy" to be annihilated. Competition in endeavors that help you to be better than you were yesterday, for example, can be both great for your individual growth and exhilarating at the same time. The difference is that your important relationships should never be the place where you are competing to "win" as a fundamental rule.

Today, most relationships are an equal partnership, yet we still invisibly operate from the default win-lose dynamic when there is a disagreement. In modern times, instead of having a preassigned winner (the Power Player), we have evolved to fight for the win. Physically, intellectually, emotionally . . . Who wins? Who loses?

Let the games begin. This is how it has been for decades.

To be fair, compromise was an effort at evolving from the old dynamic of domination, which was even worse. In domination, one person is assigned the Power Player spot and thus dominates every time. At least with compromise, no one "dominated" every time. Everyone got an equal chance to fight for the win-lose. That was progress.

In an effort to try to keep the peace, the idea of compromise was created. Let's try to be "fair" and alternate who wins and who loses. This time, your brother gets to pick the show, but next time you will get to pick. Or, just go with me to this wedding I need to go to, and next weekend you can stay home and watch the game while I go to my sister's without you.

In an effort to collaborate or cooperate with each other, people started trading or compromising to keep things fair. Sometimes you win, sometimes you lose . . . that was deemed as fair.

Compromise was certainly fairer than domination, that's true. It was a step in the right direction. What was progress then, however, has become primitive now. Now that you know compromise breaks down the relationship in the long term, you can do better. Both you and your partner deserve better.

The Destroyer of Relationships: Compromise

There is another invisible problem with compromise that no one seems to be talking about for some reason. Compromise never solves problem #1. It only solves problem #2.

Meaning, when Spouse A and Spouse B disagree on how something should be handled (problem #1), they may try to convince each other to agree. If that doesn't work, they argue their points or use other tactics. Eventually, if they can't reach an agreement, they compromise: one spouse gives in to the other in exchange for something else of value or to make the fighting stop.

Here's the issue with that. The compromise never resolved the disagreement in perspectives on problem #1. So, problem #1 is going to resurface in another similar form. It's only a matter of time. The compromise only provided momentary relief from problem #2, which is the problem of, "Since we can't agree, who gets their way on this one?"

Let that sink in.

That's why compromise doesn't fix anything. Compromise doesn't improve relationships. That's another one of so many reasons why people feel like the couples work they did failed them or made things worse. Compromise is not really solving the conflict in perspectives; it is just trying to pick *who wins this time*. It's both primitive and insufficient.

Meanwhile, in each compromise, one person feels like they lost or were devalued. Bricks go into the wall, likely on both sides. And in a long-term committed relationship, the clock is ticking on when the original issue is going to pop up again.

Compromise invisibly erodes relationships in the long term. Your relationship is either being broken down or being built up in these little moments of your day. It wasn't really about the "big" fights. Those big fights were usually the culmination of these continuous, smaller erosions before you ever got there.

People have been doing the win-lose compromise dynamic for so long that they have now even run to the end of their skill set in deciding who wins and who loses.

TAKING SIDES

This is where "taking sides" comes in. People love to tell *their* side of the story to whomever will listen. When they do, they are often seeking someone who is going to take "their side." Someone who will essentially cast a vote for "their way" (so they are the "winner").

For instance, Jill might tell her friends about a disagreement, and they might all see it Jill's way and tell her that she's right or she's being reasonable.

Brian might tell his buddy what he's been dealing with at home and his buddy might take his side, telling him that his wife is being unreasonable or crazy.

Randi might call her mother-in-law to complain about her husband, and her mother-in-law might take her side and tell her son to give Randi what she wants.

Then, of course, Jill, Brian, and Randi all go back to their spouses and tell them, "So-and-so agrees with me that you are just wrong!" Every person that you get to take your side is like your own personal jury box, casting a verdict for your win.

It has become not only socially acceptable to bad-mouth your partner to see if people will take your side, it is now commonplace. Some people get addicted to telling everyone their story and gathering votes for "their side," then throwing that back in their partner's face as if to say, "See, all these people are on my side. This proves that you are wrong."

You don't need a degree in rocket science to understand that bad-mouthing your partner is a destructive pattern in *any* relationship. It rapidly breaks down your relationship. It puts many bricks into the wall for each instance, not just one. It can even take down a marriage over time.

Let me ask you this. When you bad-mouth your partner to someone in the hopes that they will take your side, what do you win?

You win a result where you and this other person are on one side of the battlefield and your partner is on the other. It drives separation between you. Even worse, it invites someone else,

The Destroyer of Relationships: Compromise

outside of your relationship, *into* the coveted marriage relationship so that they can *judge* it. This is a recipe for disaster!

The committed love relationship is supposed to be a loyal partnership between two people. The minute you bad-mouth your partner, you have not only broken rapport, trust, and alignment, but also prioritized someone else over your partner for their "side-taking." You have a bond with someone else that is placed higher than the bond with your partner in that moment. It is a betrayal, and it breaks down trust.

It's an invisible destroyer of relationships, and it works in the dark, unseen. Bad-mouthing a partner has become so common, it is portrayed in movies, television shows, and jokes. But in real life, there's nothing funny about it.

Taking sides has become so normalized that people don't even think twice about butting into someone else's situation and casting their vote.

For example, your sister calls you and tells you that Mom is upset with you and that you need to call Mom and smooth things over. That's called triangulation. Triangulation is when a third person, who is not directly involved at all, butts in and takes sides.

In this example, the issue is between you and your mom, but your sister triangulated by taking Mom's side and telling you to call her. Triangulation is a destroyer of relationships. But people don't even see it. It has become so normalized to take sides in the win-lose dynamic that people don't even stop to ask themselves, "Am I directly involved in this?"

It's a principle of Relationship Development *not* to take sides and not to triangulate. In our Relationship Development community, we also don't allow anyone to speak badly about anyone else.

How do you do *that*? What does that even look like, you ask? Now you're asking great questions that can free you!

In the example above, let's say that your sister was on the phone with your mom, when your mom started complaining about you and what you did wrong.

Here's what your sister could say, from Relationship Development, to be supportive of Mom without taking sides or triangulating:

Mom: "Your sister is infuriating. She still hasn't called me since Sunday to apologize. Would you please call her and tell her she needs to make this right?"

Sister: "Mom, I'm sorry you're going through this. Since this is between you and her, I encourage you to speak directly to her about it. How can I support you in doing that?"

Mom: "I said it. Would you please call her and tell her that she needs to apologize to me?"

Sister: "I'm actually not involved in this, so I'm not going to call her for you, but I'm happy to support you in figuring out how you best want to speak to her yourself."

Mom: "What do you mean you're not involved? She's your sister. Don't you even care that your own mother is upset?"

Sister: "I do care, Mom, that's exactly why I'm offering my support to *you*. But this upset is not between me and my sister; it's between you and your daughter. If you don't want to reach out to her, that's your choice. And if you do want to, I'm here to help support you in doing that. I know you would prefer for me to butt in and try to convince her to do what you feel is best, but I'm not going to do that. Would you like to talk about how *you* are going to handle this or how I can help you figure that out?"

Yeah, this is not my first rodeo. It takes some skills, but once you get the skills, it becomes effortless. Refusing to take sides keeps the peace more than butting into things that don't directly involve you.

You might be thinking, *My mother would be furious if I said that*, or that it might turn it into a fight between you and your mom where there was no fight between you before.

And it may. Some folks will not like your refusal to pick up the rope that they threw at you and your refusal to tug-of-war with them. But after a few instances of this, people will give up coming to you for side taking, interfering, and bad-mouthing because you are not having any of it.

I've seen it hundreds of times. Eventually, the path of genuine peacefulness is yours when you step out of the win-lose dynamic.

Taking sides is deeply ingrained in the Demand Relationship paradigm that has been handed to us. It's everywhere you look. Usually, people will tell their story in a way that showcases their "side" so others "naturally" take their side.

People bring this dynamic into their long-term committed relationship. It shows up as a pattern where you keep trying to convince your partner to take your side, too, to give up their way and to just agree that *your* way is the "right" way.

When this stops working for them, some people will head to a couples counselor for that person to be the professional side-taker and "settle their differences" that way. They both plead their case to the third party and ask them for a "ruling" on who was right and who was wrong. Who was being reasonable and who was unreasonable? Who was the winner and who was the loser? Then the counselor picks a side and determines who must compromise.

This is another reason why we believe couples work is destructive. Couples work, by definition, *is* triangulation. It's a method that instigates blame, speaking badly about the other person, and taking sides, all of which break down a relationship.

> **PRINCIPLE:**
> Compromise is just an agreement to repeat the win-lose over and over. Compromise destroys long-term relationships.

If the relationship breaks down every time someone wins and the other loses, then it is a loss for both partners, every time.

It's like the old saying that you may have won the battle but lost the war. You may have won that argument, but your relationship took another hit. You lost a little bit more of the connection you had to your partner. You may be winning a lot of arguments, but you are losing your partner more and more each time.

Even if you win your way, ultimately you lose them. Every loss is a loss in rapport, appreciation, respect, support, alignment, connection, and trust. Every loss is a loss for the relationship.

Saying that you won when your partner lost is like saying, "Your side of the boat has a hole in it." If you shoot a hole in your partner's side of the boat that you are both sitting in, you are both going down. The "ship" of relationship is sinking.

That is why Paul and I say, in long-term relationship there is no such thing as win-lose. Every win-lose is really a lose-lose because your relationship is being destroyed.

> **PRINCIPLE:**
> In a long-term relationship, there is no such thing as win-lose. The win-lose is actually the lose-lose.

What is the alternative, you ask? There is only one answer... the win-win.

What is the win-win? What does that look like? How do I do that? And if we can't agree, how can we possibly get to the win-win? (Turn the page.)

CHAPTER 15

THE WIN-WIN

If we can't agree, how can we possibly get to the win-win?

In Relationship Development, we use skill sets to keep going until we reach the win-win. When people stop at the win-lose, it's just an indication that they ran to the end of their skill set needed to create the win-win.

The win-win is one of the things that people initially struggle with the most. When people don't see eye-to-eye, I find that it's often very difficult for them to even believe that a win-win is possible.

It's not just "people" that have a hard time wrapping their minds around what I mean by a win-win. I went to thesaurus.com and looked up synonyms for win-win and these are a few of the words that came up in the search:

bargain, concession, settlement, cop-out, sellout, fifty-fifty, trade-off, half measure, happy medium, accommodation, adjustment, and *middle ground.*

None of those mean win-win. All of those are synonyms for the win-lose. Take that in for a moment. As a people, we are so deeply conditioned for the win-lose thinking that the win-win is practically inconceivable. Sadly, even the thesaurus cannot accurately define win-win. So, don't be too hard on yourself if you find it difficult to wrap your head around this at first.

So then, what is a win-win? A win-win situation is where the outcome is a *win* for both people. Where both people feel authentically good about the outcome.

You have absolutely experienced this in real life. You have been in situations where you spontaneously said, "That's a win-win!"

I'll give you an example. Dean goes into his office and tells his manager, Nora, that he needs to change his day off next week from Tuesday to Friday because his doctor's appointment got moved. Nora looks at the schedule and says, "I'll see what I can do for you, Dean."

Ten minutes later, Donna walks into Nora's office and says, "Nora, is there any way I can have off on Tuesday for my kid's parent-teacher conferences? I can come in for an extra shift another day if you need me to."

Nora responds, "You're in luck. Dean can cover you on Tuesday if you can come in on Friday for his shift."

Donna smiles and says, "Done and done!"

Nora declares, "That's a win-win."

It happens all the time. I bet you have experienced the win-win many times in your life. You *do* know what it is. In the example above, who is the loser? No one. Who feels bad about the outcome? No one. That's a win-win. Both people genuinely feel happy with the outcome. The win-win happens accidentally all the time. You just view those moments as happy coincidences.

The difference is that most humans do not (yet) have the skill set to create the win-win outcome from a disagreement between "my way versus your way." If the win-win doesn't organically happen, and the win-lose does organically happen, most humans do not have the skills to transform a win-lose into a genuine win-win.

We teach that skill set. It is not just possible, it's been done. Let's look at an example.

SUSAN AND TED

Susan and Ted's son, Ben, lied about completing his chores before he went to his friend's house. Ted thinks Ben should be grounded for lying. Susan wants to talk with Ben and help him get his chores done next time. Susan and Ted have argued about this multiple times.

> **Susan to Ted:** "If you keep bringing that kind of punishment to the kids, you will damage your relationship with them. These kids will never tell us the truth if they just keep getting punished for it. You're teaching them to hide things from us."
>
> **Ted to Susan:** "I have a job to do. It's to get these kids ready for the world outside this house, Susan. If you keep coddling them, they're never going to survive in the real world."

Sometimes Ted throws his hands up and lets Susan have her way. Other times, Susan bites her tongue while Ted gets his way. But they are both unhappy with the outcome, and it keeps driving a wedge between them.

This is a common example that many, if not most, parents have faced. In these situations, most people default to the win-lose. You try to convince the other person to see that they are wrong, and that you are right. If *they* would just see how wrong they are, this would be so much easier, right?

If you fail to convince them, you might try other Demand Relationship tactics, try to get others involved to take sides, and so on.

So, in the example above, what would be a win-win? Really think about it. What is a solution that you could offer, where it would be a win-win? Remember, a win-win is where both people are genuinely happy with the outcome.

Usually, this is where people get stumped. Don't feel bad. This is where counselors, therapists, and everyone else gets stumped too. It's okay. There's nothing wrong with you. Creating the win-win solution is a skill set. It's just a skill set you haven't learned yet. But it can be learned.

Because most folks run to the end of their skill set to keep going until they create the win-win, the most common outcome is that people default to the win-lose. And because that feels so bad, in the future they start using tactics like escape, avoidance, and prevention just to make sure this doesn't even come up again.

In real life, what this looks like is this: You get to a stalemate on a topic that you simply cannot agree on. So, you add that topic to the "we can't talk about that" list and you try to avoid it, escape it, and prevent it from coming up again. Meanwhile, this adds more bricks into the wall between you. And this starts building your belief (however false) that the two of you just can't be together or that you are just "too different."

False belief: There's something about the two of us together that makes it so that we can't be together.
Truth: I ran to the end of my skill set to keep going until I reached the win-win.

That's a life-changing distinction to have. Marriages end, every single day, over the false belief that there is something about the two of them together that makes it impossible to get along.

It shocks us when our students tell us about their experiences with other relationship workers, counselors, and therapists, how they are handing divorce prescriptions out like they are Halloween candy, citing "irreconcilable differences" as the reason. "Irreconcilable differences" just means that the person labeling you also ran to the end of *their* skill set to help you. That's all. In all the years that Paul and I have been helping thousands of people, we have never once said that.

There are loads of skill sets, tools, and strategies in our toolbox for developing a win-win solution; let's start with one of them here.

THE RELATIONSHIP DEVELOPMENT TOOL: THE ORDER OF ALIGNMENT™

First: The WHY

Second: The WHAT

Third: The HOW

Most people disagree with their partner at the HOW level. They fight about HOW something should be done. My way for how to do this versus your way for how to do this. My way to load the dishwasher versus your way to load the dishwasher.

When you disagree and desire to find alignment, do not start at the HOW level. The order is to align at the WHY level first, the WHAT level second, and the HOW level last.

Using our example with Susan and Ted and their parenting disagreement above, the couple was disagreeing at the HOW level. Ted wanted to punish their son, and Susan wanted to help their son. Those are both *hows*. Either Susan or Ted could implement The Order of Alignment tool to solve this. Here's an example of how that works.

Step 1: Float up to the level of WHY.

Let's say that Ted is the one in our program getting the training on these tools. He could schedule a time to talk with Susan so they could come to a solution for their family. When they sit down to chat after the kids go to bed, Ted could start with step one by saying something like this:

> **Ted:** "I know we both want the best for our kids, and we've disagreed on how to do that. I'd like to try to get to a win-win on this, where you feel good, I feel good, and it's also best for the kids. If it's okay with you, can you share with me a little bit about WHY you feel that helping Ben with his chores is the best thing for him? Why does this way forward mean so much to you?"

Susan: (yells at Ted) "I see the way that Ben shuts down when you yell at him and ground him. He's slipping farther and farther away from us. He goes up in that room and shuts the door and doesn't come downstairs. He's lying because he knows he's just going to get into trouble. If we keep doing this, when the shit really hits the fan and he's in big trouble, he's not going to call us, Ted. He could be drunk at a party somewhere, and he won't call his dad to come get him. Ted, he could get into a car and drive like that instead of calling us because of a stupid punishment." Then Susan starts crying.

Ted: (comforts Susan) "Sweetie, I'm so sorry for how upsetting this is. We are going to solve this, together. I promise you. I won't give up until this is truly solved. Susan, I want him to call us too. I want him to make good decisions. Of course, I want Ben to be safe and to feel like he can call me when real trouble comes around."

By floating up to the level of WHY, maintaining his state, and reassuring his feminine partner, within minutes, Ted already created alignment at the WHY level with Susan. They both want their son to call them when the shit goes down.

In the years that I have been doing this work, I have found that, the majority of the time, two people can easily align at the WHY level. That alignment is not only a place to start toward figuring out the rest of the puzzle but also can build tremendous rapport.

If you don't have rapport, you have nothing. When you create alignment at the WHY level, you build rapport. The moment that Ted aligns with Susan's WHY, she will feel a huge sense of relief.

Think about it. If you genuinely felt that your partner had YOUR why in their heart, would that bring you a sense of relief? Would you feel closer to them? Would you feel less resistance and more hope to move forward and try to solve things?

> **PRINCIPLE:**
> No one does anything without a reason.

Most of the time, a person's reason is their WHY. They are grasping at a HOW only because that's the only way they know or believe they can get the result that fulfills their WHY. The WHY is what's in their heart. The WHY is the driver. The WHY is where the passion comes from.

Most of the time, you can align at the WHY level. And most of the time, you can, at least, appreciate the good intention in the other person's WHY.

Let's go back to our example with Ted and Susan and look at Ted's WHY.

This is Ted's WHY for wanting to punish his son . . .

Ted: "If Ben doesn't learn how to be responsible, he won't be ready for life. It's my job to prepare him for the world. I don't really care that he went out with his friends and didn't mow the lawn before he left. But if he doesn't learn this now, he's going to end up lying to his boss about something at work that he didn't do and lose his job. He's never going to learn how to *do what he has to do before doing what he wants to do.* And I will have failed him, as a father, by not preparing him."

While Susan might not be able to personally relate to any of Ted's perspective, and she might not think any of that is important (since she's feminine core and doesn't process the same way), she can appreciate Ted's positive intent for their son. She can understand that Ted is just trying to do his job to prepare his son to be a man when he's older and when Ted's not there.

This is alignment at the WHY level. Which brings us to a critical principle.

> **PRINCIPLE:**
> Alignment does not equal agreement.

You do not have to agree with someone to align with them. People use the words *alignment* and *agreement* interchangeably, but they are not the same thing. Let me explain.

Agreement means: I also see it the same way you do. I see it for myself the same way that you see it for yourself.

Alignment means: I understand the way you see it for yourself. I get it. Even though I don't see it the same way for *myself*, I do understand and validate that you see it that way for *yourself*. I don't have to see it the same way for myself or agree, but I can understand your perspective for you and I align with your view for yourself.

You may need to read this a few times (or a hundred times) to get this. An example of this may help.

In our example above, Susan doesn't think that there is any correlation between her son mowing the lawn and her son failing to hold a job or failing as a man. It's not her view of the world. She doesn't think like that, doesn't see the correlation, and doesn't value it.

You could probably ask any father if he values it and sees the correlation, and the answer will most likely be "Of course." In fact, he might raise an eyebrow as to why you are asking about something that is so obvious that it doesn't need to be discussed.

However, maybe Susan can appreciate that all humans are wired differently and that a masculine being can often see circumstances very differently than she or even her feminine friends would.

Susan can align with her husband instead of agreeing. She can align by saying, "Although I do not also see it that way and I won't pretend that I do, I'm not masculine core and you are. I can appreciate that from the masculine perspective, that is important. I align with that for you."

Alignment is like validating the other person's perspective for them. You may not hold the same perspective for yourself, but you validate it for them. You are not validating it for you; you are validating it for *them*.

Aligning at the WHY level is just validating that both people have a perspective or intention that can be understood. It doesn't mean that one person's WHY is somehow correct or "wins."

You are also not agreeing to anyone's "how" just by aligning with their WHY. (Read that again.)

Aligning at the level of WHY is just step one.

It can take a lot of work. Just accurately identifying your WHY is a skill set that has to be learned, let alone navigating the WHY alignment conversation. So, have compassion and show yourself and your partner some grace as you try to implement this.

Step 2: Align at the level of WHAT.

At this level, you need to get clear and accurate on the outcome that you are trying to get to. WHAT you want as an outcome is important to identify. This level is complicated, because sometimes the WHAT that you or your spouse is trying to get to is a Demand Relationship "WHAT." In that case, our tools will not work for you.

For example, if Ted's WHAT was, "I want my child to listen to me every time I speak," then that's Demand Relationship. We can't help you get to the outcome of demanding compliance. If you are going through this process and find that either you or your partner's WHAT is a Demand Relationship outcome, then instead of working on the alignment, switch gears to help navigate through breaking the Demand Relationship mindset.

If the WHAT is identified as something that is NOT Demand Relationship, then keep going with the alignment.

For instance, in our example above, Ted's WHAT might be, "I want our son to learn that we first do what we have to do and only *then* can we do what we want to do." And Susan's WHAT might be, "I want our son to feel like he can call us, no matter what, even if something really bad happens."

Those are both achievable WHATs. Notice that Ted did not say, "I want our son to be responsible." We can't control another person. We can't make someone "be responsible." But Ted's WHAT was, "I want our son to learn." That's always possible. You can teach your child something but you just can't make them use it, especially when you are not there.

Same with Susan. She did not say, "I want our son to call us." You can't make someone call you. She said, "I want our son to feel like he can call us." Well, you can always use skills to build a level of rapport where someone feels like they can call you. Can you feel the difference in those examples?

It's common for the two WHAT items to be completely different for each spouse. Here's where you need a certain level of Relationship Development skills to navigate. If you are still stuck in Demand Relationship thinking, you will only see that the two WHAT items are different, and the win-lose (competition) thinking may start to creep in.

Be careful not to do Demand Relationship, or you will break down the relationship with your approach. I encourage you to start using the word *and* as a tool.

Meaning Ted and Susan can help their son learn how to do what he needs to do, then do what he wants to do, *and* also help him feel like he can call them if something really bad happens.

Those two things are not mutually exclusive. You can attain both outcomes. Yet, if we didn't do this in the correct order, Ted and Susan would still be arguing over their "my way versus your way" disagreement and completely miss the opportunity to achieve both WHAT outcomes for the good of their son.

Step 3: Design the level of HOW.

> **PRINCIPLE:**
> "There are a million ways to happy."
> — Tony Robbins

There are a million HOWs to achieve any given WHAT outcome. It's a fact. While you are busy holding on with a white-knuckle grip to the one HOW that you are fighting for, you don't see the dozens of other ways to get the outcome you want.

In the beginning of Ted and Susan's example, it looked like they were headed for a stalemate. They disagreed and believed they would never agree. Yet, here we are, looking at the HOWs to meet their WHATs.

Ted's WHAT is that he wants his son to learn this principle: first we do what we have to do and then we do what we want to do. What are all the different HOWs to achieve that outcome? Can you think of a few?

As an example, here are seven different and simple HOWs that I came up with:

1. **Stop judging.** When Ted judges, he breaks rapport with his son. People don't listen to people who judge them. So, he will need to stop judging if he wants his son to want to learn from him.

2. **Build rapport.** If Ted has no rapport with his son, his son will not follow his lead.

3. **Explain the benefits.** Outside the moment, Ted can share some of the reasons he values personal responsibility so much in his own life, giving his son a glimpse into his perspective.

4. **Set up natural consequences** as part of the family systems. Instead of punishments

for not following orders (which is Demand Relationship), set up related consequences for Ben for what happens when chores are not done by a certain reasonable time. For instance, if he doesn't mow the lawn by Thursday night, then he doesn't get to go out on Friday until both the lawn is mowed and Friday's stuff is done. And if the lawn is not mowed by Saturday morning, then he will need to take on some tasks for his dad on Saturday, because Dad mowed on Friday night, and so on.

5. **Anchor in success.** When Ben successfully does what needs to be done, Ted can anchor it in for him to increase the energy around the positive result. Like saying, "Hey, Ben, great job getting that lawn done before the movie on Thursday night."

6. **Evolve with change.** Increase your trust and appreciation as the desired result becomes a pattern. As Ben shows that he's starting to internalize the responsibility, Ted could loosen the restrictions around Ben's activities or reward him with more trust. That's what a job would do. If you're trying to help him learn, then build in rewards too, like saying, "That's two months of getting that lawn mowed before going out. Mom and I want to make your curfew an hour later on Saturdays because you are demonstrating ownership and personal responsibility elsewhere."

7. **Be understanding of failures.** If Ben is generally getting his chores done but then has a struggle, be a team player instead of a dictator. Maybe Ben is running late on Thursday because his car broke down on the way home from school, and he doesn't have time to mow the lawn and get to

the party on time with his friends. He comes to you and says that he promised his friends that he would bring the cups, and if he's late, they will suffer too. Is there any way he can mow the lawn tomorrow so he can be there on time? Ted could thank Ben for coming to him with that and tell him to absolutely go to his friend's house and do the lawn tomorrow.

That's just seven different HOWs to get the brainstorming started. See, there are many different HOWs to get the WHAT outcome that you desire and meet your WHY. Some HOWs will be better than others. There may be some that you don't want to do. That's fine. But there are many ways to do something beyond the one way that you thought this needed to be.

If you can't think of multiple HOWs, then you just ran to the end of your skill set, that's all. We teach our students to bring their WHY and WHAT to our group and ask for other students to collaborate and brainstorm a list of HOWs to get started.

Next, we could make a list of ways to help Susan achieve her outcome with Ben to give her many HOWs to choose from. Then Ted and Susan can implement several HOWs that help them to both prepare their son to be responsible as well as cultivate a relationship with him that encourages him to reach out to them when the shit hits the fan.

The key is this: the HOWs can always change if you are aligned at the WHY level. Floating up to the level of WHY is the first step in building a strong win-win scenario.

EXAMPLE: THREE PIECES OF THE WIN-WIN FOR TED AND SUSAN

1. During a family meeting about chores, include Ben in the collaboration on setting up the family systems.

2. Implement the "no questions asked program." Tell Ben that if he's ever in a tough situation and needs to get out of there, no matter what it is, he can just text his mom or dad the poop emoji on his phone, and they will come get him wherever he is, with no questions asked and no punishment.

3. Ted and Susan agree to chat again in 30 days to assess how things are going and to adjust anything that's not working out.

That is an example of how to take a stalemate disagreement to a win-win solution. Instead of avoiding it, putting it on the "we can't talk about this" list, or giving up, with Relationship Development skill sets, you can keep going until you reach the win-win. But the only way that works is when you start at the WHY level and don't get stuck at the HOW level.

> **PRINCIPLE:**
> The win-lose is based on competition and separation. The win-win is based in collaboration and unity.
>
> **PRINCIPLE:**
> The win-lose breaks down the relationship every time. The win-win builds up the relationship each time by increasing the rapport, connection, alignment, appreciation, support, and trust.
>
> **PRINCIPLE:**
> Humans have been conditioned to win in the win-lose for thousands of years. The win-lose thinking is deeply wired into us.
>
> **PRINCIPLE:**
> The win-lose in long-term relationships is actually the lose-lose because nobody wins when their partner loses.

You can use skill sets to create a win-win, even in situations that seem like there is no way for both people to be happy. If you are stuck, you are likely starting at the HOW level and battling over "my way versus your way." While there are many skill sets involved in being able to get any situation to a win-win, they all start with the first step, which is to get to the WHY level.

Take a disagreement that is stuck in the win-lose between you and your partner and answer these questions: What is your WHY? WHY is your way important to you? WHY do you need this?

It may take some work for you to discover your true WHY. In helping students through this process, very often the first 5 to 10 minutes of their response to my WHY question is them explaining or defending why their HOW is the right way or telling me WHAT they need to happen. Getting to the WHY is not always easy.

Most humans operate at the HOW level. I would guess that the majority of the human world right now is disagreeing at the HOW level, and they haven't risen past that level, which is why the disagreements remain unsolved.

If you aren't clear on your own WHY and WHAT, then you will have little to no chance of brainstorming additional HOWs. The HOWs are only HOWs that get you to your WHAT and fulfill your WHY, so you must be clear on those to solve this.

If you want to create a win-win, then you must be able to design multiple HOWs that not only attain your WHAT and fulfill on your WHY but also attain your partner's WHAT and fulfill on their WHY.

I've asked countless humans to explain to me what their partner's WHY is. The majority of them will give me an answer, and when I dig deeper, I find out that it is just a guess, and they really have no idea what their partner's WHY is.

A win-win solution is a solution where both people are happy with the outcome. If you are not clear on your partner's WHY, then you cannot design something that is a win for them.

THE Missing PIECE

> **PRINCIPLE:**
> If you do not clearly and accurately know your partner's WHY and WHAT, then you cannot design a WIN-WIN.

Question for you: If you had a clear and accurate WHY and WHAT in front of you, on a piece of paper, for both you and your partner, do you feel like you might have a chance of coming up with three or four HOWs to achieve those outcomes and fulfill on those WHYs? Maybe.

Let me ask you this way, then: If all you have on the paper in front of you is "your way" and "their way," do you think you have a higher or lower chance of coming up with a win-win than if you had both WHY/WHAT lists on the paper in front of you?

I'll tell you that in my experience, if all you have is "my way" and "their way," you have almost no shot at coming up with a win-win. And that is why people think the win-win is impossible. It is not only possible but also proven because it's been done countless times. However, when you are stuck at the HOW level and don't have the skill set to do it, then it's not possible for you, yet. That's all.

We started with an example of a father who wanted to punish his son for lying and a mother who wanted to talk to the son and help him. And when I shared that story, you took sides. And at that point, it seemed like the only way to settle it was for one of them to give in because there was no way for them to see eye-to-eye on this one.

And yet, here we are. After going through just this small piece of the process, using skill sets and getting a Missing Piece (The Order of Alignment), we are much closer to a win-win on something that looked impossible before.

By the way, about taking sides: Which parent turned out to be right in the end? And which one was wrong? Was the dad wrong for wanting his son to learn to be responsible so he was prepared for the real world? Or was the mom wrong for wanting her son to call his parents when trouble came around? Which one of them was wrong?

> **PRINCIPLE:**
> No one does anything without a reason.

Neither parent was wrong. They both had good intentions for their son. Without applying The Order of Alignment Tool, how many years would be wasted fighting over their disagreement? Imagine how many unqualified and unequipped folks would happily butt in and take sides or judge one of them as just being unreasonable and needing to compromise.

When we stay stuck in the win-lose, *everyone* loses. Including our kids. Ted and Susan's son, Ben, is much better off having the guidance of two parents who love him, both preparing him for the world, than he would have been if only one of them contributed to leading him.

If Ted gave in and just let Susan handle it, would that have benefited their son more? Nope. If Susan gave in and just let Ted handle it, would that have better prepared Ben for the world? Nope. It turns out that both parents have something great to offer, and there's a gift in getting multiple perspectives instead of just one.

It's like the quote from Aristotle: "The whole is greater than the sum of its parts."

Stopping at the win-lose destroys relationships, and we are losing out on the gifts that come from bringing more pieces of the puzzle into the picture.

But what about those times when we just can't agree? How do we get on the same page when we do not and will not see eye-to-eye? (Turn the page.)

CHAPTER 16

THE PATH TO CREATING ALIGNMENT, EVEN WHEN YOU DON'T AGREE

Imagine, for a moment, that you got a job at a brand-new coffee shop in your town and that today is the grand opening. You and one other person, Chris, show up for your first day of work at 6:45 A.M. You and Chris have never met before, have never worked at a coffee shop before, and are the only two people there to run the place.

At 7 A.M., the doors open for the first time, and 25 people who were waiting outside fill the coffee shop. People are barking their orders at you, telling you that you're not doing it right, and demanding that you hurry up.

You start making drinks and assume that Chris is going to ring them up at the register so you can make coffee for the next person in line, but when you look up, Chris isn't at the register. In fact, he isn't even behind the counter with you.

So, you hurry over to the register, ring the next person up, and then jump back to the line to make the next cup of coffee. You notice Chris is in the back room, so you yell to him, "Can you please come help me here? At least ring up the customers, so I can get these drinks made."

Chris comes out from the back room to see what you're yelling about, his arms full of muffins. You quickly realize that there are food items on the menu. People are ordering food, and there's no food in the case to give them. You realize Chris must have been in the back getting food.

You go back to making coffee. Chris is ringing up a customer. You are both barking orders at each other and yelling for things when you need help.

You go to grab a donut for someone from the back, and when you come back, you realize that Chris had already grabbed the donuts as well and was ringing up that same customer. You don't even remember seeing him go to the back and grab them.

The crowd never lets up. It seems like there's always a line of people, and every moment feels like chaos. Finally, it's closing time, and you lock the front door. You and Chris slump into a couple of chairs, exhausted. There's coffee inside your shoes, and your apron is covered in something sticky.

After a few minutes, you stand up, take off your apron, smile, wave good-bye to Chris, and say, "See you again tomorrow!"

Wait, what?

Let me ask you, would you stand up, walk out, and show up the next morning to do that all the same way again? Would you keep showing up like that, day after day, with the same chaos and frenzy?

Probably not.

Maybe you would have quit after the first day. Maybe you're thinking, *I wouldn't have even opened those doors at 7 A.M. if no one was there who knew what they were doing.* Or maybe once the day was done, you would talk to Chris about what to do differently tomorrow to not repeat that horror show.

Regardless, the likelihood that you would stand up, smile, and plan to repeat this experience again without talking to the other person about how to get the workload done without the chaos is highly unlikely.

And yet, that is what most people do in marriage today, every day. Marriage is a lot like the coffee shop. You run into your day with a million things going on. There are demands from the kids, animals, household, work, school, activities, and, oh yeah, you guys gotta eat at some point too.

No wonder we end up barking at each other throughout the day. We walk into it, assuming that everyone will just do what needs to be done the right way. We get frustrated with them when they aren't where we expect them to be, doing what we expect them to be doing. It's chaotic, frenzied, unpleasant, and unfulfilling. And then at the end of the night, we just drag ourselves to bed and plan to show up tomorrow for the same gig without solving anything.

We wouldn't keep doing that at the coffee shop, and yet, here we are repeating this pattern, day after day in our family, marriage, and household (our most precious assets).

THE INVISIBLE ALIGNMENT PREDICAMENT™

Paul and I call this dynamic the Invisible Alignment Predicament. It's when you think, "Just because we fall in love, we're going to see parenting the same way." Or "Because we love each other, we are going to run this household the same way."

The Invisible Alignment Predicament shows up in three common ways:

Assumption 1: We're going to see this the same way.
Assumption 2: My partner will know what to do here, so I'll follow their lead.
Assumption 3: My partner will do things my way (and won't have a different opinion or view of their own to interject).

Have you had one, two, or three of those assumptions at one point in time?

PRINCIPLE:
You do not accidentally align on things just because you fall in love.

Most people in a long-term relationship end up with a list of things that they don't see eye-to-eye on. While there are some things that you do accidentally align on because you happen to see them the same way, over time, you also discover the list of things that you do not accidentally align on.

A list begins to form of topics that you don't agree on. You become aware that you can't get on the same page on topics like spending, household responsibilities, parenting, work, how time is spent, how we interact with each other or with the kids, and more.

The typical response is to try to push or convince your partner to see it your way. If they could just see why they are wrong and why your way is actually right, then they could get on the same page about this, and life would be a lot easier and smoother.

For instance, you might say to Chris, "Look, the only way for this to work is if one of us makes drinks and the other handles food and the register. So tomorrow, I will take the drink orders and you handle the food and the register, and this will go a lot smoother."

But what if Chris responds with, "I don't think so. If we just alternate customers and see that customer through the entire process from order to drink to register, it will move more people through the line."

That's how this usually goes, right? Spouse A starts by telling their spouse what needs to change. And if spouse B agrees, then we have no problem.

But what about when spouse B disagrees? That's when one partner will try to convince the other. Maybe you focus on showing them what they are "missing" or not getting about the situation so that they "get it" and see why your approach is the way to go.

You might say to Chris, "Actually, it is quicker to do the same task over and over and stay in one place. That's a fact. Moving from place to place will be slower and more chaotic, so you are wrong. We need to divide and conquer."

The Path to Creating Alignment, Even When You Don't Agree

This usually invites the other person to try to prove their side. It's not a conversation to the win-win, it's a "convincing match" between two people.

Chris might reply with, "In the time it takes you to make one drink, I can ring out four people at the register. It takes less time to ring someone out at the register than it does to make a drink. So, while you are trying to make one drink, the line is backing up, and I'm not ringing anyone out at the register because they are all still waiting for a drink."

Aha! Who is right? Who is wrong? It feels like a stalemate. We can't both get our way. So, who wins?

Again, this is where most people are stuck today.

Perhaps you ask them questions about "their way" and then poke holes in it and show them why their reasoning is flawed or their understanding of the situation is off, hoping that if they can just see it the way you do, they will come to the obvious realization that you are right.

This leads to the "My Way versus Your Way" tug-of-war. I'm sure you have been in this situation many, many times.

People start out focused on pushing "their way" forward. And for some folks, that approach never stops. If you have been at this with the same person for a certain number of years, eventually this can get exhausting, and one or both partners just don't want to argue about it anymore. Plenty of people end up either giving in or giving up.

Then, there are times where you just feel like you cannot give in. Maybe you feel like you constantly give in, but you just can't do it anymore. Or maybe it's just this topic that you can't give up.

You might even be open to being "wrong" about "your way" as long as someone else can show you a way that makes sense. But you know in your heart that your partner's way is not right, so you're not just going to agree to it just to keep the peace.

I imagine you have been in several of these situations at one time or another.

There are a few dynamics going on in this tug-of-war situation.

> **PRINCIPLE:**
> Your white-knuckle grip on your side of the rope causes the other person to match the intensity of your grip on their side of the rope.

Trigger: white-knuckle grip on your way → Boomerang: white-knuckle grip on their way

For disagreements where you have a white-knuckle grip on "your way," you are creating the coordinating Boomerang from the other person. They are pulling harder on their side of the rope to balance you out.

Take the common dynamic where one parent is more "authoritarian," and the other parent is more of a "coddler." The more authoritarian that one parent becomes, the more coddling or gentle the other parent becomes to balance it out.

When one partner ups the intensity on their white-knuckle grip of saving money, the other partner increases their intensity of resistance to being starved of the things they want to spend on.

It's a predictable pattern with a predictable outcome.

> **PRINCIPLE:**
> Your white-knuckle grip on "your position" is triggering the other person to increase their intensity on their resistance to you or to fight you harder.

This is usually when people freak out at the thought of loosening their white-knuckle grip on their position because in their mindset, that is the first step toward losing their position. Right? If you loosen your grip on the rope, you lose the tug-of-war, right?

It's very common and understandable. This is Demand Relationship thinking. And it's accurate thinking for the win-lose dynamic of Demand Relationship. If you stay in the win-lose, then loosening your grip will not help you fight for the win. You're correct.

But I'm not talking about staying in the win-lose dynamic of Demand Relationship. I'm talking about stepping into Relationship Development. So, let's take this one piece at a time.

Think of something that you and your partner disagree on. You have a side on this topic, correct? You know what "your way" is and how you want things to go, yes?

Okay, good. Let me ask you a question. Why?

Can you articulate to me why you are so passionate about needing your way? I'm not challenging your way. I'm genuinely curious. Please write it down on a piece of paper or just pause for a minute and articulate it to yourself. I'm giving you a moment to just explain your side to me. Tell me why your way is right or better or needed and why this is so important to you.

Now, I'll ask you this question differently to get another dimension on this that we need in order to solve things. What would be the problem if it wasn't done your way? I'm really asking. Can you please explain it to me? What are all the problems with not doing it your way or the way you think things need to be done?

The two questions I just asked you about "your way" are as follows:

1. Why?
2. What would be the problem if it wasn't done your way?

I hope that you answered those questions for yourself so we can get visibility and clarity on this topic. We need both of these to solve it.

Your answers to the two questions above represent your needs, your fears, your Triggers, your blueprint, and your meanings. You are using "your way" to get your needs met and prevent your Trigger, fears, or negative experiences from coming up.

Said differently, you are using "your way" as a vehicle to get to pleasure or avoid pain, or both.

And while you might be thinking, *Duh, of course I am,* keep in mind that it's Demand Relationship. When you are trying to use something or someone outside of yourself so that you can be happy or get your way, it is putting Demand Relationship into the Loop. You are heading into the situation with an agenda, to get something you need for you. The Boomerang of that is going to be nasty.

EXAMPLE: SPENDING VERSUS SAVING (RALPH AND VERA)

Ralph is trying to save money and make sure that they spend less. Vera is very frustrated with Ralph's fearful saving and feels stifled.

Ralph's perspective: Ralph's way to protect his family is to always have 12 months of living expenses in their savings account. He also doesn't need much and thinks it's foolish to waste money on things like purses or coffee. His wife already has plenty of purses she doesn't use clogging up their closet, and he bought her that expensive coffee maker last year that's sitting on the counter, unused. There's a right way and a wrong way to spend money. They live in a nice house, and Vera wears nice clothes. It's not like he asks her to live in crap just to save a buck. It's just about being reasonable with spending and not being ridiculous.

Vera's perspective: Vera's way is to spend reasonably for the life they lead. She works hard and has worked hard for 25 years. They give so much of their lives to work, the kids, and the house. They have plenty of savings in the bank. She can always get another job within six months and has proven that in the past. Anything more than six months in the savings account is just being irrational. She's not making them poor by stopping for coffee or ordering another purse when the season changes. She didn't work this hard to deny herself reasonable spending like this. What's the point of having excess money in the bank and depriving yourself of joy in life? So, you can die with a full bank account? It's ridiculous.

So, I'm guessing you already have a side in this. Be so careful of what you are so certain of. Let's dive in and take a Relationship Development approach to this.

Remember the Relationship Development Principles: no one is wrong, we're not taking sides, and we're working toward a win-win. Let's get clarity and visibility into Ralph and Vera's disagreement.

RALPH'S PERSPECTIVE

Question #1: Why? Why does Ralph need his way? While there are many, I'll pull out two items as an example here.

- Ralph told us that he's trying to protect his family.
- He has meanings and judgements about what is needed versus what is unreasonable. He commented on Vera's purses and her coffee. Since he doesn't have any need for these things, he is evaluating whether she should need these things based on his own blueprint of needs versus excess.

Question #2: What would be the problem if spending didn't go your way but instead it was done the way your partner wanted to do it?

- For Ralph, eventually, they would be broke. They could lose their home, and he would have failed to protect his family. It's basic math. Eventually, one of them is going to have a job change. It's just part of life. And when that happens, if they can't recover their salary within a year, they would have spent everything they have saved for the last 25+ years just to make it through one year. Their monthly bills would eat away that savings account faster than she can imagine. He wouldn't be able to keep them in that house, and then Vera would be seriously miserable.

- As much as he wants to make her happy and give her everything her heart desires, in the end, he's willing to be the bad guy and have her pout over a purse today so he doesn't fail her and have her devastated later. He could easily live in a shitty part of town in a tiny apartment. He doesn't care; he'll be fine. He's not doing this for himself; he's doing this for them. Vera would be beside herself if she had to move out of this house, and he's got two kids to protect. He's only saving this money for them so he can give them what they really need.

VERA'S PERSPECTIVE

Question #1: Why? Why does Vera need her way? While there are many, I'll pull out three items as an example here.

- Vera wants to enjoy her life without what she considers excessive spending restraints for no reason.
- Vera considers herself very responsible and not extravagant or excessive in her spending.
- Vera is sick of being controlled by Ralph's fears and exhausted from feeling judged because Ralph doesn't think she needs something that she wants.

The Path to Creating Alignment, Even When You Don't Agree

Question #2: What would be the problem if spending didn't go your way, but instead it was done the way your partner wanted to do it?

- For Vera, she would be miserable and feel trapped.
- Life would lose its joy.
- She would be no different than one of the children, doing whatever Dad said or else.
- She would have worked so hard her whole life only to keep living like the broke girl she used to be. What was the point of getting out of being broke if she was just going to be forced to live in survival for the rest of her days?
- Eventually, her resentment of Ralph would escalate and her thoughts about how different it would be if she was legally free of him would grow.
- In the end, if this continued, he might get the thing he is the most afraid of. He's going to lose at least half of his money when Vera divorces him so she can live her life freely.

Since this is one of the most common kerfuffles between partners, you probably resonate with some of what was shared about either Ralph's or Vera's perspective on spending. Maybe you even got a glimpse into the positive intention that the other person might have but has never vocalized?

No one is wrong here. Both of those perspectives have positive intent, and both are very understandable given that person's blueprint, wiring, life experience, and needs.

So, what do we do when we disagree? If no one is wrong, but they both can't get their way because their "ways" are opposites, then what do we do?

The answer: We use Relationship Development skill sets to create alignment so we can find the win-win for the team. This is where most folks believe it's impossible, when your way and their way are mutually exclusive. They think there can't possibly be a win-win. Well, I'm about to demonstrate how I do this, day in and day out. So please stay with me.

Before I can show you the HOW, I need to explain the WHEN.

INSIDE THE MOMENT VERSUS OUTSIDE THE MOMENT™

Solving this does not happen inside the moment of the kerfuffle (during the moment of conflict). It only happens outside the moment of the kerfuffle. There are two sets of tools in the Relationship Development toolbox: Inside the Moment tools and Outside the Moment tools.

Inside the Moment tools are just to help you mitigate the damage of the kerfuffle and keep things from sliding farther down the downward spiral.

Outside the Moment tools are designed to help you solve the dynamic so that it doesn't keep happening again and again. The only way you can truly solve a dynamic is by using Outside the Moment tools and being willing to do the work Outside the Moment of the kerfuffle. If you refuse to do that, then you are just fighting inside the moment, and it can't ever be solved.

Inside the moment, people are focused on either winning or keeping the peace. Outside the moment, our focus and intention are on solving the dynamic. We need the perspective we gain outside the moment to do this successfully.

Creating alignment and designing the win-win solution can only happen outside the moment using the tools designed for that (read that again).

THE STEPS TO ALIGNMENT

Remember the tool I taught you, Face It, Own It & Solve It? We start with that. Simply by writing this out and looking at the clear and accurate answers to the questions above, we are facing the issue. Again, instead of just fighting over $200 spent on this or that, we face the issue, outside the moment of a kerfuffle, with the intention of solving the dynamic for the win-win.

Owning it means taking personal responsibility. This is where you find where you are trying to control someone or something else to meet your need or quell your unrest. So, if Ralph was doing the work, he would be focused on solving his unrest around his need to protect his family so that he can come to the conversation from a peaceful place.

If Vera was doing the work, she would be focused on solving her Trigger around being controlled and missing out on joy. She would be solving some of her Triggers that she is trying to use spending to solve for her.

That is their personal Trigger work to do. And it's not because they are WRONG or unjustified in any way. But if you are trying to control something outside of yourself to calm something inside yourself, you are setting yourself up for failure.

Remember: you do not have control over anyone or anything outside of yourself. And as you can see from their answers above, their patterns of trying to use spending to satisfy their needs or Triggers is ironically leading them toward the very destruction they are trying to avoid.

PRINCIPLE:

When you are in unrest, you add unrest to the situation.

PRINCIPLE:

If you are trying to use something or someone outside of yourself to meet your needs or quell your fears and Triggers, then you will enter any conversation trying to control the outcome so that you get the win you need.

When you need to control something outside of yourself, then you are not really showing up with curiosity and openness and collaborating to find the win-win. Instead, you are showing up with an agenda to see how easily you can get them to agree to the part that *you* need, and hopefully throw something their way that they want, which you are happy to give them without losing what you need.

That's negotiation (and it's Demand Relationship).

When you need to control something outside yourself, you are not showing up to design the win-win. You are showing up to negotiate so you feel satisfied.

That's the win-lose, which is ultimately the lose-lose. This is why you are struggling to see how to create the win-win. You cannot create the win-win because you are not heading into the conversation to create the win-win. You are heading into the conversation to try to get what you need.

That is why we always start with the YOU work first. Always YOU before YOU RELATE. You must do the work on your Triggers, needs, and fears before you enter the "you relate" conversation.

How can you meet your needs internally in a way that is sustainable, and good for you, without needing to control someone or something outside of yourself? How can you heal the false beliefs and replace them with truth? How can you solve your Triggers so you can be free and peaceful? This is the work. We have an entire event dedicated to just that work. It's really important.

When you have mastered that, then you can enter a conversation having owned your part and be more ready to collaborate on the win-win solutions.

EXAMPLE: RALPH'S YOU WORK RESULTS

If Ralph was the Relationship Development student, this would be some of the YOU work that he would do before doing the YOU RELATE inter-actions with his spouse.

- There are lots of ways that I protect this family in addition to money. I physically protect them by being in this house. I teach them about navigating the world and prepare them for it. For the next 30 days, before I go to bed each night,

I'm going to write down five ways I protect this family so I can focus on achieving that.

- I'm going to map out the family budget and create three additional budgets of what we would drop our expenses to if our income dropped. I will create a plan for when certain expenses would be dropped if our savings hit a lower number. I will present this to Vera as a starting point for planning our budget and request a financial meeting once per month to review where we are.

- As long as we are not in a position where we need to drop our expenses, I will practice appreciating Vera's joy in the things she purchases. When we do not have a budget problem, those things are not a threat to my family, and I have to stop reacting as if they are. Her purses and coffees are not *dragons* for me to slay to protect my princess. She gets joy from them, and I need to practice seeing this through her eyes.

- I can protect my family without controlling them. I can't control everything. I have to let them live their lives. If something happens, I trust myself to take action. I will focus on navigating what comes up instead of trying to prevent a problem by controlling others.

Wow, can we just appreciate Ralph for a minute? That's good work! Not only will that level of personal responsibility allow him to enter the win-win creation from the energy and mindset needed to succeed, but can you already feel his stress levels going down? How much more joy do you think he will bring into his day-to-day experience of life by doing this work to shift his old blueprint and elevate this new way of thinking?

EXAMPLE: VERA'S YOU WORK RESULTS

If Vera was the Relationship Development student, this would be some of the YOU work that she would do before doing the YOU RELATE inter-actions with her spouse.

- I am going to validate my own success. I did work my ass off to get myself out of poverty, and I'm proud of who I am and what I have accomplished. Each morning, for the next 30 days, I will write down 10 things I am proud of myself for.

- Nothing I could purchase will ever satiate the hole I created in myself when I was broke and wanted everything. I have to heal that deprivation myself. I'm not missing out on anything. That part of my life is over. I'm going to do the work to take myself out of a deprivation and panic mode and recognize where I am today.

- No one can ever trap me. I can always say something. I am an empowered woman, and no one can make me do anything I don't want to do. It is a lie to believe that I could ever be trapped. Every minute of every day, I can say or do anything I want to do to create the life I want for myself and my children.

- I can decide, right now, that there is no risk of my marriage ending over my feelings about this. There are a million moments between today and giving up on my marriage. There are hundreds of things I can try to solve this before giving up. I would have to consciously decide not to say something, every moment of every day, for years in order to be so resentful that I give up and divorce him.

- My life is my responsibility. I have to stop looking to Ralph for permission for what I can or cannot do. I don't need his permission. I am his partner, and he sees me that way.
- Ralph only has the best of intentions for our family. I need to make a real budget with him and show him the numbers every month so that we can meet his need to protect these kids and this house.

By the way, phenomenal work here from Vera too, yes? Can you imagine what kind of a difference it would make in her day-to-day life, just to shift her old thinking and blueprint to something more like this? Do you think that her old reactions might be able to shift to new responses if she were to heal and solve some of the Triggers she identified that are still with her from her past? That is worthy work right there.

Either one of them could do this work and show up to lead in the conversation to create the alignment and design the win-win solution. We haven't even gotten to the tools and skill sets for the alignment piece, but do you already see how much solving is already happening just by taking personal responsibility for your own unrest and solving those pieces first?

The next step, for either one of them, would be to use The Order of Alignment tool from the last chapter to start figuring out the WHY level, WHAT level, and then lastly, the HOW options.

In Ralph and Vera's example, Ralph is the one doing the skill set training with us, so he comes to Vera to schedule the conversation with her. This is the first HOW that Ralph suggests to meet Vera's WHY and WHAT.

RALPH'S COLLABORATION CONTRIBUTION

- I created three budgets that show the changes to expenses that need to happen if our salary/income dropped to certain levels.
- I'd like to go over those budgets with you and see if we can create a plan that is triggered into action by the numbers, instead of our own fears or feelings.
- So, if income dropped by 25%, expenses in group A would drop off. If income dropped by 40%, expenses in group B would drop off . . . and so on.
- Then I'd like to schedule a monthly financial meeting so we can look at the actual numbers together and make any adjustments that we think are needed.
- With this plan in place, there logically is no need for me to change any of the day-to-day spending or react to it.
- In the meantime, I'm working on my Triggers and rewiring my reactions to spending to go from scarcity to appreciation.

VERA'S COLLABORATION RESPONSE

- Some of your numbers are incorrect, because some of these expenses don't continue year after year. I'll adjust these, so you have an accurate picture.
- I love a plan triggered by actual numbers. That's fantastic. I suggest that we create a group of expenses that drop off if our income drops by

15% instead of waiting until 25%. That's a big number and if that happens, we would definitely stop spending on certain things. We should just map that out.

- Ralph, I realize now that you are missing a huge piece to our financial puzzle. My life insurance policy has a cash value equal to two years of our mortgage payments. I did that on purpose. If one of us loses our job, even if both of us lose our jobs, we can stay in this house for two years without touching our regular savings account. Or if we get a new job, we can always replace the cash in the policy. I set that up a long time ago, but this is why I did it. You don't have to worry about us losing this house, Ralph. I'm so sorry this caused you so much stress and pain all these years. I really didn't know that you didn't realize why I had that policy.

Here's the thing: I've been doing this a lot of years, and if there's one thing I know for sure, it's that in a real win-win conversation, if you don't unmask something that is completely off the other person's radar, you're probably not doing it right.

Usually, one person assumes that the other person knows, understands, or sees something that they don't. This is the Boomerang of the Invisible Alignment Predicament.

It could be the fact that you don't know that your spouse has three job offers on the back burner in case they ever lose their job or you had no idea that the silverware thingy in the dishwasher lifts out so you can put it on the counter to unload. Know this: there are revelations to be had when we sit down and speak to each other without Demand Relationship.

> **PRINCIPLE:**
> The Invisible Alignment Predicament creates kerfuffles inside the moment (like the coffee shop example).
>
> **PRINCIPLE:**
> Collaborating on systems and processes, in advance and outside the moment, for our marriage, household, and parenting creates more calm and harmony inside the moments.

It often starts out the same way, where two people disagree at the HOW level and there's no single solution to make both people happy. This is where most humans are right now. They are at the end of their skill set at that very point of disagreement. This also seems to be where couple counselors and other relationship workers are stuck too. They ran to the end of their skill set to solve that disagreement. So, they support your false belief that the two of you just can't get along or "you're just too different," and so on.

This is why most humans today falsely believe there are only one of these three outcomes available to them:

False belief #1: There's something wrong with me (what I want is unreasonable or a problem).

False belief #2: There's something wrong with them (what they want is unreasonable or a problem).

False belief #3: There's something wrong with the two of us together (we are too different or cannot agree or are just wrong for each other).

All of those are false. You simply ran to the end of your skill set.

> **PRINCIPLE:**
> No one does anything without a reason.
>
> **PRINCIPLE:**
> If you stay stuck in the win-lose, you will never solve this.
>
> **PRINCIPLE:**
> "Your way is not the only way, it's just another way."
> — Neale Donald Walsch
>
> **PRINCIPLE:**
> Alignment does not equal agreement.
>
> **PRINCIPLE:**
> The Order of Alignment is the opening to designing the win-win solution.
>
> **PRINCIPLE:**
> YOU before YOU RELATE. Always solve your stuff first so you can enter the YOU RELATE from peace and curiosity.
>
> **PRINCIPLE:**
> You are not a family of one, you are a family of (#).

We started this example with Ralph and Vera and a situation that you probably thought was unsolvable where both of them could be happy. You and everyone else thought that. In fact, when I described their story, you most likely took a side and maybe even looked forward to hearing me declare who was "right," huh?

You could put a thousand of these examples in front of Paul and I, and we will solve them. These are not unsolvable. Your false belief that some of the disagreements you are facing are unsolvable is one of the things hurting you the most right now, whether you believe me or not.

Ralph and Vera successfully reached a win-win. It's not a trick, gimmick, or magic pill. It takes work and sometimes several months of revisions and adjustments until we see what really works, but the outcome is the win-win. In the process, each of them solved many Triggers within, increasing their levels of peace and happiness. They also solved many bricks in the wall between them through the work to collaborate on the win-win. This is how Relationship Development works.

So, if the win-win is the outcome we desire, what do we do when we feel like we are losing? What if we feel as though we are always giving in to their win? What if we feel like we are giving more than we are getting in this relationship? Then what? (Turn the page.)

CHAPTER 17

THE FAULTY RELATIONSHIP MATH™

Fran hung up the phone, smiling. She was so happy with herself. Her plan was coming together beautifully. Brad's 40th birthday was going to be unforgettable. Now, with the restaurant's private room secured at their favorite casino in Vegas, it was time to move on to the tough stuff.

She had a few bids in already on some Red Sox memorabilia that she knew would be the perfect addition to Brad's collection. And she already had the brand-new Sox jersey being customized for him with a big 40 on the back. She ordered his tux, her folks were flying in to stay with the kids, and his friends had already booked their travel for the trip. The only thing left was to get the custom awards made for the "this is your life at 40" roast they planned for him. The printer needed six weeks to get those made, but she had six months until the big bash, so there was plenty of time. He was going to be so surprised!

Fran really outdid herself on this one, but you only turn 40 once, and she had been looking forward to this for years.

Fast-forward four years. Fran's 40th birthday is now just three weeks away. She starts asking Brad if she should "not" make plans for that weekend or if there's anything she should plan around. Brad doesn't say much, and she's wondering how he's going to pull off a surprise for her if he doesn't give her a reason not to make plans.

It's now Friday morning, and Fran is getting ready for work. It's her birthday—her 40th birthday. And as far as she can tell, there's nothing going on. She didn't take the day off, but she did take a half day so she could come home by lunchtime in hopes that something was going on.

Brad is already downstairs getting the kids ready for school when Fran walks into the kitchen. "Happy birthday, Mommy!" Brad calls when she comes into the kitchen. Then, the kids start singing. Fran smiles, noticing that there is NOTHING in the kitchen. No flowers, no cards, nothing in sight. As Brad is walking out the door with the kids, he gives her a big hug and says, "Have an awesome birthday afternoon, I'll see ya tonight."

Okay, Fran thinks. *Tonight. That's when this is going to happen. No problem—tonight will be great, actually!*

Fran goes to work, looking forward to her special night. Her co-workers have a cake for her, but she doesn't finish her slice because she knows she will be enjoying a way better dessert tonight wherever Brad plans to take her.

Her Mom calls to wish her a happy birthday, and Fran can't help but notice that it sounds like her Mom is at home and not on her way to their house to stay with the kids. *What is he planning to do with the kids while we celebrate my birthday? Who could possibly be staying with the kids if it's not my mom?* Fran thinks to herself.

Fran comes home after work to find Brad in his office on a meeting with nothing special lying around anywhere for her birthday. She goes up to take a bath and take her mind off things, thinking through her plan for different outfits so she can be ready for whatever might be coming.

When she returns downstairs, Brad and the kids are waiting for her with takeout from her favorite place, cards, and flowers. She smiles and hugs them and enjoys the experience with them. Partway through dinner, she asks Brad, "Are we on any kind of time schedule that I should know about? Like are we leaving to go anywhere tonight that I should be ready for?"

Brad looks at her with disappointment on his face. "No, Fran. This is what we're doing tonight. A birthday dinner with your husband and children."

The Faulty Relationship Math™

Fran goes silent. Her mind is now reeling. She waits until the kids are tucked into bed and then the rant begins. She yells at Brad and cries about how she worked for six months planning the perfect 40th birthday for him, spent thousands of dollars on him, and made everything special, and all she gets is takeout food in the kitchen!

She goes on and on, unloading about how unappreciated she feels and how it's just another day of feeling like she does everything and gets very little in return. At one point she even says, "I don't even know why I bother."

Take a moment and consider what you think about Fran and Brad. Do you feel bad for Fran? Maybe you feel like Fran does more for Brad then he does for her? How do you feel about Brad? What do you think about him? Whose side are you on?

Okay, now place your feelings and assessment aside, and let's rejoin Fran and Brad in the kitchen . . .

Brad waits until there is a long pause.

"Are you done?" he asks.

"I might just be," she responds, putting her face in her hands and crying some more.

"Fran," Brad starts, "first of all, tomorrow night, we have plans with our friends at a fancy restaurant in the city for your birthday. I know you like surprises, and that's why I didn't tell you. The last time I tried to surprise you after a workday, you ripped me a new one about how you didn't have enough time to get dressed up, so I scheduled it on Saturday instead of today. But I don't even know why I bother because there's no pleasing you anyway."

He continues, "And about the ridiculous 40th birthday party you threw for me . . . that party was for *you*, Francine, and not me. I hate surprises. I hate having all the attention on me. I hate fancy restaurants; I only do that shit for you. You also caused me a ton of stress spending $3,500 on a fucking birthday that took me months to pay off. I hate my birthday and really did not like turning 40. I certainly didn't want all that attention brought to it. All I wanted for my birthday was to make waffles with my kids, in sweatpants, at home and enjoy my family. But instead, my kids were with their grandparents, and I was in a fucking tux in a hotel trying to count how much the whole fiasco was costing me."

Glaring at her, he finishes with, "So save your 'I do everything and you do nothing' speech, Fran. You did all of that for you, not me. And I was the one who picked up the bill. But did I scream and rant about it to you? No, I kept my mouth shut because you were so happy, enjoying yourself. Which is what I've done the last 15 years of my life with you, Fran. Keep my mouth shut to keep you happy. But it's impossible to make you happy, Fran, even when I make myself miserable for you, it's still not enough."

Now how are you feeling about Fran? What about Brad? Did hearing Brad's perspective shift how you felt about their dynamic? Was it eye-opening to hear how he saw the entire thing play out?

So, how do you know who is giving more or less in a relationship? How do you know if things are fair?

Let me ask you a question. How do you know if you are in a 50-50 relationship? How do you check to see if it's 50-50 and make sure you are not sliding into a 60-40 or even to 80-20? How do you know?

You measure. Yes, that's correct. You keep a score of what you are giving and what you are getting in return. You measure what you get versus what you give. That's how you get a sense of whether things are fair. Correct?

There is a problem with this, however . . . your measuring stick is faulty.

PRINCIPLE:
Measuring what you give in comparison to what you get in relationship always results in Faulty Relationship Math.

Let's use our example to teach this principle. From Fran's perspective, she was giving at pretty much a 100/100 (perfect score), and Brad was giving to her at a 15/100 (which is pretty sucky).

The reason why that math is faulty is because both the giving and the getting are *only* being measured by Fran's blueprint. Fran gave herself a 100/100 on Brad's birthday party that she planned because, in her own blueprint, that's what you do for someone you love! In her mind, it was perfect.

Then she also measured what Brad gave back to her based only on her own blueprint, and—shocker—it came up short.

> **PRINCIPLE:**
> Measuring what you get back from others based only on your own blueprint will mathematically come up short compared to what you give.

The simple fact is that no one else is wired exactly like you. No one else on the planet is ever going to serve life up to you exactly the way that you want it. So, no matter who you are in relationship with, your score of how they give to you is always going to come up short on the measuring stick because it's not going to be how you would have done it.

Sometimes it will be a little short; sometimes it will be a lot short. But it will be less than a perfect score because they are not you.

Of course, people can surprise you from time to time and "wow" you, surpassing your expectations. But in a long-term relationship, the next time someone comes up short in how they react, speak, or do something is just around the corner. Your score of what you are getting will eventually come up short versus what you are giving.

Yet, when you give to others, you give the way you think is the right way to give. When you intend to "hit it out of the park" for someone, you do what needs to be done to achieve that, from your blueprint. And because you are the measurer, evaluator, and decider, it's typically a 100/100 score for you.

You are evaluating both your giving and what you are getting from your own blueprint. Your measuring stick for the giving and the getting is *your* measuring stick.

So, you will always score yourself higher for what you give versus what you get from others. That's why we call it Faulty Relationship Math.

FAULTY RELATIONSHIP MATH

Measuring what you give based on your blueprint: 100%
Measuring what you get based on your blueprint: less than 100%

When you are focused on measuring, the math results will continue to disappoint you. Your *giving* number will always look higher than your *getting* number, and it will leave you feeling bad.

You're doing math in a game that is rigged for you to feel like you're losing.

> **PRINCIPLE:**
> Measuring and scorekeeping math will never work so that you feel good.

What people have been searching for in relationships, for decades, is someone who can "give it as good as they get it" (Demand Relationship). But if the measuring system is faulty, it will never happen.

When the faulty math was invisible to people, they blamed the other person. They thought that the other person was "selfish" or "incapable of love" or added some other judgemental and false label.

It's a predictable pattern with a predictable result.

Trigger: Faulty Relationship Math → Boomerang: feeling bad

> **PRINCIPLE:**
> When the Trigger going into the Loop is invisible to you, you blame the person instead of the Trigger.

Then, when it keeps happening over and over, people generalize their blame and say things like, "All men are jerks," or "All women are crazy," or "People are awful." It's not the other people. It's the faulty math that is the problem.

You just don't see the invisible Loop. It's been a Missing Piece.

> **PRINCIPLE:**
> Your misery is being created by your own yardstick.

I should know. Measuring and scorekeeping was one of the most difficult things for me to break when I was first doing this work. I was a gold-medal scorekeeper. And in my book, everyone sucked and I was awesome, and I was sick of it. It made me bitter and miserable.

Once I did the work, I figured out how to appreciate others for how they are wired, to allow others to give to me in the way that they organically do, and to allow their giving to satiate my needs and wants. My life changed dramatically. I retired my measuring stick. My own levels of peace and happiness skyrocketed. Like the Grinch, my heart grew three times as a result. And my relationships transformed too.

Measuring and scorekeeping in your relationship with your measuring stick breaks down the relationship. Because it's the "rules of the ruler." Your measuring stick, your rules.

Let's use our example to demonstrate this. Fran wants Brad to score her at a 100% on the 40th birthday experience she gave him. And she's measuring the birthday he gave her at 15%. Fran measures both according to her blueprint, so she comes up with the Faulty Relationship Math that she's giving way more than she's getting.

Don't gloss over that, please. Take a minute and give this the serious focus it deserves. Fran's Faulty Relationship Math has her thinking that she just might even be done with her marriage! This is a very big deal with very serious and painful consequences. This faulty math is incorrectly ending relationships every day of the year. And there are children in those homes. So, this matters. It matters a lot!

Question for you: If you asked Brad, would he score the Vegas birthday experience Fran gave him at a 100%? Nope. What score do you think he might assign to that birthday?

Understandably, he might score it at 15% because she was clearly trying hard to make it special for him, as misguided as she was about the execution because he didn't want any of it. Alternatively, he might even score it as a negative number, because the cost and the stress that it created lasted long after the party was over.

And what about the birthday that Brad had planned for Fran? She gave that a 15% but how would Brad score it? Maybe Brad would give himself a 100% because he was, once again, sacrificing himself to give Fran a fancy birthday out with her friends, even though he hated it and didn't want to do it.

From his perspective, he planned that fancy dinner out with friends for her, which, by the way, is something he feels she wasn't able to do for him (think about that for a moment). That sacrifice makes his birthday for her a 100% on his measuring stick.

See how this relationship math is faulty? You can't be the evaluator of both the giving and the getting from your own blueprint.

You will always wind up feeling like you give more than you get.

But it's not accurate. The math is faulty.

Plus, measuring and scorekeeping is Demand Relationship, which breaks down a relationship.

Often, one or both people start to feel like they are being taken advantage of or mistreated. Or they feel judged and criticized by a set of invisible rules from someone who can never be made happy. Over time, in a long-term relationship, as these disappointments put more bricks in the wall between you, resentment builds and connection fades.

Most people are stuck in this measuring and scorekeeping pattern, trying to get their partner to give more to them so they feel like they are getting as much as they give. They end up pushing them away, shutting down, or withholding from them if they won't.

Over time, both people wind up feeling exhausted, unappreciated, and hopeless.

The math is faulty. Measuring and scorekeeping is Demand Relationship, and it's breaking down your relationship. It will never work to give you the experience that you want from your relationships.

So, this begs the question, What does work? I'm so glad you asked!

Throw out the measuring stick.

RELATIONSHIP DEVELOPMENT SOLUTIONS FOR MEASURING AND SCOREKEEPING

Solution #1: Stop grading everyone on how they are measuring up to what you want.

Solution #2: Start getting visibility into your partner's blueprint of their world. Start looking for how they are giving in so many ways based on how they are wired. Learn to appreciate the giving they are doing and feel great about it.

It's like when your three-year-old gives you a picture for a present and you cannot make out what the scribbles are, but they are beaming with pride when they tell you it's a snowman flying to save a bunny. You appreciate how hard they worked on that. You feel loved that they would give you something that means so much to them. You allow that to satiate your feelings of love inside you, even though it might not be the kind of gift that you would give to them. That is how you learn to accept, allow, and appreciate others for how they are wired.

It's a much happier life when you learn how to see all the giving your partner has been offering to you for years that has been invisible to you before now. They are showing you how much they care in their own way. When you can see it and feel it, everything changes.

Solution #3: Shift how you are giving and start giving to them for how they are wired and what they need.

Solution #4: Take a look at some of the things you want to get from your partner and ask yourself why. Is it really a gift you are looking for, or is it a demand? Are you trying to get them to give something to you that you need, just to meet a need you haven't met for yourself? Or, is it to appease a Trigger or fear you haven't solved?

Sometimes, what we want is, in itself, Demand Relationship—for instance, wanting the "special birthday" so that I feel special, wanted, and appreciated for a day. That's my Trigger, inside me. I'm trying to use something outside of myself to avoid a Trigger or pain inside me of not already feeling special, and that's Demand Relationship. That leaves me feeling bad.

Do the work to feel happy and peaceful within. This way, you are not trying to get people to give to you in a specific way so that you feel good.

Solution #5: Do the work to evolve yourself so that you *can* receive from others without *needing* to receive from others.

I'll use myself as an example on this one. I used to have huge expectations around my birthday. When we were first together, I wouldn't tell Paul what I wanted, since the tactic that was modeled for me growing up was not to say anything and then observe what people give to you.

It's the old "he loves me, he loves me not" relationship garbage. This primitive approach is how relationship was done and certainly continues, for many, today.

Well, Paul is a simple guy, and he had no idea that I was any different than him. So, 30 years ago, he didn't do much for my birthday or our anniversary, and it was always a huge disappointment for me, every year. I looked forward to those holidays so much because I wanted to feel celebrated, special, and loved, and like he would never leave me.

But back in those days, I would have thought that only a crazy person would say to their boyfriend, "Hey, can you tell me that I am special and loved and that you will never leave me?"

The truth is, I was unhappy within myself, and I didn't feel truly special. I looked forward to holidays, birthdays, and anniversaries to feel the elusive happiness or specialness that I desired. So, when that didn't happen, I was crushed.

Fast-forward to today. Every day, I feel whole. I love myself, and I feel special. I'm proud of the woman that I am, and I always feel good about what I give to others. So, when one of our students sends an e-mail to our team to give to me, thanking me from the bottom of their heart for saving their family and telling me how much they love me, I feel honored, and I appreciate it deeply. And *I don't need it.* I wasn't on empty before I got that e-mail, and I wasn't sitting around waiting to hear if my students are grateful for all that I do for them. I was at 100/100 before anyone interacted with me.

I also don't need anything from anyone outside of myself to feel loved, happy, special, and certain.

And yet, Paul tells me every day of my life that he loves me deeply and cannot live without me. I've done the work. I've implemented the Relationship Development tools. I've learned about how Paul is wired. I know how to give to him for his blueprint instead of mine. Not out of pleasing, but because it genuinely feels great.

The irony is that when I used to need to get things from others, I never felt like I was getting.

Think of it this way: Have you ever been in a situation where you knew someone wanted something from you? Maybe they were using guilt on you or pressure or trying to get you to do or say something to them. How much did you feel like giving them what they were trying to get from you? Not so much.

When we need things from others, we rarely get it. People can feel us coming a mile away. We kind of "stink" of demands/neediness.

But when we stop needing or demanding from others, without closing off from the world, an interesting thing happens.

Today I show up to give to others and I'm open when interacting with people. Ironically, I no longer need anything from others, and yet, people pour gratitude over me all the time. And I deeply appreciate it, receive it, and connect with them in those moments. I take it in. I really do. And then I flow it back out into the world, from a place of love.

It's a predictable pattern with a predictable outcome.

Trigger: demand what you want to get from others → Boomerang: come up short/empty

Trying to get what you need from others is Demand Relationship. It breaks down relationships *and* leaves you feeling empty.

I remember when I started learning about how Paul was wired. I discovered that in Paul's blueprint, protecting me is one of the primary ways that he gives to me and provides for me.

I never really thought about "him protecting me" in terms of our romantic relationship, so I certainly wasn't giving him "points" for that in my scorekeeping. Why would I? I don't want it, so it doesn't "count."

When I started to really watch how Paul was giving to me, I saw how many times in a day he was protecting me. From putting my cough drops in his pocket before we leave the house to how he walks near me in the street to following up on my paperwork to make sure it gets filed on time.

Honestly, I used to get pissed off at him for all those things. I used to tell him to "stop treating me like a baby" or to "stop trying to control me." I can remember one time when I said to him, "I'm a big girl, you know. I became successful at my job all by myself, I don't need you to run my life."

Uggh. It makes me sick now to think that I said those things. I am the most important thing in the world to Paul, and his life's purpose is to make sure I am protected at all times. From protecting my physical safety to protecting me from late filing fees, he is always on it, like a dog on a bone. And I didn't see it. My measuring stick didn't account for it. And worse, I was giving him negative "points" for the interactions I was labeling as insulting or controlling.

Once I learned how he was wired, I started to see the love that I wanted so badly pouring out of him every time he put my cough drops in his pocket or checked to see if my paperwork was filed on time . . . I saw his love for me. I saw it for what it truly was from him, his way of demonstrating that I was the most important thing in the world to him. And I allowed myself to feel it every time he did those things for me.

I started rewiring myself to receive love the way Paul was organically wired to give love. Imagine how often I got to feel love doing that! It was every day, many times a day.

In addition, I learned the skills to ask for what I wanted and shared with Paul how I am wired. I never demanded it, but eventually as the Brick Wall Between us came down and the appreciation from Paul toward me for transforming our relationship grew, he started asking me about what I wanted and what he could do for me to make me happy.

So, it's at this point that many people think, "Oh, so I'm always going to be giving in my relationship, and I'm never going to get jack shit from anyone?"

That's not what I'm saying, but I get it. It's a common Demand Relationship assumption.

Allow me to briefly explain how this one piece works.

YOUR TREE MIGHT BE DEAD

Love relationships are like a tree. No matter how creatively or forcefully you try to get it to give you fruit, if the tree is dead, it cannot give you fruit.

If you want fruit from the tree, you need to care for it, tend to it, revive it, feed it, water it, give it sunlight, let it grow, and most importantly, stop killing it.

When it starts to show signs of life, instead of immediately going to the tree and demanding fruit or trying to get the tree to take care of you, continue to nurture that tree. While you may have stopped the tree from dying, it's not vibrant enough to bear fruit, yet.

When you do this consistently, the tree will grow strong and be so abundant that it will grow fruit. Then, two things will happen:

Thriving tree result #1: You can go to the tree and ask for fruit, and it will happily provide for you.

Thriving tree result #2: It will start dropping fruit on you, without you even having to ask for it.

Marriage is a lot like this tree. You keep focusing on the fruit you want to get, but what is invisible to you is that the tree has been dying in its current environment because of the skill set level of the two participants.

I'm well aware that people misunderstand what I'm teaching and mistakenly think that I'm telling you that you can never get fruit from your tree, you can never ask for what you want, and you are going to have to do everything while your partner does nothing.

I'm not saying that. I'm never saying that. I'm merely showing you the truth: that you cannot demand fruit from a dead or dying tree.

In relationship, you absolutely can ask for everything you want . . . if you have done the work to create the relationship that is ready to give it to you and if you have the skill set to ask in a way that inspires someone to want to say yes to you.

The Faulty Relationship Math™

YOUR TIMING DOES MATTER

When people feel like they are not getting what they need from their relationship anymore, they try Demand Relationship tactics to try to get their partner to give them what they need. And very often, it is invisible to them where they are on the Your Tree Is Dead Spectrum of development.

YOUR TREE IS DEAD SPECTRUM™

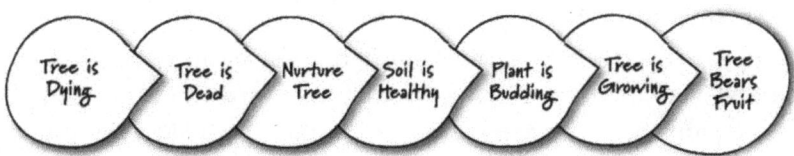

You can get everything you want and more from your relationship, but not if it's dead or dying. Do the work to revive the tree, and it will give you all the fruit you desire and more.

Even if this relationship doesn't turn out to be the forever love relationship you desire, at least you have learned how to be a tree grower! That is a skill set that you can take to any relationship.

For my 50th birthday, Paul planned a surprise party for me at my favorite restaurant. While we were finishing up dinner, he stepped away to set up his laptop so he could play something on the screen. It was a compilation video he made for my birthday! It started out with dozens of pictures of us through the years, celebrating my life.

Then, it transitioned into video clip after video clip from my friends, sharing how much I mean to them. There were videos from more than 40 people in the compilation. For months he had been coordinating that, in addition to all our work. Reaching out to people, organizing the videos, and editing it all himself so that I wouldn't find out about it.

It was such a magical night; I could barely process the whole thing. It was a happiness overwhelm moment for me. He did all that for me. I never asked for anything. That was his plan. He dropped so much fruit on me I could barely get back up.

It's not that you can never get what you like or want—of course you can, and you will. It's just that demanding it, scorekeeping, or seeing life only through the lens of your blueprint is not the way to get it.

And if you *need* to get it, then there's nothing anyone outside you can give you to satisfy that need.

Paul makes no secret of the fact that the only thing that matters to him is me and the kids. He would happily sacrifice himself without a second thought in order to protect me or make me happy. The only reason he regards himself at all is because he knows very well that living life without him would cause me more pain than anything else. Every word and action from him reflects that his only focus is on me and what is best for me.

And yet, nearly 30 years ago, I stood in the doorway to his home office asking shyly if maybe he would be done with work soon and want to hang out? Knowing before I even asked that work was the only thing he was aware of, and he would certainly not be choosing me . . . again.

Magnificent relationships are not found, they are created. It has nothing to do with love. It has only to do with a skill set we never had before. We created our relationship, and so can you.

YOUR ACTION LIST

1. Stop the measuring and scorekeeping.
2. Learn how your partner is wired so you can understand their blueprint.
3. Adjust your giving to others to give for how *they* are wired, instead of how you are wired.
4. Practice receiving from others and seeing their giving through the lens of how *they* are wired. Allow their giving to satiate you.

5. Look at your needs and do the work within yourself to free yourself from needing to make someone or something outside of yourself comply with a need you have inside yourself.

6. Use Relationship Development skill sets to bring your tree back to life, so that it starts dropping fruit on you.

7. When your tree is thriving, use Relationship Development skill sets to share ways that your partner can give love to you and contribute to your happiness, without attachment.

8. Become the happy, whole, peaceful, and loved version of yourself so you don't need the world to give you something that you haven't figured out how to give to yourself, yet.

PRINCIPLE:
Measuring and scorekeeping is Demand Relationship.

PRINCIPLE:
Allowing, appreciating, and understanding others is Relationship Development.

PRINCIPLE:
Measuring what you get versus what you give by your own blueprint will always result in you coming up short. It's Faulty Relationship Math.

PRINCIPLE:
Demand Relationship breaks down relationships.

PRINCIPLE:
Relationship Development builds up relationships.

Hopefully, by now you are starting to see a new possibility for new results. But what do you do when you don't trust your partner, or your partner doesn't trust you? What if betrayals and disappointments have broken the very trust your relationship was standing on? Can trust even be rebuilt? And if it can, should you even bother? (Turn the page.)

CHAPTER 18

THE REBUILDING OF TRUST

A TALE OF TWO TRUSTS...

Story #1: Maria and Valerie

Seven years ago, Maria's world turned upside down when her wife, Valerie (Val), took a new position at work without talking to her first. The job required that their family move overseas for three years. Maria supported her wife in moving. And after talking it through, Maria also agreed that taking this position was the absolute best thing for Valerie and for their family.

She didn't disagree with the decision, but the fact that Val said yes and made that commitment without talking to Maria caused a break between them that Val has been trying to repair for seven years.

Maria would say things like, "I forgive you. It's fine. I don't disagree with the decision. I don't regret moving here, and I understand." But then something would happen, and Maria would suddenly be overcome with distrust of Valerie. She would ask her a million questions, trying to predict if there was something that Val was hiding from her.

When there were fights, even about something completely different, at some point, Maria would yell something like, "Well, I can't trust you, so who knows what else you're not telling me."

Then of course, there were the jabs at Val's expense. Maria would say things like, "Why even ask me where I want to go for dinner? It's not like you would consider my opinion anyway."

It was one of those comments that set Valerie off most recently. She sat Maria down after the kids were in bed.

"Maria, I love you and the kids, and I've dedicated my life to providing for your lives. I have apologized a million times, but it's never enough. Why don't you trust me?"

Maria offered the usual, "I do trust you, but I'm just scared that something like that is going to happen again. You spend so much time away from me, and I have no idea what's happening. When I ask you, your answers are two words long, so I'm in the dark here."

"This will never work if you don't trust me, Maria." Val stated. "You say you trust me, but you really don't. You question me constantly. No amount of time is enough. In seven years, I've not given you any reason to distrust me, but that goes unseen and unheard. You treat me like a criminal, and there's nothing I can do to satisfy you. I can't go back in time and change what happened. If you can't trust me, I don't see how we can stay together. Make your decision."

Story #2: Leslie and Mark

It's been two years since Leslie ended the affair she was having, but she still feels distant from her husband, Mark, every day.

They go out to dinner and take vacations. They talk about work, the kids, and their friends, but even driving in the car, sitting inches from each other, she still feels like they are miles apart.

He already knows why she wound up in a relationship with another man. His travels, his focus on his job, and his 80-hour workweeks, all left her raising kids in a giant house all alone. She never meant for the relationship to be anything more than a friendship, but the truth was that while she barely saw her husband, having someone to support her each day and really "see" her was filling the void of a dying marriage.

Not a day goes by that she doesn't regret what she did. Looking back, she can barely recognize the version of herself that she was back then.

She and Mark both saw the affair as their "wake-up call" to prioritize their marriage, and while it was not Mark's fault by any means, he knows that he played a role in creating the marriage that left Leslie feeling like there was barely a marriage to hang on to back then.

Mark forgave her. His family is the most important thing to him, and he wanted a second chance for them.

During this last argument, Mark again made a comment about Leslie's "lack of integrity."

"Mark! I cannot go back in time and undo what happened. I have apologized a million times, and yet you still punish me! What more do you want from me?" Leslie yells at him.

"Save your apologies, Leslie. I don't need them. It doesn't change the fact that you made a choice to cheat. That's who you are. It's a fact. You lack integrity. It doesn't matter how sorry you are afterward; it still happened."

"Then why are you still with me?" Leslie questions him. "Why stay in this marriage and punish me? Why are you still here?"

"Because my family is the most important thing, and we said we were going to try to put the past in the past where it belongs and move on," Mark answers, for the millionth time.

"Well, that's not really working, is it? Mark, if you can't trust me from today forward, then you are the one taking down this marriage, not me. Either trust me for who I am today, or let's just let each other go," Leslie says, and she walks out of the room.

I'm guessing you picked your sides in these two battles? Yeah, I'll get to that in a minute.

First, let's step into the shoes of the spouse who can't find a way to trust their partner, like Maria and Mark.

It's painful and scary to not be able to trust your spouse. Over time, it becomes difficult to function in everyday life. You try to let it go, but eventually it builds up to the point of questioning why you even bother with the relationship. The betrayals and disappointments are like pouring cement over the brick wall between you, and it seems like everything that is said or done is flavored by the mistrust.

You wind up snooping, questioning their stories, and looking for ways to prevent another blindside moment where your world comes crashing down. Every time you do, you hate yourself for it and then hate your partner more for driving you to this point. It's brutal and exhausting, and, in time, it can cause you to feel like you don't even know who you are anymore.

How about the one who is labeled as untrustworthy, like Valerie and Leslie?

When your spouse, the one person in the world who is supposed to be on your team, doesn't trust you, it feels unbearable. You spend your life apologizing, but it's never enough. You wind up getting accused of other things that you never did, but you can't defend yourself because that brings up all the things they don't trust you about.

No matter how much you do to try to make up for it, you can't undo the past, and it's still there every day, haunting you and ruining your life.

Even if you made good, you are still serving a life sentence with your partner, branded as untrustworthy. Everything is used against you, and all you can do is take it and hope that it helps your spouse feel peace. But it doesn't work.

You are harder on yourself than your spouse will ever be. You hate yourself for what happened, but that's nothing compared to knowing that you caused your partner to suffer. You would let them go, but they tell you that would just make it worse, so you are trapped.

This does not feel like a marriage. It's a prison, and you are the prisoner. You wonder every day, "When is enough, enough?" But it's never enough, and there's no end in sight.

The fact is, when trust is lost in a relationship, it's hell for both people.

What do most people do when trust is broken?

They tell the other person to "apologize and promise me that it will never happen again." But even when they do, it doesn't work.

The Rebuilding of Trust

When the other person apologizes, it doesn't work to solve anything. When the other person promises it will never happen again, it doesn't fix things.

So, the person apologizing will eventually make a demand of their own, like, "You have to trust me." But that still doesn't fix anything.

This is where people are stuck today. They already tried to say all the things you can say to apologize, promise, repair, forgive, and let go. And they are still stuck with a lack of trust that they feel inside.

That's because both dynamics of "apologize and promise" and "forgive and let go" are Demand Relationship with the other person. It's a demand based in nothing.

No human being can promise what the future will be. This is why, even after someone promises you it will never happen again, you still watch them, ask questions, and check up on them. Because a demand-based promise doesn't solve the very real distrust.

And no human being can say the words, "I forgive and I'll let it go" and experience it inside themselves, because those words do not solve the distrust. Even with the best of intentions, they are demand-based and empty promises.

I get it. You want to forgive and let go. And you want to apologize and promise. But the fact remains that trust and distrust do not get solved by those words. It's not my opinion. It's a predictable pattern with a predictable outcome.

Demanding trust does not work. That's not how trust works. But since Demand Relationship is what has been modeled to us for centuries, we keep repeating this ineffective pattern.

In addition to that, all the things we do along the way—the snooping, the questioning, the snide remarks, making them wrong for everything, the pleasing, the compromising, the judging, and the blaming—is Demand Relationship that further breaks down the relationship. None of that rebuilds trust. It just takes a fragile relationship and breaks it down further.

When the Demand Relationship approach to rebuild trust fails, people give up. They either declare that "I can never trust you" or "You're never going to trust me." And they end the relationship.

You cannot build or rebuild trust through Demand Relationship words. Neither demands nor empty promises can build or rebuild trust.

So, the question becomes: Can trust even be rebuilt?

The answer is: absolutely. Trust can be built or rebuilt.

Next question: So how do you do it?

I'm so glad you asked!

Answer: It's a predictable pattern with a predictable outcome.

Okay, this is going to be a little bit of a mindfuck. Are you ready?

> **PRINCIPLE:**
> Trust is actually a BOOMERANG.

Trust is the effect or symptom of something else. It's not something you can demand or give; it's a symptom or a side effect. You already know this because, inside, you feel when you either trust someone or you don't.

So, what is the cause of trust or mistrust? What causes that feeling to happen as the effect? What is the invisible Loop that we are missing?

THE RELATIONSHIP DEVELOPMENT TOOL: THE SPHERE OF INFLUENCE®

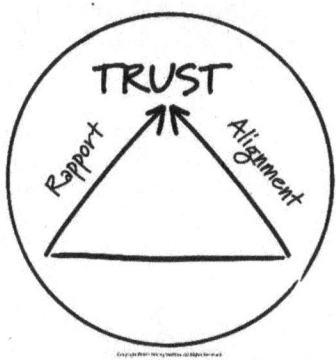

The Missing Piece is that rapport and alignment create trust. The lack of rapport or alignment breaks trust. Your internal feeling of trust or mistrust is the result of the levels of rapport and alignment in the relationship. Rapport and alignment go into the Loop and trust (or mistrust) comes out of the Loop.

Trigger: rapport and alignment → Boomerang: trust

I'm using the terms *rapport* and *alignment* to mean the following:

Rapport is the feeling of friendship, connection, bonding, comradery, or kinship that you have with someone.

Alignment is when you have mutual understanding, reach a win-win, see eye-to-eye, or happen to agree on something.

Just like with every other Loop pattern, when the Loop is invisible, people try to fight with the Boomerang to make the other person give them the Boomerang they want.

That's what most humans are doing with trust. Everything I described to you above, like people demanding to be trusted or making people promise it will never happen again, are examples of fighting with the Boomerang and wanting trust to come out of the Loop.

However, the rapport and alignment are still broken. You can't demand that trust come out of the Loop if the rapport and alignment going into the Loop are broken. Trust can neither be demanded nor declared. It actually does not work that way in human dynamics.

Trigger: low or no rapport and alignment → Boomerang: lack of trust

> **PRINCIPLE:**
> Trust can neither be demanded nor declared.
>
> **PRINCIPLE:**
> In Demand Relationship, people try to demand trust or declare trust with words, but neither works.
>
> **PRINCIPLE:**
> In Relationship Development, you use skill sets to increase the rapport and alignment, then over time, increased trust is the outcome or result.

Let's look at this Sphere of Influence diagram again.

I'll use Maria and Val's example to explain the elements in this dynamic.

When Valerie made a decision without talking to Maria first, she broke rapport with Maria, and she broke alignment with her as well.

Breaking rapport: Maria felt betrayed, blindsided, and like her world was turned upside down in a way that she couldn't control or see coming. Those are not things that people feel about their friends or people they have rapport with. When someone makes you feel that way, there is a loss of rapport between the two people. Even if it's a misunderstanding or a mistake, it still breaks rapport, and that needs to be healed or repaired.

Breaking alignment: At the same time, Valerie broke alignment with Maria in a big way. From Maria's perspective, not consulting her on a move overseas that included their children is a big demonstration that they are not a team, and they are not in this together. That decision left Maria feeling unvalued, even though Maria and Val were absolutely aligned on the decision to move being the best decision for their family. It was the decision to say yes, without first discussing it with her wife, however, that broke the alignment between them. Even if it was a mistake or an inadvertent misunderstanding, the alignment was now broken and needed to be repaired, healed, and rebuilt.

Think of a relationship that you have with someone who you really trust. Would you say that your level of rapport with them is on the high side or on the low side? And would you say that you are aligned with them on a few different things that really matter to you? And because of that, you gift them the precious outcome at the top of the triangle in our Sphere of Influence diagram above . . . trust.

The Relationship Development solution for rebuilding or building trust is to increase (or rebuild) rapport and increase (or rebuild) alignment using Relationship Development skill sets, not using Demand Relationship tactics or manipulation.

In situations where the trust was broken and rapport and alignment were damaged, using the Relationship Development skill sets to repair, heal, and rebuild rapport and alignment over time is required before trust can begin to form again.

RAPPORT

Let's talk about rapport. What is it and how do we build it up? Rapport is that feeling of connection or friendship or that good feeling between two people.

Sometimes we develop rapport with someone by getting to know them and becoming friends over time. Other times, we build rapport with someone in an instant by discovering something we have in common.

Like when you are traveling in another country, and you run into someone who is from your hometown. You typically have instant rapport with them. There's a smile, and you say, "Hey! I'm from New Jersey, too! Ay-oh! Get outta here!"

No amount of rapport-building skills or techniques, however, can overcome the consistent breaking down of rapport that comes from Demand Relationship tactics.

For example, when you use Demand Parenting with your kids to get them to do what you need done, rapport-building tactics will not work. If you are actively breaking rapport with them consistently, they won't see you as a friend inside their Sphere of Influence. You will be outside their sphere, and they will have to protect from you or plot around you. No one considers the person trying to control them as a trusted friend.

You must stop doing Demand Relationship with someone if you want to rebuild rapport. That is a fact, and there is no fancy way around it.

ALIGNMENT

Alignment is when you have mutual understanding, you have a win-win scenario, or you happen to agree or you are able to see things the same way.

Most people mistakenly think that to have alignment you have to have agreement, but that is untrue and holding a lot of people back. You may accidentally align with someone because you happen to agree with them about something, but agreement is not required for alignment to occur.

Accidental alignment looks like this: "Yeah, I'm also thinking we should just grill on Sunday and keep it simple when everyone comes over." In that situation, the two people are aligned on grilling on Sunday, but the alignment was really just an accidental agreement.

> **PRINCIPLE:**
> You do not have to agree with someone to have alignment.

You can align even when you do not agree. For instance, Paul is always prepared for any scenario. I'm not wired like that at all, but I understand that he is. He has a water sensor with an alarm on it in our attic so that if the HVAC up there creates too much condensation, the alarm will alert him, and he can handle it before there's a water damage issue in the house. I'm telling you right now, in a million years I would not think of that, I would not do that, and I wouldn't put time or energy into that. I also know that putting that sensor there is how he takes care of us and this house. It's part of how he's wired. He sees something that should be done a certain way to be done right, and he does it. I align with him on the attic sensor. I don't also see it the same way for myself, but I absolutely understand and see that, for him, that is the right choice.

The difference between alignment and agreement is that when you agree with someone, you see it the same way for yourself as they see it for themselves. Alignment means that even though you don't see it that way for yourself, you understand and validate their perspective for themselves.

I don't have to suddenly become someone who would put a water sensor in her attic. And I don't have to agree that it's a good idea. I also don't have to pretend that I would also make that choice.

All I need to experience is the understanding and validation that it is right for Paul to put that sensor up there. And it really is. I can imagine him not putting that sensor in there and then keeping all that worry in the back of his mind, checking the attic every month for water and beating himself up if there's a problem that got out of hand before he became aware of it. I know that's what it would be like for him if he didn't have that sensor. I don't want that experience for him. So I very much align with that sensor. Even when it wakes me up at 4:15 A.M., saying, "Water sensor, attic," and scares the shit out of me (true story). I still align with him on that attic sensor, because it's right for him, and I see that it's right for him.

I'm guessing you chose a "side" in this attic sensor thing, huh? Maybe you're reading this and thinking, *Shit, I need that sensor* or maybe you're thinking, *That sensor sounds like overkill to me.*

Here's the thing. In a long-term relationship, there are thousands of these "attic sensor" moments. And most humans are completely hung up on "my way versus your way" and figuring out who's "right." I say this: who cares?

The fact is, I would never think to put a sensor in the attic for excess condensation from the HVAC. Add that to the list of loads of things I will never think to do and never would do. But Paul is wired to think of all those things and make sure he does them all. He won't sleep until they're done. So, it kind of feels to me like we're perfect together. He thinks of those things and does them, and I don't and won't. We're two pieces that fit together perfectly. We don't need to agree. We don't need to be the same.

Because of doing this work, I learned how to stop resisting who he really is and learned how he's wired so I can support him and align with him on things that matter to him. He's my person. It brings me tremendous joy that the freaking attic sensor can give my husband peace of mind. I'm not kidding. I've seen my husband take the weight of the world on his back. If there's anything that I can do to help make his load lighter, that's my job and pleasure. And the number one thing I can do is to stop giving him shit about what's important to him and what he needs to do for how he's wired. And I have done the work to be authentically happy to do so.

TIME

Rapport, alignment, and trust require time. It is a key element in this dynamic. Short amounts of time do not typically build trust or create influence. If you just met someone at the store and they were buying the same cookies as you, you might smile and say,

"Great choice," but you probably wouldn't trust them to look after your kids. You just met them. There's not enough rapport and alignment to reach the top of the triangle, where the diamond of trust is.

How much time is enough? It's different for different folks based on both the programs in their brains and their life experiences. Some people are very trusting early on and only lose trust when rapport and alignment are broken, causing the diamond of trust to topple off the perch between these two supports.

Other people are more cautious and need many occurrences or longer periods of time to build up rapport and alignment before trust results.

Either way, trust or lack of trust is a result (a Boomerang).

When a relationship takes a big enough hit or enough small hits through time, where rapport and alignment are lost, trust falls off that perch.

And you can't just demand it back. It has to be rebuilt. Here's the principle.

> **PRINCIPLE:**
> Trust is not the element that gets rebuilt. Rapport and alignment get rebuilt, and trust is the result.

Boom. The world is stuck and suffering right now because people are trying to build trust by working on trust. But that is not how it happens.

Trust is the Boomerang, and you cannot fight with the Boomerang that is already in motion and try to change it.

You build or rebuild trust by working on rapport and alignment. Those are the two levers that you have available to pull.

Back to our example. Mark lost trust for his wife, Leslie, when she had an affair. Leslie's actions caused both a break in rapport and in alignment. Causing Mark that kind of pain was a big hit to the rapport he felt for his wife. And the alignment was pretty much shattered since Mark certainly didn't align with his wife's decision to have an affair.

Leslie's decision to have the affair left Mark feeling betrayed and seeing her differently. In his blueprint, only someone who lacked integrity would make that kind of decision, so he labeled her as lacking integrity. It had been impossible for him to trust her with this lack of integrity "stamp" of how he saw her.

Just telling Mark that she's sorry didn't do anything to rebuild the rapport or alignment. There were still Bricks in the Wall between them, and the affair just poured cement over them.

In addition, Mark had broken rapport and alignment with Leslie long before the affair. She felt alone and unsupported all the time. She did not align with his decision to work so many hours or travel away from their family. She never expected his career to take her husband away from her at such a fundamental level. She felt that way for over 10 years before having an affair. And she still feels that way, but she can't say or do anything about it because she's the "wrongdoer" and has to take her punishment. But deep down, she still feels like she suffered a long time before this affair ever happened.

Using Relationship Development skill sets, tools, and strategies, Leslie or Mark could go brick by brick and solve the issues between them. Each time they solve an issue, rapport is built and alignment is created.

Using our other example from this chapter, Maria lost trust for her wife, Valerie. Valerie lost rapport when she made Maria feel that she wasn't important enough to consult on such a big decision. And Valerie broke alignment when she blindsided Maria with something that Valerie controlled without giving Maria a voice. It was a decision that changed the course of Maria's life, and Valerie made it for her, leaving Maria feeling powerless. That is a break in alignment.

Just telling Maria she was sorry didn't rebuild the rapport or create alignment. There were still bricks in the wall. And the distrust just poured cement over them.

Using Relationship Development skill sets, tools, and strategies, Maria or Valerie could go brick by brick and solve the issues between them. Each time they solve an issue, rapport is built and alignment is created.

ONE BIG LEVER

Remember, there's another big lever that you can pull to build more rapport and increase alignment. Stop doing Demand Relationship. Demand Relationship breaks rapport every single time. There are not enough tools in the world to build up rapport if you are going to continue to break it with Demand Relationship. It's like trying to fill a bucket with a hole in the bottom.

RELATIONSHIP DEVELOPMENT: 7 STEPS TO INCREASE RAPPORT & ALIGNMENT

Trust building step #1: Stop doing Demand Relationship.

Trust building step #2: Use the skill sets to solve the bricks in the wall.

Trust building step #3: Take personal responsibility to stop judging and blaming.

Trust building step #4: Create a win-win, create alignment, and stop perpetuating the win-lose (which breaks alignment every time).

Trust building step #5: Stop making the other person wrong for how they feel.

Trust building step #6: Heal yourself so you can be at peace.

Trust building step #7: Use the Relationship Development 5-Step Forgiveness Process™ to heal the past and free yourself to move forward.

Look at that list for a moment. Do you think that if someone did all seven steps for you and your relationship, consistently, over the next six months to a year, that you would feel the trust start to rebuild? Do you think if they did all seven of these steps for you and your relationship for two years that you could be rock solid and have complete trust?

Here's the great news: the strength of our relationships does not come from never having fallen; it comes from how we handle the fall and rebuild.

There's a form of Japanese art called kintsugi, where the cracks in a ceramic piece are filled with gold because the flaws in an item are to be celebrated and the cracks can become the strongest parts when mended.

Many of our students over the years report that their marriage and relationships are stronger than they ever were before the breakdown because they are doing real work that creates rock-solid strength as its outcome.

This isn't about "love" or even "feelings." It's human dynamics. They've just been invisible up until now.

The result of stopping Demand Relationship and building up the rapport and alignment through time is TRUST.

It only takes one person to implement the skill sets, tools, and strategies to build or rebuild trust.

For instance, when Luisa came into our program, she thought she could never trust her husband, Ryan, again. She started our program to get the skill sets to navigate co-parenting with him and to heal their relationship for their two kids and her own sanity. She could never see staying married to someone she didn't trust.

Through doing this work and now seeing all the pieces that were invisible to her for so long, she felt hopeful for the first time. With consistent work to solve the bricks in the wall between them, she started to feel the rapport growing and alignment building. It took time, but today she has saved her marriage, and she would tell you that Ryan is the one person she trusts most in this world. It wasn't about the initial fall; it was the steps she took with him every day during the rebuild that built a new level of rapport and alignment and formed their rock-solid foundation.

> **PRINCIPLE:**
> Demand Relationship breaks down relationships.
>
> **PRINCIPLE:**
> Relationship Development builds up relationships.
>
> **PRINCIPLE:**
> Demand Relationship breaks rapport, alignment, and trust.
>
> **PRINCIPLE:**
> Trust is a Boomerang. You cannot demand nor declare trust.
>
> **PRINCIPLE:**
> Rapport plus alignment through time results in trust.

There's work to be done and many conversations to be had. But what about if we argue every time we try to have these conversations? How can we build anything up if we keep spiraling down every time we talk? How can we talk about these things without fighting?

As I've said before, in my experience, about half of all arguments between couples are a result of the masculine and feminine processing differences causing kerfuffles.

I've also said that while the other half of the kerfuffles may not be caused by the masculine and feminine differences, the moment we start trying to talk about solving those kerfuffles, there are masculine and feminine communication differences that add to our issues.

Meaning we start fighting about how we are fighting. While Paul and I could teach about these differences for days (and we do), I'm going to share one that will help you get significantly better results next. (Turn the page.)

CHAPTER 19

THE DIFFERENCES IN MASCULINE AND FEMININE COMMUNICATION

Back in 2013, there was a video that went viral by Jason Headley called "It's Not about the Nail." In this hysterical video, a woman is shown overwhelmed and complaining to her husband about her struggles. When he tries to interject to solve what she's struggling with, she yells at him that she doesn't need him to fix it; what she really needs is for him to just listen!

At that point, the camera turns, and you see that she's got a nail stuck in her forehead. Then the camera turns back to the husband. He's struggling with the "just listening" approach and says back to his wife, "See, I don't think that is what you need; I think what you need is to get the nail out . . . " He doesn't even finish his sentence before she explodes on him by saying that he "always does this!" and he "never listens."

If you haven't seen it, just search for it online. It's worth watching. In the video, Jason brilliantly depicts the very real dynamic between the masculine and feminine, where she's trying to talk and he's jumping in to "fix it." It's really funny and very well written.

There have been millions of movies, TV shows, and songs depicting the same dynamic: women who just want to talk about it and men who just want to fix it.

While this real dynamic is very well depicted in many formats, let me be the first to tell you that the widely accepted conclusion about this is completely false.

Most humans see this dynamic and walk away with the common misconception that "women just want to talk and talk and talk, and they don't want anything fixed."

And that men "can't listen; they just want things fixed."

Both of those conclusions are flat-out wrong.

These false beliefs are also divisive and cause kerfuffles. But make no mistake: the dynamic that is portrayed is 100% real. What's causing this real dynamic has been invisible to humans for thousands of years, which is why no one understands what is actually happening. It's been another Missing Piece, and I'm going to give you that piece, right here, now.

It's not true that the feminine core beings don't want anything solved. That is for sure false.

Every feminine being I have ever worked with has a long list of shit that she would like solved, and she's very certain that she wants it all solved. It's complete bullshit that she doesn't want it solved. (Can I get an amen, ladies?)

And yet, every masculine being on the planet has found himself in the position of trying to help a feminine being solve something and feeling her wrath when she lashes out, saying that she doesn't need him to solve it and why can't he just listen.

You will often hear the feminine say things like:

- "Don't tell me what to do!"
- "I don't need you to tell me what to think!"
- "You're not even listening to me!"

Often the masculine will say things like:

- "Why the hell do you ask me for my opinion if you don't really want to know?"

- "Why don't you just ask XYZ, because I already know you're not gonna listen to me anyway?"
- "This is a waste of freaking time!"

This dynamic causes pain on BOTH sides.

So, what's going on here?

There's a big piece missing that is causing a very real and painful kerfuffle. I'll explain this dynamic using a tool from our Relationship Development Method.

THE RELATIONSHIP DEVELOPMENT TWO-PART FEMININE CONVERSATION FRAMEWORK™

Feminine core beings have two conversations:

Conversation #1: The Processing Conversation
Conversation #2: The Solving Conversation

Neither the masculine nor the feminine know about this (yet), so it has been an invisible Loop causing kerfuffles. Hear me out, and I'll explain what's going on.

Conversation #1: The Processing Conversation

One of the reasons why the feminine can remember so much so easily is because the feminine core being's brain stores emotions with information. When information is stored in the brain with emotion, it increases your ability to remember it.

When the feminine thinks something through that co-exists with big emotion or upset, she often needs to process and release the emotion she has about the topic first before she begins logically sorting through the information. The feminine does this organically.

She usually prefers to process and release her emotions by "talking it out" with a trusted supporter. But if she has to do this alone, she will do this in her own thoughts or in a journal.

THE PROCESSING CONVERSATION PHASE LOOKS LIKE THIS:

During this conversation, she's just getting out her feelings and thoughts about what happened. She's just talking it out. Unloading everything that she's been holding in her mind and heart about it.

She instinctually knows she's not ready to make any decisions yet or solve things. It's too early in the process. She hasn't even "thought it through" yet.

That's why you will often hear the feminine say, "I don't even know what to think about this" or "I haven't even decided what I think about this yet."

It's because she hasn't completed the Processing Conversation to release the energy and emotion yet and get all her thoughts "out."

Think of it like having a big tub of LEGO blocks and dumping them all out on the carpet to see what you have before assessing the contents, sorting them and figuring out what you want to build.

It's difficult to assess and sort the LEGOs when they are all still inside the tub. She needs to dump them all out first. That's similar to what a Processing Conversation is. She hasn't yet assessed, sorted, and organized her emotions and thoughts, she needs to dump everything out first.

WHAT SHE NEEDS DURING THE PROCESSING CONVERSATION

She needs to get it all out, without interruption.

She really needs to release it without being judged, criticized, edited, or challenged.

It's very beneficial to the process for her to have a trusted, supportive listener who validates her during the Processing Conversation phase.

If she is interrupted, judged, criticized, or otherwise feels blocked from completing her Processing Conversation, then the processing phase will be incomplete, and she will not likely feel ready to move into the Solving Conversation.

Usually, the feminine being has no idea that this is what she is doing and has no words to describe this. It's just part of her organic processing. Feminine to feminine, this happens organically, all the time.

I encourage the masculine to get good at the Processing Conversation support role. I'll show you more on how to do that. The better you are at this, the faster and easier she will move into the Solving Conversation (the part the masculine is organically wired for).

Conversation #2: The Solving Conversation

Once the Processing Conversation is complete, she can easily move into the Solving Conversation. She'll know when she is ready to move into figuring out how to solve the situation or issue.

Depending on the complexity of the situation, the Solving Conversation may be two sentences, or it might be a separate conversation that takes a lot of time.

Once she is through the Processing Conversation, she may navigate the Solving Conversation independently and easily know what she needs to do. Other times, she might seek external opinions or validations.

In my experience, she will not even be able to tell you if she's going to need external help finding a solution until she gets through the Solving Conversation herself.

It can be hard to imagine what these conversations look like, but you have participated in them thousands of times. Let me show you an example. It will be easiest to observe it first feminine to feminine, because there won't be kerfuffles breaking up the pattern.

Sara and Lilly are at work and both end up in the kitchen at the same time to get a cup of coffee.

Sara: "Hey, Lilly, what's up?"

Lilly: "Not much."

Sara: "Lilly, what's going on? I know something's up. Just tell me."

Lilly: "Are you sure? It's really nothing. I can handle it."

Sara: "Stop it. Come on. Give it to me."

Lilly: "Okay. Look, I'm super grateful for all my mom's help. I am. I'm not a bitch. I completely know that I wouldn't be able to do half the things I do here if my mom didn't take my kids every day. I get it. I'm super grateful for her."

Sara: "And . . ."

Lilly: "And I'm losing my mind, Sara. She is driving me nutty. Legit batty."

Sara: "There it is. Come on. Out with it."

Lilly: "Okay, remember when I told you that William wants to take swimming lessons, and we talked about going to that place on Main Street with the instructor that Emmy likes?"

Sara: "The one with the blue hair?"

Lilly: "Yes, the blue hair. Her name is Vicky, by the way. Well, William loves it, and he's been doing great. And then one day, he got scared in the water and there was this whole thing, and he started crying. My mom brought him home. No big deal, right?"

Sara: "Yeah."

Lilly: "Right, so the next time William didn't want to go. He started crying as soon as my mom said it was time to pack the bag."

Sara: "Because of the thing that scared him?"

Lilly: "Yes, exactly. So, he doesn't want to go. She fights with him for like half an hour, and now he's in his room crying and she's calling me, telling me the entire saga, like I can do anything about it."

Sara: "Why doesn't she just drop it and let him stay home?"

Lilly: "Thank you! That's exactly what I said. I told her, 'Mom, it's just swim, it's not worth it. He can do it later if he wants to. It's not worth getting him upset and you upset over this.' So, she yells at me that these kids need to learn responsibility and yadda, yadda, yadda. Meanwhile, Natalie gets off the bus, and everyone in the house is angry, so she also calls me, saying that I have to apologize to Grandma because they are all crying."

Sara: "Oh. My. God!"

Lilly: "I know! So, I call my mom. I tell her, you're the adult here, Mom. Don't tell my kid to call me about this. You're stressing them out, and now you're stressing me out, too!"

Sara: "What did she say?"

Lilly: "She told me I'm ungrateful, the kids aren't learning how to be responsible and respectful, and, oh, apparently my brother's kids are so much easier. Never mind that they live five states away, and she sees them five days a year."

Sara: "Geez, this is a shit show. I'm so sorry, Lil. That's just ridiculous. What are you going to do?"

Lilly: "I don't even know. I mean, the kids love my mom, right? So, it's not like I'm going to stop having her be with them. But I can't keep settling shit every day when something goes down."

Sara: "Of course."

Lilly (lets out a big breath): "Maybe I'll just have a family meeting and include my mom. We can talk about the swim thing, and she can feel like she's part of the process. This way, we can also hear William out about what he wants to do."

Sara: "That's great. I bet she'll really like that."

Lilly: "Yeah" (another deep breath). "I'll just add that to the pile that is my to-do list. Am I right?"

Sara (laughing): "You got this, Lil."

Lilly: "Hey, thanks for listening, Sara, you really are the best!"

Sara: "Stop it right now. How many meltdowns have you navigated with me? Like a million. Please. You spew, I got your hair, girl."

Lilly (laughing): "Nice imagery. You're such a lady, Sara."

Sara: "You know it!"

They both laugh, grabbing cookies from the counter and heading back to their offices.

Okay, let's break this down and show the two conversations of the feminine in motion. In the first few sentences, it's already begun.

Sara: "Hey, Lilly, what's up?"

Lilly: "Not much."

Sara: "Lilly, what's going on? I know something's up. Just tell me."

Lilly: "Are you sure? It's really nothing. I can handle it."

Sara: "Stop it. Come on. Give it to me."

When Sara asks Lilly "what's up," she's demonstrating her instinctual knowing that Lilly is carrying something with emotion. Lily responds by downplaying it, not wanting to be seen as a burden (very feminine response). And then Sara gives Lilly permission to proceed by telling her, "I know something's up. Just tell me."

By the way, you get bonus points if you noticed that Lilly tried to brush her off again (double politeness factor) by saying "It's really nothing" (which means it's something) and "I can handle it" (which means "I don't want to burden you with my problems").

Okay, the next section of the dialogue starts the Processing Conversation, when Lilly is "getting it out," and Sara is being the trusted supporter. If you look back at Sara's dialogue from

"And . . . " all the way to "What did she say?" it's all supportive, validating, and encouraging for Lilly. Everything Sara says is nonjudgemental and she doesn't interrupt Lilly's process.

The dialogue takes an important step forward here:

Sara: "What did she say?"

Lilly: "She told me I'm ungrateful, the kids aren't learning how to be responsible and respectful, and, oh, apparently my brother's kids are so much easier. Never mind that they live five states away, and she sees them five days a year."

Sara: "Geez, this is a shit show. I'm so sorry, Lil. That's just ridiculous. *What are you going to do?*"

The statement from Lilly above is when Lilly gets to the point in the process where she can identify the problem.

Notice how Sara validates Lilly's predicament by compassionately validating what a shit show that is and implying that Lilly doesn't deserve that by calling the comment from her mom ridiculous. These are all very helpful for the feminine to feel that their supporter is "on their side."

Next, Sara transitions the conversation with the statement, "What are *you* going to do?" Notice that Sara did not start telling Lilly what she thinks. She did not tell Lilly what Lilly *should* do. She asked her, "What are *you* going to do?" This is critical.

Sara knows that her role is supportive, not directive, and that she needs to encourage Lilly, not tell her what to think. She's giving Lilly the space to think it through and come to her own conclusion first.

Sara waits until she is asked, if she's ever asked, to weigh in.

That gives Lilly the opportunity to easily transition into the Solving Conversation phase.

Lilly: "I don't even know. I mean, the kids love my mom, right? So, it's not like I'm going to stop having her be with them. But I can't keep settling shit every day something goes down."

> **Sara:** "Of course." ← (validation)
>
> **Lilly** (lets out a big breath): "Maybe I'll just have a family meeting and include my mom. We can talk about the swim thing, and she can feel like she's part of the process and hear William out about what he wants to do."
>
> **Sara:** "That's great. I bet she'll really like that." ← (validation and encouragement)

Lilly is able to move through the Solving Conversation in two quick pieces. First, she establishes what she's *not going to do* (she's not going to have her mom stop being with the kids).

Notice how Sara validates that for her with the golden phrase: *"Of course."*

Then Lilly comes up with the idea independently to include her mom in the planning so she can move things forward.

Sara validates that idea and gives reassurance. Everything said after Sara says, "That's great. I bet she'll really like that" is the dismount of the conversation. It's Lilly's way of thanking Sara and assuring her that she really helped her. And it's Sara's way of reassuring Lilly that she's not a burden and that she deserves the support, like reminding her that she's done the same for her many times.

I know that was a lot to take in. You may need to review that many times to get some of the details, and that's okay.

Remember, the feminine being has two conversations. The Processing Conversation is first and usually must be completed before the Solving Conversation, which comes second. Now let's take a look at the masculine's conversation.

THE MASCULINE CONVERSATION

Typically, the masculine does not have an external Processing Conversation with someone. Generally, the masculine does not value emotion in problem solving to begin with and tries to eliminate emotion as quickly as possible. Most masculine beings easily and instinctively remove the emotion from the logic. As a result, they are not typically storing substantial emotion with their information. Since there is little to no emotion stored that needs to be processed and released, a very different dynamic is created for the masculine being.

The masculine being is also an internal, autonomous processor. So, he will do the "thinking it through" processing within his own thoughts. He's not "ready" for any external conversation from his blueprint because he hasn't processed it himself, yet. Nor would an external conversation be necessary.

It's not that the masculine doesn't process; it's that he generally won't have a conversation for the processing phase. He will go through that by himself, autonomously, and he generally assumes all other beings do the same.

The masculine thinks and speaks on the logical level. His only focus is on solving the challenge so it can be done and over.

Even if the topic is something that the masculine has strong feelings about, which is rare, he will shut those feelings off to get to the solution on the topic so that it can be over. Masculine to masculine, this is referred to as "Suck it up" or "Shake it off." That means, shut that emotion down and get the job done. And he can do it, because he's not wired like the feminine.

KERFUFFLE FROM THE MASCULINE AND FEMININE PROCESSING DIFFERENCES

Since neither the masculine nor the feminine being knows about this processing difference, the masculine is applying masculine meanings to what he observes the feminine doing, and the feminine is applying feminine meanings to what she sees the masculine doing.

The Predictable Pattern Loop is invisible, and it's causing a massive amount of unnecessary kerfuffle, day after day.

The masculine assumes that when the feminine starts speaking, it's a Solving Conversation. The masculine has no corresponding external Processing Conversation need, so, without training, he is unaware of the feminine being's need in this area.

As a default, the masculine enters a conversation with the feminine, expecting it's a Solving Conversation since that's his modality. With any other masculine being, it would be.

So, she starts processing (conversation #1) as any feminine being would do, and he's participating as if it's a Solving Conversation (conversation #2) as any masculine would do . . . and BAM! The Boomerang back is the "I don't need you to fix this. I don't even know how I feel about it yet, geez!" response.

Can you say *kerfuffle*?

This is why there's such a big clash! It's not that the feminine doesn't want things fixed, and it's not that the masculine can't listen.

The truth is, neither of them knew which conversation they were in at the time. Is it #1 or #2? The feminine is wired to organically begin in conversation #1. The masculine typically only has conversation #2, so he wouldn't have any idea about conversation #1.

This is just a TIMING difference. She's not ready to have conversation #2, yet, and he thinks all conversations are #2s!

Without clarity into this dynamic and training to navigate it, they both run to the end of their skill set, and it results in a huge kerfuffle.

In over a decade of working with thousands of students, Paul and I have discovered many of these masculine and feminine processing differences that specifically apply to differences in communication, conversations, and collaborations.

Meaning, when we try to talk to each other, say something to the other, or work on collaborating on something, there are specific differences between the masculine and feminine processing that inherently cause kerfuffles.

So, even if it wasn't a masculine and feminine difference that caused the initial issue you need to talk about, once you start trying to talk about it, these differences will often come up, creating a new issue.

This is happening every day in masculine and feminine interactions, especially in the workplace.

The Differences in Masculine and Feminine Communication

Here's an example:

Allison walks into the office where her manager, Victor, and his boss, Winnie, are going over some contracts.

"Oh my God, oh my God, oh my God," Allison says. She's wringing her hands and pacing the room, and Victor and Winnie both stop what they are doing, realizing that something has happened.

"What's up?" Victor asks.

Allison is still pacing. "The shipment is missing. It's just missing."

"Don't worry, Allison," Victor starts. "We'll find the shipment. We can call Albert and—"

"No!" Allison stops him, "I already called Al. He can't find it." Allison mumbles something else that Victor can't quite make out.

Victor picks up the phone and calls down to the warehouse. "Give me Bobby, I need to get a shipment out. It's an emergency," Victor says into the phone.

Immediately, Allison grabs the phone from him. "Never mind, Carol. Ignore Victor." And she slams the phone down.

She now turns back to Victor, raising her voice, "I already had Bobby send another one out, but it will never be there in time. Diana is going to get off that plane tomorrow, and there are going to be zero products at the venue for her. Nothing! She's going to freak out and it's all going to come back on me. Even though I told her that we needed three more days of a buffer when she wanted to put that last round of changes through, that won't matter."

Tears start rolling down Allison's cheeks as she's pacing the floor.

Still angry that Allison grabbed the phone out of his hand, Victor stops himself from what he was about to say after seeing Allison crying. He is standing there, confused, when Winnie gets out of her seat.

Winnie goes over to Allison, holding her by the shoulders, and in a calm voice says, "Okay, okay. It's going to be okay. Look at me. Take a deep breath. We'll do this together. We're going to help you. Okay, Allison? This is not your fault. You did nothing wrong. Shipments get lost. It sucks. And yes, Diana will probably yell. Okay, so what? She'll yell at all of us. I'll stand right next to you. It's going to be fine. Okay?"

Allison lets out a deep breath and sits down. She pauses for a minute. Victor watches as she clearly shifts from crying to calm in a surprisingly short moment of time.

"Germany!" Allison yells as she jumps up and startles everyone.

"What about Germany?" Victor says.

Allison continues, "We sent prototypes to the German distributor for a presentation on Tuesday. I can have those redirected to Diana in France and send the new shipment to the German office in time for their Tuesday meetings."

"Crisis averted!" Victor celebrates. "Maybe next time start with the Germany idea and don't give me a heart attack like that," he says as he starts laughing.

Unfortunately, those kerfuffles are all too common. And in this case, Allison is likely to walk away feeling like Victor is an insensitive jerk. Victor is likely to walk away feeling very confused with thoughts like, "What the heck was that?" and simultaneously offended at how Allison treated him. The more these masculine and feminine differences remain unseen, the more breakdown will continue to fester in the day-to-day interactions between them.

Nobody did anything "wrong" here, and it is very unfortunate that so many unnecessary kerfuffles are being caused by The Missing Pieces in our understanding about relationships with others.

HOW DO WE SOLVE THIS?

As with all our Relationship Development solutions, either the masculine or the feminine can solve this for both of you. I'll demonstrate some solutions for feminine core beings first and then masculine core beings after that. Please use the ones that are best suited for you.

RELATIONSHIP DEVELOPMENT SOLUTIONS FOR THE FEMININE CORE BEING

Feminine solution #1: Take ownership of your need to process. This is valid, and there's nothing to apologize for. Intentionally ensure that you allow yourself the time and space to have a Processing Conversation before trying to solve it.

Feminine solution #2: Outside the moment, explain the concept of the two conversations of the feminine: the Processing Conversation and the Solving Conversation. Set him up for success so he understands this difference and what role he can play to truly serve you.

Feminine solution #3: If you are going to attempt to have a Processing Conversation with the masculine, use a preframe to tell him when it's a Processing Conversation versus a Solving Conversation.

Feminine solution #4: Stop saying, "Can I run this by you and see what you think?" You say those words, but what you really need is a Processing Conversation first. Take personal responsibility to stop doing that and instead say what you need.

Feminine solution #5: Depending on where your relationship is on the Your Tree Is Dead Spectrum, you might be able to ask him to support you through your Processing Conversation, or you may need to strategically talk through your Processing Conversations yourself or with someone who is already wired to support you in that way. In the beginning, you might start with only bringing Solving Conversations to the masculine and build from there.

RELATIONSHIP DEVELOPMENT SOLUTIONS FOR THE MASCULINE CORE BEING

Masculine solution #1: When the feminine is sharing with you, first assess where she is in the two-part conversation framework. Is she having a Processing Conversation (conversation #1) or a Solving Conversation (conversation #2) with you?

Masculine solution #2: I'll give you a hint: she almost never starts with the Solving Conversation. When in doubt, assume it's a Processing Conversation and start from there.

Masculine solution #3: Use Relationship Development skill sets to show up for the conversation that she is actually having.

- If she's having a Processing Conversation: validate, support, and encourage her.
- Do not interject your own perspective without being invited to.
- Understand that your role is to support and encourage her to get all that emotion and energy OUT so that she can see and think it through more clearly. It is hurting her to keep it all inside. You are providing an important service to her just by doing this!

Masculine solution #4: She is not masculine. When she speaks, she will not be providing you with efficient and orderly information for you to assess. It's probably going to come out in a random fashion and that's because that's what a Processing Conversation is supposed to be. As Paul teaches, the equivalent for you is when you hear your own internal thoughts change from one aspect to another, when something is bothering you and you don't have a solution yet.

Masculine solution #5: She may or may not need your input or your help solving this. Do not apply the masculine meaning that she shouldn't have dragged you into this if she wasn't going to use your input. That's a masculine meaning, for masculine conversations. The feminine invited you in to help her process, and that's exactly what she needs from you.

Masculine solution #6: If you are not in the right mindset or if the timing isn't right for you to be able to support her in her Processing Conversation, share that with her in a caring way.

You might say something like this: "I definitely want to support you through this. Right now, I don't think my energy would be helpful for you because I'm working through some of my own shit. Can I help you with this later when I'm feeling better and can really be there for you, or do you need to get this out now?"

Most feminine beings would understand that completely. I know that is not something you would say masculine to masculine, but remember, you want to wrap what you say for your listener, so that's how you do it.

The Relationship Development solutions above, for both the masculine and the feminine, allow the individual being to authentically be who they really are and to use skill sets to inter-operate with someone wired differently so that the relationship builds up instead of breaks down.

By contrast, the primitive Demand Relationship approach is to see the difference between us, judge one as being worse, and then *try* to get them to change. This breaks down the relationship until someone gives up.

Masculine and feminine processing differences are real. And these differences cause very real kerfuffles. These kerfuffles can be solved with skill sets and tools without either person being made wrong and without either person needing to be something they are not.

Skill sets and tools can be used to create harmony and eliminate kerfuffles. Both people can feel understood and honored for who they authentically are. And each time we do this, it builds more rapport and alignment.

For instance, Larry, one of our students, shared this celebration with us. He was in the beginning of a conversation that was turning into a fight with his wife when he heard her say, "Don't tell me what to say when you don't even know the whole story." In that moment, he realized that she was in a Processing Conversation (conversation #1).

He switched gears and said, "Ah, you are correct. Sorry about that. I didn't realize you weren't done. Please, tell me everything."

Larry told us that after she shared everything with him, she was lighter and happier almost instantly.

He realized that it was going to take him some time and practice recognizing these conversations when they were initially happening in the moment. However, he was already getting better at spotting Processing Conversations, *and* the solution was already ten times easier than the fighting that used to be in its place.

> **PRINCIPLE:**
> Demand Relationship makes one person wrong and breaks down relationships.
>
> **PRINCIPLE:**
> Relationship Development uses skill sets to solve kerfuffles, without compromise and without making anyone wrong, building up relationships.
>
> **PRINCIPLE:**
> Masculine and feminine beings are wired differently and process differently.

There truly are ways to communicate without fighting. Of course, this takes real work, and it's not a trick or gimmick. This is just one of many, many tools, but the fact remains, it's a skill set and it can be learned. It only takes one person.

If you are struggling, it's not that the kerfuffle is unsolvable. It's just that you ran to the end of your skill set.

However, I have to warn you now that just "learning it" is not enough. Just taking an educational approach to these skill sets is simply not enough to use them effortlessly in real-life moments. It's not that the information isn't accurate and it's not that I'm "holding back on you." It's just that when it comes to life skills, learning is the first step, but it's not the last step if you want real results.

So, what is required to speak and operate from Relationship Development so you can get the kind of results you really desire? (Turn the page.)

SECTION 4

THE RIPPLE

CHAPTER 20

THE KEYS TO LIVING IT VERSUS JUST LEARNING IT

Think of the last time you tried to make a change. Maybe it was a new habit, like changing your morning routine to get up earlier and meditate before starting your day. Or maybe you tried to change your habit from grabbing something from the drive-thru every day to making yourself a healthy lunch instead.

How long did it last? Or better yet, when was the first moment of falter?

Did you find that in the beginning, you had gusto and enjoyed the change for a bit and then "something" came up that threw you off your new habit and back into your old ways? Perhaps you got a cold or there was a new deadline at work or one of your kids wasn't sleeping through the night or you injured your knee . . . The odds are that something came up and knocked you off your horse, so to speak.

When this happens, most humans blame themselves. "I'm not good enough." "I suck at this." "I'll never get there."

Or they blame the new change: "This is too hard." "I doubt others are really doing this." "They are full of shit." "This is impossible for regular people."

Or they say the infamous "I guess this just wasn't meant to be."

It's easy to blame. To blame ourselves, blame the other person, or blame the Universe. All that blame is incorrect. None of those things are the actual reason the failure occurred.

It's a predictable pattern with a predictable outcome. It's just that it has been invisible to you. And remember, when the Predictable Pattern Loop is invisible, we are often quick to incorrectly blame someone or something outside us.

It's critical to gain visibility and understanding into how change happens. In other words, how to get results.

> **PRINCIPLE:**
> All change happens on a spectrum.

When you are making a change for yourself or changing a pattern, the change does not happen by going from point A (the before story) to point Z (the end story) in one move.

But that's not how we have been conditioned. Most people today want the magic pill, the quick fix, or the silver bullet. In fact, many humans will go so far as to say that if it can't be solved (A to Z) in one move or moment, then it doesn't work. They will call it a scam or bullshit.

Think of any legendary athlete. They didn't become that great from one moment or idea. Think of any accomplished chef, scientist, or artist. They did not get there in one moment or idea.

I understand that people want a magic pill, but if you look through time, you will see that the greatest people in history practiced, learned, and developed over time to be great. Think of the movie *Ocean's 11*. They built a team of experts with decades of expertise and mountains of knowledge. And even the greatest experts knew that they needed *months* to prepare. They built a life-size replica of the vault they were breaking into so they could practice, among other things. They rehearsed it over and over and over again.

Anyone who has achieved anything great started out sucking at it, but they knew it was worth it to keep going to become great.

So, let's say that I can't cook, but I want to become a great cook. Not to have my own restaurant or anything, but I just want to be able to cook amazing meals for my family without destroying my kitchen or stressing everyone out. I want that effortless enjoyment of preparing a great meal and enjoying the experience with my family.

First of all, can I even become a great cook? Is it possible?

Sure, why not? It's a learnable skill, right? I mean, of course there are some people born with the genius inside them, but if I want to be able to cook an incredible meal for my family without stress or breakdowns, I can learn how to do that, right? Sure I can.

Okay, so what would I need to do? Really answer that question. What are some of the things I would need to do to become a great cook?

Were any of these things on your list?

- Get a cookbook or get some recipes
- Learn to cook (maybe take lessons or classes)
- Get the right tools for the kitchen (if my only tools in the kitchen are my phone to order in, I might need to buy the right tools for what I want to achieve)
- Practice, practice, and keep practicing

Now, let's say that I get a cookbook or find some recipes, but when I try to prepare them, everything is burned and gross, and I ruin the pot in the process too.

What do you think I should do then?

Should I give up? Is it impossible for me to learn to cook? Is "cooking" as a thing impossible for people to learn? Is cooking "a scam"? Is it just "not meant to be"?

Perhaps I need someone to teach me the stuff I never learned before, like how to dice an onion, how to properly sear a steak, or how to do some fundamental things during the cooking process. That seems reasonable.

And I may have started with trying to roast a turkey when I can't even make a grilled cheese sandwich, so I may need to work my way up to the turkey by learning smaller things first, right?

Why is that? The recipe is written in the book. Even though I've never actually used the oven that's in my kitchen, why can't my turkey turn out the way Julia Child's turkey turned out?

Were you thinking something like, *There's a lot more to it than just the recipe*?

Well, that applies to more than just cooking. It's the same with relationship work. There's a lot more to it than just the principles I could explain and squeeze into this book. That doesn't mean the principles in this book are not valuable nor does it mean they are wrong. It just means that there's more to it.

Think of this book like a collection of recipes for someone who's never made a grilled cheese sandwich before. This is where we begin. This is not where we end.

That's the reason people like to watch a cooking show. They need more than the recipe. They want to see the technique, the materials, how it progresses, and what it is supposed to look like during each phase so they know if they're on the right track and how to recover from a mistake and more.

It's why people can't just read a book about basketball and then go out on the court and play with the Chicago Bulls. There's more to it than just reading "about" it. Understanding it is the FIRST step. It's a critical step and a valuable step, but it's not the only step. All change happens on a spectrum.

THE SPECTRUM OF DEVELOPMENT™

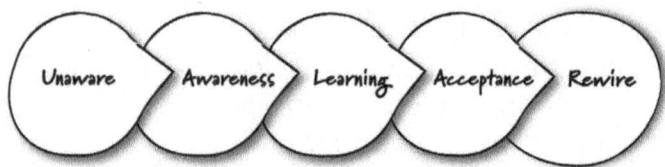

At a high level, there are five main phases along the Spectrum of Development.

Phase #1: Unaware: This represents the phase before you knew about the change you want to make. When you are in the "before story" of yourself. Maybe you haven't even heard of it before.

Phase #2: Awareness: This is when you become aware that there's a change that could be made. You didn't know it existed before and now you know that there is such a thing as the change you are considering. Like when you became aware of Demand Relationship and Relationship Development.

Phase #3: Cognitive Understanding (Learning): This is the phase where you dive into everything there is to learn about this new change or opportunity. You study, you learn, you read, you take classes, you get questions answered, you fill in gaps, you try to interpret it, you get course corrections from someone more advanced in the study, and you get trained by the teacher or expert with the knowledge of the subject. In this phase, you go from being the newbie to being knowledgeable in the subject.

This phase requires you to go outside yourself, to get answers from people farther along the path than you. You must get answers to the questions you have and resolve those questions so that you can use this knowledge. This is the journey of the mind: to learn, explore, and answer the unknown. You must learn enough about this to understand it so that you can apply it.

Phase #4: Acceptance (Emotional & Energetic): In this phase, you have an inner journey. It's about coming to a genuine acceptance within yourself. It's solving the snags within you that still want to go back to the old ways. It may be the moment that you realize that getting up early to meditate is giving you the experience of your day that you want, and sleeping more is not.

It's the end of the inner struggle between the old way and the new way. It's the journey when you realize, within yourself, that the old way you have been doing things is genuinely no longer what you want.

It's when you solve any internal snags you have had to becoming the change. In Relationship Development work, this is where you resolve the inner chatter that keeps saying, "Why should I do this when they are the ones who need to change?" If you are not emotionally and energetically congruent to the change that you say you want to make, then your 95% mind will not rewire in the next phase.

Your nervous system will not open to something it knows you don't really want deep down. It will protect you from that.

You can't just use willpower to master this phase. Willpower or pushing will never get you to acceptance. You can't fake this phase. The work here requires real perspective shifts and solving the very real snags that exist within you.

Phase #5: Blueprint-Level Rewiring (95% Autopilot Mind): This is the phase of rewiring the 95% Autopilot Mind from the old pattern (unwanted) to the new pattern (wanted). When you get through this phase, your new pattern is on autopilot, and you no longer have to *"effort"* to get the results you want.

This is where you achieve results without having to try anymore. It has become your automatic pattern.

In relationship, we must do this phase so that, in our everyday interactions, we don't have to keep trying to think through all the different tools and things to say before saying it.

Speaking happens too fast to think every time for the rest of your life. You can exert effort in the beginning, but eventually, you need to develop the automatic skill set to talk Relationship Development and use the tools habitually so that you get the results effortlessly.

LIVING IT VERSUS JUST LEARNING IT

People who love to learn or love doing growth work are usually stuck in phase 3 on the spectrum. They keep learning and learning, but their life doesn't change.

They go from thing to thing, thinking, *Maybe the next book will have the real answer.* But it's not just about the book; it's the fact that you must go through phases 4 and 5 if you want your life to really transform.

We have been trained that "knowledge is power" and falsely believe that learning it is enough. But it is not.

Phase 3 gives you knowledge. Phases 4 and 5 give you transformation. There is a massive difference.

You can stop at phase 3 for things like memorizing the state capitals for a quiz. But if you are doing lifework, something that needs to be wired or rewired into the 95% mind, then you must successfully navigate the Spectrum of Development through phase 5.

How?

Paul and I created our 4-Step Breakthrough Formula™ to help our students get through the five phases on the Spectrum of Development, so they can achieve the 95% rewiring of the Autopilot Mind with Relationship Development skill sets and tools.

Curriculum and training: You will not guess your way to the transformation that you want. And doing what you've always done won't work either. You must get training that has proven to be effective in real life.

This book is an excellent start to getting real, actionable, and effective answers. While I couldn't shove everything you will need into this book, it's a foundational and necessary first step in your training.

Application and Q&A: In lifework, learning is not enough. You have to implement what you are learning. It's in the implementation phase that the questions arise.

Having the ability to get complete and accurate answers to your questions so that you don't stay stuck is what will allow you to make it through all the phases and rewiring for the results you want.

It's a proven pattern that when humans don't have access to complete and accurate answers, they typically wind up asking well-meaning friends, who also don't have accurate answers, and that just leads to stagnation, backsliding, and giving up.

This happens in any transformation journey on the Spectrum of Development, whether it's athletic, creative, scientific, or human dynamics. There will be questions along the journey and WHO you have to answer them will determine your destiny.

Community: Who you surround yourself with will impact your results, every time. Think of it this way: if you are determined to break the chains of Demand Relationship, yet everyone in your world is doing Demand Relationship 24/7, how hard do you think it will be for you to effectively stop doing Demand Relationship yourself?

Whereas if you are surrounded by a tribe of Relationship Transformers, all living from Relationship Development, speaking the same language you are, and navigating the same journey you are, how much easier do you think it will be for you to start living from Relationship Development and practicing your skill sets? That's the difference that the right fit community makes.

Immersion to rewire: You already know that if you want a breakthrough in your 95% mind, Immersion is one of the three ways to get from the 5% Thinking Mind into the 95% Autopilot Mind.

So, when you "know" something but you struggle to "live" it, don't be so hard on yourself. Transformation doesn't happen instantaneously. There's a predictable pattern that creates a predictable outcome.

You *can* do it. There's nothing wrong with you. It's just that there was a piece missing from what you thought was required to get that result. And that's my job... to give you The Missing Pieces.

Before I send you out into the world with this, I have three tools and five next steps that you will need as you set out on your journey. I know, I know, but I have to give you these. (Turn the page.)

CHAPTER 21

THE TOOLS FOR YOUR NEXT STEPS

Before I send you off into the world to start using this material, I want to give you three tools and five steps that you will need on your journey.

THREE TOOLS FOR YOUR NEXT STEPS

Next Step Tool #1: Educated Blame™

Since you have been reading this book, I'm willing to bet that you have had multiple experiences of seeing Demand Relationship in others around you. You notice it now when someone else is doing Demand Relationship, correct? Maybe, like many of our students, you feel like you see it everywhere now.

One pitfall of seeing it everywhere is that sometimes students will start telling other people, "Hey, you know what you are doing is Demand Relationship and . . . " Or they will experience Demand Relationship from others and tell them, "Don't do Demand Relationship with me."

Either way, whether you are pointing out to others the Demand Relationship that they are doing wrong or telling others to stop using Demand Relationship with you, both are what Paul and I call Educated Blame.

Educated Blame is when you use what you learn cognitively to blame others for what *they* are doing, or you choose to use your new knowledge as a weapon to blame or shame others for how they are "showing up" with you.

Educated Blame is Demand Relationship. You are doing Demand Relationship when you do that. You are seeing other people, evaluating what you would rather see them do or say, and telling them how they can change so that you can be happy or peaceful.

Instead of Educated Blame, which is Demand Relationship, change how you are showing up in your life. Live your life as the example. Change your words when you speak. Change your thoughts. Change your skill set level when you inter-operate with other humans. Stop blaming others and instead shift yourself. Remember, with Relationship Development skill sets, you don't need anyone else to change for you to be happy.

Next Step Tool #2: Right-Hand/Left-Hand™

Many, many years ago, before Relationship Development was even an idea in my mind, I was surrounded with folks who were doing personal growth work. As I watched them navigate their development journey, I noticed a pattern.

They would have a big breakthrough in their development and make a change that brought them fulfillment and happiness. Then, in their excitement, they would go into their regular lives and basically spew all their new development work all over their family and friends. As you might guess, this didn't go over well. In case you need me to tell you, people don't love it when you vomit all that you are learning and your growth all over them.

I kept seeing this pattern where people would take one of two paths. Either (1) they would shrink back to their old ways, letting go of their new growth and happiness so that the people around them would be more comfortable. Or (2) they would tell the people in their life, "Screw you if you don't like it." They would hold on to their new growth and distance themselves from the people in their lives who didn't "get" them anymore.

Unfortunately, an overwhelming number of experts and mentors in the growth space encourage the latter choice. They will say things like, "Not everyone will come with you on your road to success" or "The path to greatness is less traveled for a reason" and to "only surround yourself with positive people who support what you're doing."

Oh boy. That is tragic advice. And it's not their fault. They mean well. All they have is the same Demand Relationship skills that everyone else grew up with. They are just supporting you in the "get on board with me or I have to separate from you" phase of Demand Relationship since they, too, have run to the end of their skill set in this particular area.

I've watched many people isolate themselves on their Island of Personal Growth because they lacked the Relationship Development skill sets to co-exist with people who are wired differently or on a different path than they are.

So I created a tool to help my students with this. It's called Right-Hand/Left-Hand™, and here's how it works.

You have three groups of people in your life.

Group #1: Tribe: They are like-minded people on a growth path who care about your journey and are supporting you.

Group #2: Family and friends: They are on a journey of their own, and they are not into growth or development work.

Group #3: Toxic people: These are people who will find a way to make things worse for everyone, and they are committed to staying that way.

Listen to me: your partner, friends, and family are not toxic just because they are not into growth. People often label everyone as "toxic" if they are not supportive. It's inaccurate, unfair, and immature. We don't have time to chat about toxic people in this book, so we are going to focus on the other two groups of people, since they are the majority of humans with whom you inter-act.

Friends and family: Your friends and family are probably the largest group of people in your life. They have been around through many phases of your life. They have positive intention for you, even if they don't have the skill sets to build up their relationship with you or support you. They are not into growth. So what? They are just trying to get by in life, and they are doing the best that they can with the skills that they have.

Tribe: Your tribe are the people who get you. Those are the folks who are on the journey with you. They are the ones whom you can call up and say, "Hey I'm doing a juice cleanse for fourteen days! Want me to send you the link to it?" And they are like, "Yeah! Let's do this!"

It's easiest to be your real and best self with your tribe. They are the ones who will celebrate your wins and catch you when you fall. They are also the ones who will hold you accountable, and if you are not living up to your potential, they will get behind you and kick your ass all the way up that mountain to the pinnacle, if that's what it takes.

To make it easier to understand this next piece, do this exercise with me for a moment, please. Put both of your hands out in front of you, palms up.

Now imagine that, in your right hand, you're holding your Friends and Family group. Your Tribe group is in your left hand. Now, clap your hands together hard.

Here's the truth; pain happens when you don't know which hand you're in and what your role is.

The kerfuffle happens when you are with your Friends and Family group and *you* inter-act *as if* you are with your Tribe. You want your friends and family to see you, support you, and talk with you like your tribe does, and it Boomerangs back in kerfuffle. (You can put your hands down now.)

It's a predictable pattern with a predictable outcome. But when the Loop is invisible to you, you incorrectly blame the other person.

Trigger: your incorrect expectations of friends and family → Boomerang: kerfuffle

It's not that your friends and family are bad people because they don't get the growth work you are doing. They just don't want to hear about the book you're reading, and they really don't know how to support you.

It's not about them at all. It's about how *you* are interacting with them.

Pain happens when you are with your Right-Hand people and expect them to be Left-Hand people.

The kerfuffle is usually a result of you feeling unsupported and them feeling judged. It's Demand Relationship, and it breaks down the relationship, even when you don't intend to.

This happens when you talk about your growth stuff with them. Or when you tell them how to solve their complaint with something you learned from your growth work. Right or wrong, it can make them feel like you are either somehow better than them or they feel bad about themselves because you are genuinely elevating yourself "past" them (creating separation). Either way, they don't like it. Here's the tool we created to solve this dynamic.

The Steps to the Right-Hand/Left-Hand Tool™

Step #1: Which hand are you in? Before you enter a situation, know which hand you are in. Is this person a Right-Hand (Friends and Family) person or a Left-Hand (Tribe) person to you?

Step #2: Know your role. Navigating the interaction from within your role is the critical piece.

Your role with your tribe: When you are with your tribe, your role is to inter-act the way you have been. Share your vision, talk strategy, give and seek support, and share challenges. Talk about growth work, seek insights, and get and give support and validation. Go for it.

Your role with your friends and family: When you are with your friends and family, there are two parts to your role.

Part 1: Lead by example: Don't *talk* about your growth, just live it. Live as the example, with humility. Just be who you are without talking about it. If you have grown, then act like it. If you have new Relationship Development skill sets, then use them in real life instead of talking about them. Stop offering unsolicited advice and unasked-for help. Lead by example.

Part 2: Give unconditional compassion: Show up with unconditional compassion for them for exactly who they are and exactly where they are in life. This is a tough one. It requires skill sets and work.

Every human on this planet needs more practice and exercise in giving unconditional compassion to other humans. Instead of needing others to be something they are not or needing them to change something about themselves, just give compassion. Most humans will live their entire lives and die without experiencing unconditional compassion from another person. You could be that source for your friends and family.

Giving unconditional compassion is not easy. But here's the thing, you have a Tribe. You have support in your life. You have answers, solutions, tools, and skills that others don't have. You are growing. So, fill yourself up from your Left-Hand Tribe, and you will have satisfied what you need inside you to be able to give to your Right-Hand Friends and Family without looking for something in return.

You may also need to manage the amount of time that you spend in situations where you are the giver of unconditional compassion. There's a point at which your giving runs out, and you wind up pleasing. You need to manage yourself before that happens. Maybe you end up being somewhere for four hours with Friends and Family because that's how much unconditional giving you feel you have. Whereas in the past, you would have spent the whole weekend with them out of a feeling of obligation (pleasing).

The key to you being able to give unconditional compassion is that you must have a strong Left-Hand Tribe. If you are completely unsupported anywhere in your growth and development, it would be much more draining to be so unconditionally giving when you are with your Friends and Family long term. In fact, if your Friends and Family Group is your only group, you will likely keep looking to them for support and validation, which will only cause more kerfuffles.

If you want to strengthen and expand your Left-Hand group, don't despair. We welcome you to join our community of Relationship Transformers. Get access to join us at the end of this book.

Next Step Tool #3: Measuring and Tracking Your Progress Tools

On this journey of breaking the chains of Demand Relationship and showing up from Relationship Development, you will need many tools, including tools to check in and measure your progress so you know where you are on the spectrum.

Here are two Relationship Development progress tracking tools you can use.

PROGRESS TRACKING TOOL #1: 30-DAY NO-JUDGEMENT CHALLENGE

When you look at the Demand Relationship versus Relationship Development Chart, you will notice that Judgement is in the center of the chart, dividing the two sides. (You can get a copy of our chart in the Book Bonuses at the end of the book.)

You are getting pulled into Demand Relationship when someone says or does something and you would prefer that they say or do something different. You will usually reach for a Demand Relationship tactic to get the change you want.

For instance, you walk into the kitchen and notice that your spouse left a dirty platter, bowl, and grill tools on the counter after they grilled a steak for themselves. You are frustrated that you do everything. You can't stand how messy they are and how thoughtless they were to leave their dirty dishes out. You would really prefer that they wash their crap and put it away after they cook something. Now you find yourself resentfully washing the dishes and putting them away (and yeah, maybe you did slam them a bit so someone would hear that you are cleaning up their mess).

Let's slow that moment down, so I can show you where the judgement happened. The moment you first saw the dirty dishes left out was the moment of observation. You are observing the facts or taking in the data.

Then, the judgement happened. In a split second, you were aware of "what is" versus what you would prefer it to be. Clearly you would prefer that there not be dirty dishes out and not be a mess left in the kitchen. This judgement moment happens in that split second, after the observation.

It all happens inside us. After we observe, we evaluate what we observe and compare it to what we prefer. That is the moment of judgement.

Like when your kid comes downstairs wearing the same sweatshirt she's been wearing for four days and you tell her to march back upstairs and change into something clean. Your brain observed her sweatshirt. In a split second, you also processed the fact that it hasn't been washed and she's worn it for the last four days. Those were all observations. The judgement happened when you decided that you would prefer that she wear a clean clothing item to school. Even before you told her to go change, the judgement happened in a split second.

When we stay in *observation*, we can more easily use the Relationship Development skill sets on the Relationship Development side of the chart.

The moment we go into *judgement*, we slip into Demand Relationship and reach for a Demand Relationship tactic to try and change the situation. Like going into the over-responsibility of cleaning the dishes, the passive-aggressive displeasure of slamming the grill tools, or ordering your child to change.

PRINCIPLE:
When we stay in the seat of the observer, it's easier to operate from Relationship Development.

PRINCIPLE:
When we go into judgement, we are already slipping into Demand Relationship.

You need to break your pattern of judgement. The better you get at staying out of judgement, the better (and faster) you will get at operating from the Relationship Development paradigm instead.

So, for the next 30 days, I invite you to take the 30-Day No-Judgement Challenge.

Catch yourself each time you slide into judgement. Remember, awareness is a phase of progress on the Spectrum of Development, and we need to bring more awareness to our patterns of judgement that keep pushing us into Demand Relationship.

You can keep a journal or make notes in your phone, but try to stay out of judgement, and take notice of the times that you do judge so that you can work on breaking those patterns.

PROGRESS TRACKING TOOL #2: PROGRESS CHART FOR SPECTRUM OF DEVELOPMENT

On any journey, it's imperative to have a map. That's how you know where you are going and how close you are to getting there. Paul and I make maps that we call Progress Charts for the skill sets that we teach our students. This helps them to know where they are on the Spectrum of Development and helps us to see what their next step is on the path to the result they want.

Here is the one for No Judgement so you can see where you are on the spectrum as you implement. For each phase on the spectrum, I describe what your experience of life looks and feels like so that you can see where you are operating from and know the phase you are currently in.

Relationship Development Progress Chart for the No-Judgement Skill Set

Phase 1: Unaware: I am unaware that I am judging; this is just how I think (and how all people think).

Phase 2: Awareness: I've heard of the concept that my own judgement might be contributing to some of the results I'm experiencing.

Phase 3: Cognitive Understanding (Learning): I am clear that my judgement is what puts me into operating from Demand Relationship. I know that my judgement is CAUSING a good deal of what I don't like in my life and relationships. I know that my judgement is not a FACT because it comes from my personal unique perspective.

I know that my judgement is MY personal responsibility and no one else's. I understand that when I judge others, I am already wrong because they do not have the same blueprint as me. I know that the opportunity to rewire my blueprint to stop judging is for me and benefits me.

Phase 4: Acceptance (Emotional & Energetic): I believe, in the depths of my being, that no one human has any place judging any other human. I have no snags about that. I feel that being the observer is the best quality of life I can create for myself, regardless of what it does or doesn't do for my relationships; it's who I want to be.

Most of the time, I am congruent with my belief that my judgement is only mine and that it is hurting me and my relationships. The positive outcomes of living as the observer are something that I can feel and want deeply. Every time I operate as the observer instead of judging, it creates more desire in me to have this as my center of gravity in how I operate.

Phase 5: Rewiring of the Blueprint (95% Mind): Inside the moment, I no longer FEEL judgement first and then talk myself back from it. Inside the moment, I feel myself peacefully observing the other person (or myself) as the observer.

I operate as the observer. I no longer perceive things as they relate to ME. Instead, during my interactions with everyone around me, I perceive the information they give to me as data points.

I am able to incorporate what I observe of others to better lead and serve in my relationships with them. My center of gravity is to operate from the seat of the observer 80% or more of the time.

Using this Progress Chart over the next 30 days, you can check in from time to time to see where you are on the spectrum of progressing toward judging less and observing more.

Speaking of the next 30 days, I have some steps for you to follow as you set out on your journey to becoming a Relationship Transformer.

5 NEXT STEPS FOR YOU AS YOU SET OUT ON YOUR JOURNEY

ONE: Do the work. Do the work to break Demand Relationship and show up from Relationship Development. Don't do it for your relationship. Don't even do it for your partner. Do it for *yourself*. Do the work because of who you are becoming as you do this work. Do this work because you love and respect yourself more when you do this. Do this work because you are becoming happier and feeling more authentically yourself with each step forward. Do the work.

TWO: Change the trajectory of your legacy. This is about so much more than you. Every step forward you take into Relationship Development, remember, you are breaking the chains of Demand Relationship for your family's legacy. You are freeing your children and their children from the chains of the destructive past. If we don't do this now, we saddle our children with the burden of doing it.

Don't get me wrong, if you don't do the work of stopping Demand Relationship, your kids will. That's the infinite beauty of their generation. When they need to know the answer to something, they take out their phone, and after a quick Internet search, they have the answer. They will find us, and we will be there for them. I guarantee it.

But I bet you don't want them to have to figure this out after years of pain, like you did. Instead, you want things to be better for your kids than they were for you, right?

Well, you have the power to change the trajectory of your family's legacy. When you stop doing Demand Relationship and start doing Relationship Development, in real life with them, they will model the Relationship Development you demonstrate. The alternative is perpetuating the old Demand Relationship thinking and enduring the suffering that goes with it. It's your choice. You have the opportunity, right now, to break the chains for your family!

THREE: Be a Relationship Transformer. From this day forward, step out of the old identity of being unaware of this paradigm shift, and step into the new identity of being a Relationship Transformer! You are the one who will get the training, implement the strategies, use the tools, be the community member, and set the example for others.

FOUR: Share the love. If this book has served you in any way, please be part of the mission of Relationship Development and share this with others. Whether you gift the book to a friend, send them the link to get their own, or just tell people how much you love this book, it all makes a difference. At the end of the book, I've given you the link to the website for this book and ways you can easily share it with others.

Everything you do to share this message is helping our mission to let every family know that this solution is available for them. No one should have to suffer in darkness anymore. Let's shine the light! This ripple has reached you. Join it. Share it. And help us turn this ripple into a wave.

FIVE: Work with us. We are right here. We have a bottomless toolbox of solutions and daily support to help you. We have training programs and events to serve you. Whether you just do our online classes, do an online event with us, or want to join RelationshipU, which includes the opportunity to work with Paul and me directly, we are here to help. The resources for reaching out to us are in the back of this book. You can always go to RelationshipDevelopment.org as well.

Before you read the last chapter, I just want to take a moment and let you know that I truly mean it when I tell you that we are here to help. It would be wildly irresponsible of me to show you the great discovery that I made, tell you about the invention that we created to solve the problem, and then say, "See ya, good luck! I hope you figure this all out on your own!"

As long as I'm alive, and hopefully long after, you will never be alone. That is my commitment to you. We will always be here for you. As we say in the Relationship Transformer Community, "You've got this, and we've got you."

Hopefully, you are seeing how powerful this book is. And that this book alone can give you a different destiny than you would have had without it. I know it's hard for you to imagine, but the hardest part of writing this book was figuring out what to put into it and what to leave out.

I estimate that this book represents less than 1% of the content we have built over the last 14 years. It was daunting to look at our content library and figure out what we could squeeze into this book without making it a thousand pages.

Yet this book is an extraordinary foundation for doing Relationship Development work. The students who read this book before doing the training with us will be light-years ahead of the students who didn't have this book as their starting point. You will get even faster results than the students who came before you. That's the blessing of the evolution of this work. And it's our honor and blessing to share it with you.

All we ask is that you pay it forward to help another human and family. (Turn the page.)

CHAPTER 22

THE RIPPLE

We've been led to believe that one person can't make much of a difference. The thought that "one person can't change the world" is a common one.

Well, what if I told you that this whole thing, my discovery and everything I've figured out, all began with one five-year-old boy who started a ripple.

FROM PAUL MARTINO

I was taking our son to kindergarten one morning, and before he got out of the car, he asked me, "Daddy, what does divorce mean?"

I calmly asked him, "Where did you hear that, buddy?"

He said, "My friend at school said that his parents are getting a divorce, and now his daddy won't be sleeping in their house at night anymore. I don't want that to happen to me, Daddy. I need you sleeping right where you are. So, how do I not get one of those divorces?"

Tears filled my eyes, and I tried not to let it show. If Stacey had not done what she did for us, this likely would have been my son's life experience as well.

"Don't you worry," I told him. "Divorce can't happen to me and Mommy. I'm always going to be sleeping in our house, every night, buddy." I then hugged him as I unbuckled him from his seat and sent him off to go inside to school.

Stacey: When Paul walked in the door that day, I was in the kitchen, making coffee (of course), and I knew something was wrong (but not about me this time). Paul sat down and told me the whole story. He said that seeing this happen to that family made it seem so close to home because that could have easily been our own son's life if we'd had him before our hanging-by-a-thread moment. We hugged, feeling grateful for the second chance we were given for our family.

A few days later, Paul came to me again, "Stacey, do you realize that if those parents just knew what you and I know about relationships, maybe they wouldn't be getting a divorce? Those boys could be sleeping down the hall from two parents at night instead of trying to figure out how to navigate life bouncing from one house to the other."

"I don't know about that, Paul," I told him honestly.

"Stacey"—he got that determined look in his eyes and continued—"there's gotta be a way to help them, or at least people like them. I feel like I see families unraveling everywhere I look. There must be some way for us to help them."

"Us to help them?! What the fuck? Have you lost your mind?" I jumped up from the chair I was sitting in.

He continued, "No, think about it, Stacey. You saved us. And you told me about the things you figured out along the way. I look around and nobody sees what you see or knows what you know. You are probably the only one who can help people, because you actually did it . . . and you did it alone."

"Paul Martino, you are batshit crazy. I'm not calling someone and butting into their marriage. Are you out of your mind? You think I want to be the bitch who meddles in someone's marriage?!"

Paul said, "I get that, Stacey. I really do. And I also know that we have something that we already know can help people, so how can we just sit back and watch the unnecessary suffering and not even try to do anything about it? How can we *not* do something?"

It wasn't over for Paul. It haunted him. He brought this to me many more times after that. The impact on these kids (and so many others) hit him hard each day.

Eventually, after months of conversations, I found myself thinking about it too. I would find myself driving and realize I was thinking through what I could possibly share with people to help them. I kept brushing it off because the harsh reality of navigating life with both a five-year-old and a newborn, dealing with problems at work, and worrying about paying our bills was in the forefront of my mind.

I don't really recall how many months this went on, but I do remember the night it all changed. Both kids were finally in bed, Paul and I sat down to talk at the kitchen table, like any other night, but then he said these words to me: "Stacey, I know you have something unique that can *really* help people. It wasn't me who saved us; it was you. I believe in my heart that you are the only person who can do this, and I will support you 100%. I know we both have work and now we have *two* kids and the timing sucks, but maybe we can figure out how to take the next step forward. We *can* do something to help. And if we can, then we should."

At that point I told Paul that I had been having thoughts too. I had been hearing the call to teach people what I figured out, but I was terrified to even consider it. I told him I didn't want to meddle in anyone's life. I didn't want people to hate me. Who the heck am I to butt into people's relationships? What would I even say?

Undeterred, Paul said, "Stacey Martino, this is not about you, and this is way bigger than just you and me. Most people would never make it back from the edge of destruction we faced without someone there to guide them.

"Who's going to stand up for kids in those homes if not us? Who is going to speak for the ones who cannot speak for themselves? Nobody on this planet even knows that what you did is even possible.

"What if we just start with capturing everything that you've figured out? If we can quantify it, perhaps it could be taught to people who need it."

Finally, I said, "Okay, sweetheart. Let's try to figure this out. But I can't promise anything, and I'm still scared as shit."

Paul said, "I understand. I'll do whatever I can to help. Let's just take the next right step."

It took us two years from that point. Two years of trying to map out everything I had figured out and trial and error of figuring out what will and will not work for "anyone" across the board. Testing my tactics with friends who agreed to be our testing group and failing a lot.

After a lot of trial and error and plenty of mistakes that turned into learning lessons, Paul and I finally figured out a step-by-step system that we believed anyone could follow to single-handedly transform their relationship.

As much as I wanted to share it with the people who needed it, I still struggled deeply because I never wanted to do this work. I had zero desire to be a "relationship" person (coach, expert, mentor, or whatever). I feared how people would react. I feared not being able to help. I didn't want to get involved, butt in, or meddle.

But this mission is not about me. There are children in those homes. There are kids sitting at the top of the stairs, listening to their mom and dad argue and wondering what's going to happen to them. There are kids caught in the middle of parents shuffling them from one house to the other and fighting over arrangements. There are kids with no voice, no power, and no ability to solve the pain in their lives. And it was those kids that pulled me through my discomfort to start this mission and share our discoveries, tools, and method with people.

Thank goodness I did, because the results were nothing short of miraculous. People started transforming their relationships immediately. The steps, tools, and solutions I was sharing were working for people all across the globe. Hundreds of students were implementing our tools and strategies and single-handedly saving their marriages, healing their families, and bringing harmony back to their homes. Lives were changing. There was a ripple forming.

Today, as I write this chapter, we have been serving our students through this mission-based organization's events and programs for over 14 years. There have been tens of thousands of happy families that have thanked us for helping them save their family or transform their relationship. By this point, a countless number of children have been positively impacted by the solutions that Paul and I created to help their parents. The ripple of our work has now reached all the corners of this planet.

Having been able to work with and see the transformations in the lives of so many students, Paul and I firmly believe that we have literally cracked the code on human relationships.

We have built hundreds of tools, strategies, and solutions over the years to solve whatever relationship challenges our students were facing. Our method and tools have been proven effective by thousands of humans, and we believe our success, effectiveness rates, and happiness among our students are unmatched.

In a six-year study of our students' results, our RelationshipU® students had a 1% divorce rate over those six years. Some of our students were on the brink of divorce, heading to divorce court, or told by multiple therapists there was no other option but divorce, and *still* they saved their marriage with our method, tools, solutions, and support.

I'm very happy to tell you that there's nothing else in the world I'd rather do than exactly what we do today: serve the humans who come to us for the solutions and answers they deserve to make their marriage and family everything they dreamed of and more.

And now this is in your hands. Your journey begins today.

So, as I invite you into the solution we have created for every relationship, family, and human, I remind you of the mission behind the Relationship Development Organization: the children of the world. When you have a tough day or a tough moment, remember what Paul told me: "This isn't about you. It's about those kids."

Whether for your own children, or the children of the world, we're doing this work to flip the switch on the broken relationship paradigm (and mess) that has been handed down to us, generation after generation. We're cleaning it up, together, so they won't have to.

We're breaking the chains of *our* past to create ripples of transformation for *their* future.

Yes, our lives, our relationships, our love, and our family will transform too. Yes, we will be happier than we've ever been. Yes, our relationships will become the strongest and most loving they've ever been. And, we will, from this day forward, model to our children what does work and stop perpetuating what was modeled to us, which does not work.

For Paul and me, our life's journey has shown us that this has been The Missing Piece for human relationships. And it's my greatest joy to be able to present it to you so that you, too, know what is possible when you're willing to let go of the old way and open your mind to a new way.

You deserve better. The world does too. Thank you for being the one to read this book and change the trajectory of your family's legacy forever. You've got this, and we've got you.

LET THIS RIPPLE BECOME A WAVE ...

Hopefully by now, you are seeing that Relationship Development has been The Missing Piece in humanity for relating to each other. It has been The Missing Piece in our skill set for interacting as free humans. It has been The Missing Piece in personal development for relationships with others.

It is our greatest desire that this discovery, and all our work, serve you and your family and transform your marriage; your parenting; your work, family, and friend relationships; and your relationship with yourself.

It is our greatest hope that you create a ripple with this work and live as an example that elevates your life and the lives of your spouse, children, family, and everyone who interacts with you.

Relationship Development was created to bring humans together! Not force them to stay together, but empower them to connect and inter-operate together, in peace, harmony, and love.

The Ripple

This Universe is filled with amazing humans, and love is meant to give us the feeling that inspires us to do the work necessary to stay connected. Everyone tells us that "marriage is hard work," but no one ever told us what that work needed to be . . . until now.

Relationship is a skill set, and it can be learned. It's not about you, your partner, or the two of you together. It's not about the personality-level differences. What you can't see can and will hurt you.

There is no need for us to distance ourselves from people who happen to be different than we are. We can learn the skill sets that build the bridge between us, so that we can be who we authentically are, allow others to be who they authentically are, and thrive together harmoniously.

You were never meant to find someone exactly like you and try to love them, just so your relationship would "work." It was always about becoming the version of yourself who has the skills and abilities to love who you are and who they are.

There's nothing wrong with you, or them. And you didn't pick wrong. It's just that there's been this gigantic piece missing . . . the Relationship Development Method.

I can't believe we are at the end of the book. It's been an honor to be with you on this journey. I hope you laughed when I laughed and cried when I cried. But most of all, I hope that the truth in this book was a revelation for you. That you will always carry this truth in your heart. My wish for you is that you take this beyond just knowledge, beyond living in your heart, and implement this into your life and relationships.

Let this be the beginning of something amazing and not the end of something interesting.

Until I see you soon . . . sending love!

ENDNOTES

Chapter 1

1. Mark Banschick, "The High Failure Rate of Second and Third Marriages," *Psychology Today*, accessed May 2024, www.psychologytoday.com/us/blog/the-intelligent-divorce/201202/the-high-failure-rate-of-second-and-third-marriages.

2. Wilkinson & Finkbeiner, "Divorce Statistics: Over 115 Studies, Facts and Rates for 2024," accessed March 2024, www.wf-lawyers.com/divorce-statistics-and-facts.

3. U.S. Surgeon General, "Our Epidemic of Loneliness and Isolation 2023, The U.S. Surgeon General's Advisory on the Healing Effects of Social Connection and Community," U.S. Surgeon General's Office, accessed May 2024, https://www.hhs.gov/sites/default/files/surgeon-general-social-connection-advisory.pdf.

4. BJC HealthCare, "WHO Declares Loneliness a Global Health Concern. Here's How to Recognize If Someone in Your Life Is at Risk," January 4, 2024, https://www.bjc.org/news/who-declares-loneliness-global-health-concern-heres-how-recognize-if-someone-your-life-risk.

THE ACKNOWLEDGMENTS

There are so many people to thank for helping us bring this book to life.

To you, the reader. Thank you for being the one to break the chains of Demand Relationship for your family's legacy. Thank you for sharing this book with others who need The Missing Piece.

To those who have shared wisdom with us along our journey. We are truly grateful, every day, to be on this planet at the same time as you. Thank you for the many gifts you have each brought into this world to make it a better place for humanity. Sage and Tony Robbins, Cloe Madanes, Bob Burg and John David Mann, Dr. Wayne Dyer, Dr. Bruce Lipton, Mike Dooley, Deepak Chopra, Michael Singer, Neale Donald Walsch, Esther Hicks, Dr. Joe Dispenza, Simon Sinek, Louise Hay, and Oprah Winfrey.

To those who believed in us, inspired us, and guided us along our journey. Thank you, Linda Joy, Fabienne and Derek Fredrickson, Blue Melnick and Bari Baumgartner, Lisa Marie Grantham, Amy McCready, Kaelin and Brandon Poulin, Brad Gibb and Ryan Lee, Erin Verbeck and Sarah Petty, Chris Wark, Brent Berg, Dave Lindenbaum, Bill Allen, Dan Henry, Urvi and Janak Mehta, Mark Stern, Eric Beer, Ashlan and Wallace Nelson, Krista Mashore, Alison Prince, Steve Larsen, Nikki and Jaime Smith, Annie Grace and Brian Jensen, Yara Golden and James Friel, and Collette and Russell Brunson.

To our entire team at Relationship Development Organization (RDO), who worked around our insane writing schedule for over a year to help this book come to the world. We love you and thank you for helping us to serve these families each day. Thank you to everyone on the RU Leadership Team. Thank you to everyone at both Valiant Productions and Custom Box Agency for your tireless dedication to our content and delivery.

To our early readers, who generously pored over every page of this manuscript and offered priceless insights and guidance. Thank you, Nikki and Jaime Smith, James Friel, Alison Prince, Annie Grace, and Kathryn Vasquez.

To Reid Tracy, Sally Mason-Swaab, and everyone at Hay House Publishing. Thank you for bringing this book to life. Reid, we are eternally grateful for your persistence and strong belief that this book belonged at Hay House.

To Russell Brunson. There aren't enough words to thank you for your unending generosity and huge heart. You are our mentor, messenger, brother, and friend. You've believed in us, championed us, taught us, pushed us, and guided us. In a thousand different ways, this book would not be published today if it weren't for you. And more than all that . . . you brought us home. We love you and are eternally grateful.

To James Friel and Yara Golden. Thank you for your generosity and for lending your talent, wisdom, and expertise to RDO in so many ways. We couldn't ask for two better humans for best friends. Sharing work with you is amazing, but sharing our life with you is a blessing. Our love for you is endless.

To Annie Grace. In the overwhelming moment when I realized that I was the one who had to write this manuscript (when I didn't want to do it, didn't know how to do it, and was terrified to do it), one of my greatest blessings was that God had already sent me you as a best friend so many years ago. Thank you for sitting with us with sticky notes and index cards all over the place and for developing the outline for the book with us so brilliantly and effortlessly. I am forever grateful for your contributions in helping us shape this book. But I'm even more grateful for your love and friendship and for sharing your life with us. We love you.

The Acknowledgments

To the students in RelationshipU, past and present. Relationship Development would not exist if it weren't for you. The journey to bring this mission to the world has been incredibly challenging, and yet watching your transformations continuously inspired us every day. Thank you for being part of the creation process. Every question asked over the years served as a catalyst for our further growth and the development of the solutions needed for everyone. Thank you for saying yes and doing this work for yourselves and your families. As much as I know you are grateful for us, we are eternally grateful to you . . . more than you know.

To Kathryn Vasquez. Thank you for serving as my right hand for many years now. You handle a thousand things a day at lightning speed and always with the biggest smile. You pivot on a dime and are the first to cheer "Let's go!" There are not enough words to thank you for tirelessly editing this entire manuscript and pouring your heart and soul into it. This book is even better because of you . . . and so is our world. We love you, Kat, and are endlessly grateful.

To our children. We marvel at the magnificent human beings you both have grown to be. You inspire us daily. We love you more than you could even imagine! We're so proud to be your parents and love you both, eternally. Everything we have ever done, or ever will do, is for you.

To my husband, Paul. You already know this truth, but there would be no book, no Relationship Development, no anything, without you. You have been, and always are, my biggest champion. You sat patiently through every tantrum as I yelled about not wanting to write this book. Then, you turned me around and plopped me back in front of my laptop with a kiss and a cup of coffee. You supported me and cared for my every need through endless days of writing. You distracted me (expertly) when I needed it and encouraged me when I needed it. You took on so much more for *us* just so that I could do *this*. You meticulously reviewed every word of this book, editing and perfecting it in the way that only you can. You told me you were proud of me every day, which is all I ever needed to get this done. The only thing that exists in life is you. Being near you, listening to you, hearing you laugh, touching you—that is what life is to me, and there is no life without you. Just to say I love you is never enough. It's not that you are everything, Paul, it's that you are the only thing.

To my wife, Stacey. I never cease to be amazed and inspired by what you accomplish and how you never, ever, give up! It was you, alone, who brought this mission to life and nurtured it into what it has become today.

The brilliance and passion you poured into this book is yet another example of how the love in your beautiful heart overcomes any obstacles that foolishly try to get in your way. Supporting and caring for you during this book's creation, and every other moment of any day, is *always* my pleasure and nothing less than my honor as the one chosen to do so.

You are my life, and no words will ever adequately capture how much I love you or express my gratitude for us falling in love. In many ways, you both saved my life and made it everything it is today. You are my love, best friend, and mentor all at the same time. There "ain't no mountain high enough," no foe tough enough, to keep me from you. You are, and always will be, the hero in my story.

ABOUT STACEY AND PAUL MARTINO

STACEY and PAUL MARTINO have proven that it only takes one partner to transform a relationship, any relationship!

For over 10 years, they have helped thousands of people to transform their marriages, parenting, and families (all by working with only ONE spouse)!

Through their decade+ of profound work, the Martinos have shown that couples work doesn't work, and that relationship is a skill set and it can be learned.

The Martinos invented their Relationship Development® Methodology and hundreds of proprietary tools to empower anyone to save their marriage, bring the passion back, eliminate the fighting, and bring harmony to their home.

Their RelationshipU® program has had a 1% Divorce Rate and a 99% Success Rate over a six-year study period of student results! Those results are unheard-of! And that's because . . . their methodology WORKS!

The Martinos are the founders of RelationshipDevelopment.org, where they serve students through their revolutionary online programs and life-changing events. Every day, their curriculum provides Relationship Development solutions to real-life challenges; while Stacey, Paul, and their large team of trained Relationship Development leaders provide answers and 24/7 support to the students in their programs.

Relationship Development Org (RDO) is a mission-driven organization here to serve families. RDO's mission is to empower one individual in each family with the Relationship Development skill sets to transform their marriage and parenting. We help our students to break the chains of Demand Relationship and change the trajectory of their family's legacy.

You can connect with Stacey and Paul at
RelationshipDevelopment.org

MEDITATE.
VISUALIZE.
LEARN.

With the **Empower You**
Unlimited Audio Mobile App

Unlimited access to the entire Hay House audio library!

You'll get:

- 600+ inspiring and life-changing **audiobooks**
- 1,000+ ad-free **guided meditations** for sleep, healing, relaxation, spiritual connection, and more
- Hundreds of audios **under 20 minutes** to easily fit into your day
- **Exclusive content** *only* for subscribers
- No credits, **no limits**

 **Life changing.**
" My fav app on my entire phone, hands down! – Gigi "

New audios added every week!

Scan me with your phone camera!

TRY FOR FREE!
Go to: hayhouse.co.uk/listen-free